COMPLETE GUIDE TO
DOG BREEDS

Everything you need to know
to choose the right dog for you

DIANE MORGAN

COMPLETE GUIDE TO DOG BREEDS

Project Team
Editor: Heather Russell-Revesz
Indexer: Dianne L. Schneider
Designer: Mary Ann Kahn

TFH Publications®
President/CEO: Glen S. Axelrod
Executive Vice President: Mark E. Johnson
Editor-in-Chief: Albert Connelly, Jr.
Production Manager: Kathy Bontz

TFH Publications, Inc.®
One TFH Plaza
Third and Union Avenues
Neptune City, NJ 07753

Printed and bound in China
14 15 16 17 18 19   1 3 5 7 9 8 6 4 2

Derived from *The Simple Guide to Choosing a Dog,* originally published in 2003

Library of Congress Cataloging-in-Publication Data
Morgan, Diane, 1947-
  Complete guide to dog breeds : everything you need to know to choose
the right dog for you / Diane Morgan.
      p. cm. -- (Animal planet)
  Includes index.
  ISBN 978-0-7938-3733-5 (alk. paper)
  1. Dogs. 2. Dogs--Selection 3. Dog breeds. I. Title.
  SF426.M6785 2012
  636.7--dc23
                            2011046299

The Leader In Responsible Animal Care for Over 50 Years!®
www.tfh.com

CENTRAL
Garden & Pet

PART ONE: BEFORE YOU CHOOSE

PART TWO: THE BREEDS

PART ONE

BEFORE YOU CHOOSE

1

IS OWNING A DOG RIGHT FOR YOU?

For a lot of people, getting a dog is the smartest choice they'll ever make. Studies show that dogs are not only good company and loyal pals, but that they actually help people live longer, happier, and healthier lives. Merely petting a dog lowers blood pressure, and studies show that children of dog-owning families relate better to others, have fewer learning disabilities, less aggression, more empathy with other beings, a greater sense of responsibility, and fewer allergies. (Studies at the Medical College of Georgia back up earlier research by showing that exposure to two or more cats or dogs in the house during the first year of life reduces the probability that a child will test positive for skin allergies by 50 percent.)

All this being said, it is still a bad idea for some people, even the nicest ones, to get a dog at certain times in their life. It isn't that they picked the wrong dog—the problem is that they decided to get a dog at all.

Some people get a dog because their spouse or kids wanted one, because they saw one in the movies they liked, because they thought a dog was a "status symbol," or because someone gave them one for Christmas. I have seen people give in to wild impulses when walking past a pet store. I have seen young people get a dog because they wanted some practice in taking care of something before they had a baby—as if they are anything alike. Some of these people would most likely be better with a lower-maintenance pet like a cat, or maybe an aquarium.

Owning a dog is a big decision—one that will affect the entire family.

At the other end of the spectrum are people who are not impulse buyers or impulse adopters. They think things through. They care about dogs, and they care a lot. They are open-minded, ready to learn, and haven't locked themselves into a particular breed. They truly want to find the best match. They buy books (like this one!) to try and find the best fit for their lifestyle.

This is good news for dogs. Owning a dog is a big decision—one that will affect the entire family. Finding a dog to give your heart to is one of the most important choices you'll ever make.

In some ways, it's very easy to become enamoured of a dog. They don't ask their humans to be good-looking, rich, young, brilliant, or even socially acceptable; that's why people like dogs so much. Dogs are perfectly egalitarian. Dogs never discriminate on the basis of age, gender, or race. What they do care very much about are

Your lifestyle should
dictate the type of
dog to choose.

really important things—compassion, fairness, tolerance, and loyalty.

Therein lies the difficulty. While the idea of the "perfect" dog seems attainable, it's simply not achievable. Far too many people take on the responsibility of dog ownership, and end up shocked (shocked!) when cuddly little Fido starts chewing up sofas, barking all night, and herding the neighborhood children into a tight little circle.

The problem with the human-dog relationship is that people usually get to choose the dog, not the other way around. Most dogs end up with whoever happens to decide they are cute, funny-looking, or a great show prospect. Unfortunately, these are not the best reasons to choose to a dog. Rather, your particular life circumstances should dictate what type of dog to get, or whether to get a dog at all.

What type of life circumstances? Times have changed, and raising and caring for a dog just isn't the way it used to be. In some ways, that's a good thing, and in some ways it's not. Back in the "olden" days, there was usually one person home all day who could let the dogs in and out of the house 40 times a day. People weren't as apt to have fenced yards back then either, and dogs trotted around the comparatively empty streets. Now most families have two people working out of the home, and the owners are gone most of the time. Fenced yards are necessities because it's the law in most places, and even where it's not, most people know it's not safe to let dogs wander around by themselves all day. Some people don't even have yards any more—they live in apartments, condominiums, or townhouses. There's nothing wrong with this, and lots of dogs can live perfectly happily in such a setup as long as they get enough exercise. The problem occurs when owners don't modify their wants to conform to reality. It's just too hard to keep some kinds of dogs in apartments; they aren't suited to it. Some small dogs are too noisy for peaceful apartment living, while some big ones can adjust very well.

And even though there are a lot of resources available for working owners, like doggy day care, some dogs just need more.

ASK YOURSELF THIS...

So, if dogs could choose their owners, what exactly would they ask them?

Do You Know What a Dog Is?

This may sound like a trick question, but it isn't. Although most people can recognize a dog on the street, when it comes to interacting with them, it's amazing how easy it is to get them mixed up with something else, like a human child, a wolf, or a robot. Dogs are none of these things.

Take wolves, for example. It is true dogs used to be wolves, a long, long, long time ago—but they've moved on. Wolves are wild animals. They prefer to be as far away from people as possible. Dogs are highly domesticated creatures who would die without human care. And while the genetic link with wolves is close enough for interbreeding, it's just not done, unless forced upon them by humans. Although many dogs retain some wolf-like characteristics (which we'll discuss further in Chapter 3), there is a deep chasm between wolves and dogs.

Dogs are not human children either, although they do have some qualities that remind people of children. (Most of the qualities are retained juvenile characteristics of their ancient wolf days.) They are sweet and dependent. In fact, in many ways, dogs are more childlike than human kids. They will never grow up, move out, go to college, get married, or even start a paper route. However, they don't think like people, who never seem to be satisfied with things as they are; they just don't have the same goals. Beyond love, food, and a warm place to sleep, dogs are pretty unambitious. They don't want to be great artists, don't want to

be famous, don't want to establish a charitable foundation, and have no need to "self-actualize," since they are already as actual as possible. While they look up to people as leaders and companions, they aren't kids.

Dogs aren't robots, either. They are complex, highly advanced animals. They feel pain, anger, love, and jealousy, and, like humans, are unpredictable. What works with one dog may not work with another; what worked yesterday may be useless today. No matter how well humans think they know a dog, there's always a surprise in store. I can't tell you how many times I have heard people say, "Wow, he never did anything like that before." This is one of the most entertaining parts of the dog-human relationship—dogs keep us on our toes.

Why Do You Want a Dog?

Hopefully, you want a dog primarily or solely for

Consider your environment and living situation before you choose your dog.

through-ers. Electric fences may work for some people with large properties, but it doesn't keep out nasty neighborhood dogs or teasing kids. A privacy fence is safest, but any strong, non-climbable fence will work. Even a dog inclined to stay around the yard whether it's fenced or not is at risk of being stolen or lost.

Will You Puppy Proof?

If you think you a want puppy, you'll need to get your house puppy ready: electrical cords taped to the wall; cabinets locked; trash cans secured; and dangerous plants, swallowable objects, and curtain or blind cords put out of the way. Realize that puppies explore the world with their mouths, and if they can eat it, chew it, swallow it, or gnaw on it, they will. The same thing goes for backyards and garages. Fertilizers and other chemical lawn treatments can be deadly for dogs, as can unwiped antifreeze spills—not to mention rat poisons and other rodenticides.

Where Do You Live?

Most dogs are pretty adaptable, so long as they get the right amount of exercise. In a city, that's harder to do for sporting dogs, like pointers and setters, and some of the sighthounds, like Whippets, so most of them are better off in a place where they can run and play. And while some dogs are "self-starters" in this regard, others need some encouragement to take that run. Some popular breeds, such as Beagles and Dachshunds, have a tendency towards obesity without a daily workout. And don't be fooled by size—some small "apartment-sized" breeds, such as Yorkies, make so much noise that their owners risk eviction. On the other hand, some big dogs, like Saint Bernards, can thrive in the city.

A lot of people don't know that the main consideration as to whether a dog can be happy in

a pet. Of course, there's nothing wrong with the dog show game, and tracking, hunting, and lure-coursing can be downright fun. But after the day at the show or in the woods is over, every dog appreciates some cozy down-time with his owners. Even though a Siberian Husky doesn't seem to mind the cold, he needs an air-conditioned house in the summer and really likes human companionship. Dogs belong in the house except when you are doing great stuff outdoors with them. You should love and cherish your dog, even if he can't cut the mustard in the show ring or doesn't know a rabbit from a rhinoceros.

Do You Live in a Safe Environment?

Do you have a fenced-in yard? If not, are you committed to taking your dog on long daily walks? If you have a fence, is it escape proof? Some dogs are terrific diggers, climbers, and squeezer-

the city depends more on mental qualities than on physical ones. Calm, low-key, not-easily-stressed dogs can often handle the fast pace, loud noises, and stress of city life better than high-mettled animals.

Are You Permitted to Own a Dog?

You may not even realize it, but some leases or covenant agreements do not allow dogs in the building. Do not consider "sneaking" a prohibited dog into your premises—you'll eventually get caught, and then you and your dog will be out on the street.

Where Will You Be All Day?

Once upon a time, there was usually somebody hanging around the house all day to cater to a dog's every whim—but not any more. Nowadays most owners go off to work, usually working long hours or with an extended commute. A few dogs really cannot tolerate such a long separation, and nearly all dogs enjoy as much human companionship as possible, but they are adaptable, too. As long as you can give a dog plenty of attention and exercise when you are home, most dogs can adjust. So, taking it for granted that most dogs will be left alone for part of the day, the question becomes, exactly where are they going to spend that alone time and what are they supposed to do?

If your dog is going to be left alone in the house for a long time, who is going to take him out for a morning and afternoon walk and bathroom break? Some dogs are good about holding it for a long time, but it's not very comfortable, and puppies or small dogs with tiny bladders need some relief. If you want to be a good owner, you'll have to be mindful of this and ask a neighbor or hire a dog-walking service to give the dog a much-needed break. You might consider installing a dog door to let your dog go in and out as he pleases (as long as you have a fenced yard in a safe neighborhood).

Some owners can afford a doggy day care, pet sitter, or dog walker to keep their dogs happy—that works, too.

How Much Time Do You Have?

While some dogs are pretty independent and can get along by themselves, with another dog, or even a cat, for company, it's no fun to be deprived of human companionship day in and day out. And for puppies, being alone for long periods is a real recipe for disaster. Puppies need lots of one-on-one socialization time, so you work full-time, you may want to consider going to a shelter or a rescue organization, where you can get a nice older dog who won't demand so much time and attention. (And older dogs are usually already housetrained!)

Who Is Going to Take Care of the Dog?

If the answer is, "the kids," you probably aren't being realistic. Of course the children will volunteer, even beg and bargain for a dog by promising with all their hearts to feed him, walk him, train him, play with him, and snuggle with him at night. Some kids will actually do some of

these things for more than a week; others won't, no matter what they say now. Let's face it, kids can be pretty forgetful. If you are thinking of getting a dog "for the kids' sake," please think twice. You should want a dog yourself, because chances are you are the one who will be feeding and walking him—and you're the one who will be paying the bills.

In fact, according to a recent study by the American Animal Hospital Association (AAHA), 66 percent of the respondents said that "Mom" had the primary responsibility for pet care. As for the kids, in fewer than 10 percent of the homes did the children follow through on their promise to care for a dog. If Mom is even slightly uncertain about wanting to take home a dog, then it's best to wait.

By the way, people who "want a puppy for the kids to grow up with" need to understand that the puppy will grow up a lot faster than the child. Kids are better off with older, already grown-up dogs, because they tend to be more tolerant and are through the nipping stage.

Do You Have Kids?

If there are children in your home, are they old enough to understand how to handle and treat a puppy? Are you prepared to always supervise interactions between young kids and the dog? While it's great to see a puppy and child playing together, some kids can play with a puppy until he drops from exhaustion, because the loyal puppy will continue to try to play as long as he is asked to. The children don't mean to be cruel; they just don't know when to quit and neither does a puppy.

Parents must be willing to teach the kids the right way to pick up a puppy, and to leave the dog alone when he is eating or wants to sleep. And the truth is certain dogs don't really care for kids; or some dogs love their "own" kids, but not the neighbors' kids. As a parent you should do your research and find out what breeds are likely to be kid lovers.

Are You Adaptable?

Let's face it, a dog is going to change your life. If you have rigid expectations about dog ownership, you will be in for a surprise. Or, if you want to get a dog "just like your old one," you are bound to be disappointed because each dog is an individual (even among the same breed). Adjustments will be a lot easier if you are open-minded (and open-hearted too).

How Are Your Finances?

Let's talk money—dogs can be expensive, and that's no joke. They cost more than a lot of people seem to think. Even a "free dog" ends up costing more than you might suppose. We all know that buying a high-quality, purebred puppy from a responsible breeder will cost hundreds (maybe thousands) of dollars; a sizeable chunk of change for many people. Even humane society or rescued dogs aren't free. The kind people who save the lives of these dogs have to get money from somewhere to continue their good work.

Then, after the purchase or adoption, dogs will eat up the cash. (Sometimes literally. It's not a good idea to leave money lying around—a few pennies can poison a puppy with zinc). Big dogs cost more than small ones—there's more to feed, for one thing, and boarding kennels and groomers charge more for big dogs. Even veterinarians charge more to spay big dogs than small ones.

And those dogs whose coats need special attention—Poodles, Shih Tzu, Maltese, and some terriers—really need a professional groomer. Groomers wash, dry, comb, brush, pluck, shave, scissor, clip nails, clean ears, perfume—all for a fee.

What's for Dinner?

Good food costs money. While not every owner has to go so far as to provide home-cooked meals (although this is becoming increasingly popular), you should find a commercial food that is nutritious and formulated for the dog's age or medical condition. In the dog food world, at least, there is a close relationship between how much commercial dog food costs and how nutritious it is.

How About Those Checkups?

You'll need to consider veterinary care. Choose a vet whose office is relatively close in case of emergency, who has a system ready for after-hours emergencies, and who genuinely loves dogs. It's best if the vet is familiar with the special problems of your breed in particular.

Dogs need vaccinations, and should get their teeth cleaned and get regular health checkups.

And are you prepared if your dog eats something awful or gets into an accident?

With the right care, dogs can live well into their teens. Veterinarians can treat and cure illnesses that were death sentences 20 years ago, but it's not cheap. Ultrasounds, echocardiograms, and sophisticated surgery are all expensive, albeit lifesaving, procedures. A good, really dedicated dog owner will forgo a vacation or cut back on restaurants to provide for a dog's special needs or medical procedures.

Are You Willing to Train?

Training is one of the most important aspects of a dog's relationship with people. You should absolutely be committed to training your dog, and you should train him in a positive, enjoyable way. Yelling or hitting should not be part of any training program. There's no excuse to strike a dog; it only makes him fearful or bad-tempered. This goes for housetraining, too. Owners need to be patient and not resort to behavior like screaming, hitting, or rubbing a dog's nose in his mistakes. Such owners have been improperly trained themselves and need some reminders about correct housetraining methods.

Be aware of the most current training methods and have the right expectations for your particular breed. Labradors and Goldens just love obedience, and setters can't get enough of racing around in the fields after birds. Hounds take easily to trailing rabbits. But what comes easily for some is a real hurdle for others. Understand what you can reasonably expect from your dog.

What About Your Home?

How attached are you to a "perfect-looking" home? If you can't stand the sight of dog hair everywhere, you'd better think about getting a low-shedding breed and stay away from the shedders and droolers. And while any dog can be destructive if deprived of sufficient exercise and company, some dogs are capable of eating though walls and devouring floors if bored enough.

What About Roommates?

Do you have other dogs or maybe a cat? Some dogs subscribe to the "pack" mentality: they always like to have another dog or two around for company. However, there are other dogs who cannot get along with other dogs or small animals.

Think about your current dog, and decide if he'd really like company. Sometimes people get a puppy to keep their old dog company or to cheer him up. This may work, or it may depress the older dog still further. Also, if you already have another dog, it usually turns out that dogs of opposite sexes get along better than same-sex pairs.

As for cats, some dogs will chase cats in part due to their breeding; they just can't help it. They aren't bad dogs, but chasing cats is an irresistible temptation for some. Surprisingly, households that already have two cats seem to have better luck with adding a dog than those with only one. It has something to do with the way cats organize themselves. Apparently, if there's only one cat, it tends to get into a contest with the new dog about who will be boss.

THE FINAL ANALYSIS

In the final analysis, getting matched up with the right dog is possible. It just takes an open mind, a willingness to do some research, and an honest assessment of your lifestyle. When you get the right dog, you are able to form a friendship that lasts, receive love and affection, and create a bond that is mutually beneficial for both of you—what could be better than that?

2

WHERE TO FIND THE DOG OF YOUR DREAMS

Once you've thought about it and decided that yes, you are an excellent candidate for dog ownership, you'll need to figure out how to find the dog of your dreams. But before you embark on your search, there's another decision you'll need to make, and it directly affects where you'll begin looking for your dog.

PUPPY OR ADULT?

Before you start looking, decide if you are interested in a puppy or an adult dog. All dogs start as puppies, and all puppies turn into dogs. Most people, especially most first-time dog owners, want a puppy. And puppies are wonderful! They are warm, cuddly, and extremely irresistible. Choosing a puppy has several other advantages, too. You get to train your dog right from the beginning, and you don't have to deal with the training mistakes made by former owners. If you get your pup from a good breeder, you'll most likely have a healthy and psychologically sound dog as well.

Puppies aren't for everyone, though, and while they are charming and undeniably cute, there are many reasons to consider getting an older dog. One obvious reason is appearance. A puppy, even from a reputable breeder, is always something of an unknown quantity. An adult dog, on the other hand, is there in all his size and glory. Older dogs are usually housetrained, and they have finished with the disastrous chewing stage. And despite

the old adage, old dogs can learn, and they learn quickly. In fact, they have a longer attention span and are less likely to be distracted than puppies. Additionally, older dogs are often well-socialized and understand how to get along with others—something many puppies still have to experience. Older dogs are loving and grateful to have a good home. Older dogs need less supervision than puppies, and they are instantly ready to join you on long walks and other grown-up activities. And they won't keep you awake all night crying for their mothers. Of course, there's a downside to everything. Many older dogs are given up because of temperament or training problems, so it's important to be sure you know the whole story before you decide to adopt an older dog.

If you have your heart set on a puppy, then you should start your search for an ethical breeder. If you've decided an older dog is for you, then your search should include rescues and shelters (although some breeders may have an older dog they are looking to adopt out).

Is a puppy or an adult dog right for you?

QUESTIONABLE SOURCES

There are many places to find a dog, and some are better than others. It's up to you to do your research and make sure you find a source for your dog that's breeding healthy companion animals.

Internet and Newspapers

Some people begin their search for a family dog in what seems like the most sensible place—on the internet or the newspaper classifieds. While you may indeed find a good dog in this way, you're fighting the odds. In the first place, the very best breeders don't advertise online or in the newspaper, or even in most dog magazines, because they don't need to. They already have a waiting list of knowledgeable buyers.

On the other hand, backyard breeders, puppy millers, and desperate owners who want to dump their behaviorally challenged dog on the unsuspecting public, go straight to the classifieds. Just remember: Buyer beware. Many of these people use evasive language (and sometimes outright lies) to draw in the unsuspecting public. They use words like

Not all sources for obtaining a dog are good choices.

"full-blooded" by which one presumes they mean "purebred." However, the term "full-blooded" or "thoroughbred" is not used in dog circles, so it's a guarantee that the seller probably has no idea what she is talking about. Sometimes they offer "papers," but this term is ambiguous. It might mean pedigree, it might mean national club registration, like the American Kennel Club (AKC), or it might even mean a dog license or some kind of health certificate.

A favorite term of the backyard breeder is "AKC champion bloodlines." Big deal. A lot of registered dogs have AKC champion bloodlines—if you go back far enough. But these far-off ancestors don't mean much after a couple of generations. If you are considering showing your dog, or even if you want a dog that is a fine physical example of the breed, look for a few champions among nearer relatives, such as the parents and grandparents.

In addition, an AKC championship is no guarantee of the health or character of the dog who earns it. I have known dogs with epilepsy, hip dysplasia, and personality defects who earn enough points to get their championships. Unfortunately, some breeders care more about ribbons on a wall and bragging about their "gorgeous" dogs than about health and personality. Don't fall for it. "AKC-registered" means nothing in terms of quality, health, or temperament of the dog; it simply means that the breeders have submitted the proper paperwork to the American Kennel Club. Don't make the mistake of thinking that every AKC dog is ready for Westminster. Even casual breeders who have good intentions often simply don't know enough about the perils of genetics and breeding to produce good puppies, especially these days when so many inherited diseases abound. They often fail to perform the proper genetic screening for the parents, thus exacerbating the problems.

Some people are fooled into thinking that "Both parents on premises" is a sign of good breeding. Actually it just means that the breeder had two dogs of opposite sexes. Many good breeders go across the country or have their females artificially inseminated; however, you should at least be able to see a picture of the sire.

Some unscrupulous breeders bill their maladjusted, oversized, inappropriately aggressive dogs as "extra": more Rottweiler; more Pit Bull; more Chow Chow; more German Shepherd. Most people have all they can handle with the regular specimens of these breeds, let alone anything "extra." Terms like "Needs adult home" or "Protective" often means the dog is aggressive with kids. It is a bad idea to bring home a dog with behavior problems that you may not be able to handle.

Here's my personal favorite: "Rare color." If a puppy were "rare" in a desirable way, it wouldn't be advertised in the paper. There are no rare colors or patterns in the sense that it makes the dog more valuable. There are, however, some "rare" colors that disqualify a dog from the show ring. Parti-colored Poodles, "blue Bassets," and other anomalies are not desirable, and in some breeds, have genetic problems associated with them. For example, in many breeds, white can signify hearing or eye problems. Check the list of accepted colors for your breed and don't be led astray. The same is true for eye color. With the

Understand the breed standard before you make your purchase.

exception of the Siberian Husky and a very few others, eyes should be brown. Always check the breed standard before you go looking to find out what is and what is not acceptable.

Friends and Neighbors

Some people get their pets from a friend, relative, or neighbor. And while this is a good source for an older dog (you probably know everything about the animal already), it may be a poorer place from which to get a puppy, unless that friend, relative, or neighbor is a person who is truly an expert on the breed and proves it by entering competitions like dog shows, field trials, or tracking events. That makes your friend fall into the "breeder class," which we are going to discuss next.

THE RESPONSIBLE BREEDER: A GOOD SOURCE

If you are looking for a puppy, the best way to find one is by contacting a reputable breeder. If

Puppies bred by a neighbor or friend may not meet the breed standard.

you're not planning on showing, explain that you're looking for a "pet-quality" puppy. Pet quality doesn't mean there will be anything wrong with the puppy. It merely means that in the breeder's opinion, the dog will not achieve a championship in the show ring. Eyes that are too light, wrong color nose, or ears hung too high or low are just a few unimportant factors that may limit a dog's "show-worthiness" but have no impact on how good a pet the puppy will be. Even stranger, from an outsider's point of view, is that many breeders want their line to have a certain, instantly recognizable "look." That look may involve a particular type of head, coat color, movement, or, in performance dogs, certain special abilities. If the puppy does not measure up to the breeder's particular expectations, he automatically becomes a pet-quality dog and your golden opportunity.

them how much you like their dog (they will be flattered). Ask for the name of their breeder, or if they are the breeder themselves. If so, ask if they are planning to breed in the near future and that you'd like to apply for a puppy. If they are in a hurry, be satisfied with a business card and make arrangements to call or visit their kennel.

Most exhibitors will be delighted that you take an interest in the breed and will welcome you to the circle of fanciers. However (and I hate to say it), some dog show exhibitors are just plain rude. I have seen enough of it to be able to state this as a fact. Some may be rude because they just lost, others because they see no reason to be polite to a mere spectator (as if courtesy needs a reason), others just don't know any better. If this happens to you, mumble something about "sorry to have caught you at a bad time" and find someone who will treat you with respect. A good breeder regards every contact she has with the public as an opportunity to be an ambassador for her breed, and people who don't take on this responsibility with grace are not good breeders in my book.

What to Look for in a Breeder

Here are some criteria by which to judge a responsible breeder.

Age

A responsible breeder won't sell puppies until they are at least eight weeks old (or even later for certain breeds), although she may allow you to put down a deposit earlier. The early weeks of a dog's life are critical for socialization. This is even more essential for slow-maturing breeds. Besides, breeders need the time to evaluate members of the litter for show potential.

Breed Club

A good breeder will belong to the relevant breed

Whether you're buying for pet or show, a responsible breeder will ask you lots of questions. Some of them may appear personal. Don't be offended; she is merely trying to make sure her dogs are going into the right home. Her questions should make you confident that this is a person who cares about her puppies and who has done a good job of breeding them.

A reputable breeder is the ideal place to get a purebred puppy.

Finding a Breeder

One great way to find a breeder is to attend dog shows. Even if you have no intention of ever showing your dog, going to shows and seeing a lot of high-quality dogs up close will give you a good "feel" for what dogs who meet the breed standard look like in the flesh. The parents of the puppy you choose should be of this quality. If you do see a dog you like, pick a quiet time (usually after the judging) to speak to the exhibitors. Tell

club. Ideally, she would work in your local breed rescue organization as well. If the local breed club has never heard of her, it's usually a bad sign.

Breeding Program

A good breeder has a breeding program—a specific set of goals. Ask the breeder what her breeding goals are. If you get a blank look, you've come to the wrong place—probably a backyard breeder. A responsible breeder is likely to talk your ear off about this, dragging out various pedigrees and old photos.

Cleanliness

A good breeder keeps her puppies in immaculate surroundings. A filthy kennel area means the breeder does not care about the welfare of her dogs and compromises the health of the puppies and their parents.

A good breeder keeps her puppies in immaculate surroundings.

Commitment

A good breeder keeps any puppies for which she cannot find a quality home. She will not get rid of them by giving them away to a rescue organization, shelter, or the kid next door.

Contract

A good breeder provides a written contract and will agree to take back the puppy if, for any reason the dog does not work out. This includes an unconditional health contract, agreeing to take back any puppy not found to be healthy by your veterinarian. She will also keep in touch long after the purchase. If you and the breeder live in different legal jurisdictions, the contract should include a special provision called the "forum selection clause" that states that any legal disputes between the parties must be resolved in the state or legal jurisdiction in which the seller resides. (This is advantageous to the seller, of course, but it is the only reasonable way it can be done.)

Cost

Good breeders charge what their puppies are worth. Get out your wallet, because well-bred dogs are not inexpensive, and some people will pay well over a thousand dollars or more for a show dog. Although you can certainly buy a puppy at a lesser price, the chances are that such "bargain dogs" (or their parents) may not be fully tested for inherited defects like von Willebrand's, a bleeding disorder, or heritable thyroid problems. These tests can get expensive for the breeder. The extra money you pay is well worth it in order to get a healthier dog. If the price the seller is asking is considerably lower than other area breeders, there has to be a reason, and it's probably not a good one. Some good breeders offer pet-quality puppies at a lower price than show quality. Others do not, maintaining that while some puppies are pets and some are for show, all are of equal value. (I like this approach myself.)

Health

A reputable breeder sells only healthy puppies. This means more than having all their puppy shots. It means the breeder has had the parents evaluated for hereditary problems. She should provide you with the written proof that she has done this and give you the results of any tests. In breeds where hip dysplasia (a debilitating disease affecting many larger breeds, in which the femur does not fit correctly into its socket) is common, ask to see the Orthopedic Foundation for Animals (OFA) results for both parents. The OFA rates hips as excellent, good, fair, borderline, or dysplastic. Puppies cannot be tested for hip dysplasia, because their bone structures have not sufficiently formed to tell how they will develop. Dogs must be two years old before this certification can be given, and it requires an X-ray. Another way to evaluate hips is the PennHIP™, developed by researchers at the University of Pennsylvania, which evaluates hip laxity. These tests are very important, because you can't tell whether or not a dog has hip dysplasia by simply watching him move. This disease is often masked in young dogs and does not manifest itself until later in life. (I should mention, however, that breeders of sighthounds may not have this test

A responsible breeder does pedigree and genetic research before breeding.

done because of the sighthound's sensitivity to anesthesia.)

Chances of hip dysplasia in the progeny are lowest in puppies whose parents are both rated excellent, although nothing is foolproof. Not only are certain genetic problems clustered in certain breeds, but each line within a breed may have specific health problems as well. A good breeder should volunteer this information. One question to ask a breeder is: At what age did each of your dog's closest relatives die and from what? Questions about hip dysplasia, allergies, and epilepsy are also appropriate. While these diseases are not fatal, they are debilitating and lower the quality of life. Beware of a breeder who claims that none of her dogs has ever had any diseases or a breeder who has never heard of these problems.

For breeds with heritable deafness problems like Dalmatians and English Setters, ask to see the results of the brainstem auditory evoked response (BAER) test that all conscientious breeders should have performed. The Canine Eye Registration Foundation (CERF) has similar tests for breeds that have heritable eye problems.

House Raised

Choose a breeder who raises her puppies in her home—not outside in a kennel. A house-raised dog will be better socialized when you bring him home. Living in a home environment from the very beginning will get your future dog accustomed to the sights and sounds of everyday human life— vacuum cleaners, blaring stereos, screaming and running kids. Ideally, this socialization should be accomplished before the puppy is eight weeks old. By 12 weeks, it's much harder—and by the fifth month, it's extremely difficult to "re-program" an unsocialized or undersocialized puppy. Each puppy should receive individual attention from the breeder daily.

Pedigree Research

The responsible breeder does pedigree and genetic research before breeding. Some first-time buyers are concerned by what they perceive as incest when they examine the pedigree of their prospective dog. In dog circles, this is called line-breeding. Technically, a line-bred dog is one in which a particular dog's name appears more than once on a three- or four-generation pedigree. Line-breeding is done to produce more uniformity in the offspring—in other words, to get more predictable and uniform results. However, unless the forebears are of good conformation quality and free of genetic faults, line-breeding can be dangerous. And even when the relatives appear perfect, the lessening of the gene pool, which repeated line-breeding involves, can be damaging to the breed as a whole, even while it benefits your own particular puppy.

References

A good breeder will give you references from

former customers. Be sure to call them and ask about the health and temperament of the dogs they bought. Also inquire as to whether the breeder was supportive during their adjustment period or if she was helpful if a problem came up. Of course, if a breeder had a problem with a client or dog, you're not likely to be offered that information. It is still a "buyer beware" world.

Registration Papers

A quality breeder will give you the dog's registration papers and, for a puppy, the so-called "blue slip." This enables you to apply for full registration. An adult dog will come with a full registration certificate, a white piece of paper with a purple border. (There will be a transfer of ownership form on the back.) You should also get a pedigree with your dog, which goes back three generations. You can apply to the AKC for a longer one if you want, for a fee. The papers should come with the puppy. Don't let the breeder tell you she will send them later. (I fell for this myself years ago when I purchased my first Irish Setter. The papers never came, and while I am reasonably sure my Flannery was an Irish Setter, I never did get the proof of it.)

Showing

A reputable breeder is actively involved in showing her dogs. She is proud of their quality and places them in competition with other quality dogs. Most of the near relatives of your prospective puppy should have an AKC championship or a comparable title in obedience, tracking, herding, retrieving, or field trials. Any AKC titles your dog's ancestors have won will be indicated on the papers. Some national breed clubs also award titles, which will be indicated on official certificates. Showing dogs is important for most breeders, because they want to prove

through competition that they are the best. On the other hand, a responsible breeder's primary concern is not showing dogs, but raising healthy, good-tempered puppies. Of course, she is also interested in producing a handsome representative of the breed. A breeder who raises healthy, good-tempered Basset Hounds who look like Beagles is not a good breeder.

Socialization

A reputable breeder produces well-socialized dogs. This means the dogs seem comfortable with both human beings and their littermates. The personality of the mother dog can tell you a lot, too. I would not trust a breeder who will not let you look at the mother.

Specialization

A responsible breeder specializes in only one or two breeds. If the person seems to raise dogs of every description, you've stumbled upon a puppy mill. Leave fast. Also, a good breeder does not sell her puppies to a third party, such as a pet store or a pet broker.

Temperament Testing

A good breeder has her puppies temperament tested by someone certified to do so. The temperament test rates each puppy, among other things, on shyness and aggression. Ask to see the results of the test.

Unfortunately, not everyone who shows dogs is well-informed or even cares about important health and temperament issues. Some very nice-looking dogs have a shyness or aggression problem that makes them poor choices for a family pet.

Your Instincts

Most importantly, trust your instincts. If the breeder seems evasive, uncommunicative, or noncommittal, or something feels "not quite right," there is probably something wrong.

The Application Process

The breeder will ask you to fill out an application. Questions may include seemingly nosy ones such as:

- Do you own or rent? If you rent, you may be asked for your landlord's name and phone number. Many times renters get a dog and simply hope the landlord will give in and change the rules once he sees how cute it is. That doesn't usually happen, however, and the dog ends up without a home.
- Is your dwelling a house, apartment, or mobile home? Breeders need to know how much room you have, and, for some breeds, if they need to climb stairs.
- Do you have a fenced yard? This is always a plus, and, for some breeds, practically a necessity. If you do not have a fenced yard, you'll need to do a lot of walking your pet. The application may ask you details about the fencing type and height.
- The name and phone number of your veterinarian. Most responsible breeders will give your vet a call to make sure that you are accustomed to giving your pets standard care or better.
- How many adults live in your home? How many children? What are their ages? Not all dog breeds or lines within breeds are good with young children. Others love to be in a big group of them.
- How much time will your dog need to spend alone every day? Where will he be housed during that time? If

indoors for a long period, how will his elimination needs be handled? Most dogs do best with someone home a lot, although certain breeds seem to do pretty well on their own all day. Regardless, someone needs to be responsible for taking the dog out regularly, especially if you are purchasing a puppy and he needs to be housetrained.

- What other pets do you own? How long have you had each one? Some breeds don't do well with other dogs or with cats.
- Why do you want this breed? Breeders and rescues use this question not only to determine your goals but to see if you have realistic expectations about the breed in question.

A breeder will ask you to fill out an application with details about your lifestyle.

- Where will the dog sleep at night? Obviously the breeder wants to know if your dog will be safe and happy. While some breeds don't mind an occasional night camping out, most pet dogs should be in the house with you at night.

If you get turned down, ask why. Find out what you can do to qualify or if the breeder thinks another type or breed of dog may suit you better.

Picking a Puppy

If possible, take along your whole family to help you choose the puppy of your dreams. Let everyone in the family be invested in the final decision, but listen carefully to what your breeder has to say about each puppy. Pay close attention. Your breeder has the most experience in matching the right pups for each family.

Look for healthy, active, friendly puppies. You should see how each puppy behaves with his littermates, alone, with you, with his mom, and with the rest of your family. One excellent way to assess the adult personality of the puppies is by taking a good look at the mother dog. Don't expect a mom to be brimming with joy at the prospect of large strangers poking around at her puppies, but she shouldn't be aggressive either. Watch the puppy's reactions to his littermates—it's a rule of thumb that his behavior to his littermates will indicate his responses to his humans. If the puppies have any full siblings at the establishment, examine them for temperament as well.

The temperament of each puppy will be different. The one you choose should be suited to your needs. A dog with "show potential" should be alert and very outgoing. A family pet or even a pup slated for formal obedience work may be more reserved. In general, the behavior that you see in

Take along the whole family to help you choose your puppy.

puppyhood will become more pronounced as the puppy grows.

You can also make some observations of the puppy's apparent health. A healthy puppy, whether pet or show quality, will have clear eyes, a bright coat, and a shiny, clean, slightly cool nose. His gums will be a nice healthy pink, not pale or dark red. He should feel solid to the touch; a distended belly may indicate worms. His skin should be pink and elastic with no crusty or red patches, and certainly no fleas or ticks should be visible. No diarrhea should be evident; puppy stools should be dark and well formed. The puppy should be able to walk and run without any obvious difficulty.

The Right Paperwork
The Bill of Sale

Don't leave the breeder's without a bill of sale. This is the legal proof that you have paid the breeder for your dog. It may be part of the contract or in addition to it, and it may contain some clauses required by state law. Some states, for instance, require that the seller take a dog back and refund your money if the pet becomes ill within 48 hours from the time of purchase.

The Contract

The contract should specify the price of the dog, including a deposit. The contract should state if some of the money will be refunded if you spay or neuter your pet, a proviso sometimes added for a pet-quality dog. The clause should include what proof of neutering or spaying you need to supply, when it should be done, and when the money should be returned to you.

The agreement should also designate the primary intended use of the dog, whether it is for pet, show, or performance (like obedience, herding, tracking, or hunting). It may also

How About Two Puppies?

The advantage of getting two puppies is obvious; they will play together, suffer less anxiety when leaving the litter, and provide you with lots of entertainment. But two puppies are twice the vet bills and twice the training. Interestingly, the question as to whether or not to get two puppies depends somewhat on the breed. Hounds, who are natural pack animals, are a good choice for two puppies, but it's a bad idea with retrievers and some sighthounds, like Pharaoh Hounds; the puppies may bond to each other instead of to you! There's another consideration as well—some day those two cute puppies will become two very old dogs, and you may have the heartbreak of losing both within a short time.

require the owner to microchip the puppy, although more and more responsible breeders are microchipping their own litters. Microchips can be implanted into the dog to help identify him if he is ever lost or stolen.

The contract should include a health section, with a clause that stipulates you should take the puppy to your veterinarian with 72 hours. If the vet finds the dog to be unsound, the contract should stipulate that the breeder will take the dog back for replacement or full refund. The contract should also state how the breeder will deal with any inherited health problem that might show up.

It also should certify, as a matter of course, that the dog is purebred and eligible for AKC registration. AKC registration is rather a mystery to some people, but it really shouldn't be. When puppies are born, the breeder registers the whole litter by applying to the AKC. The AKC then sends a "blue slip" for each puppy. At the time of sale, the seller must supply a properly completed AKC registration application. The buyer registers the individual puppy in his name, or the seller may wish to stipulate the registered name. The buyer is responsible for submitting the dog's registration papers by completing the application and sending it in with the required fee. Once a dog is actually registered with the AKC, his name cannot be changed (officially). But don't let that stop you. If your dog's official name is Lord High Muckey Muck, but you want to call him Barney, that's fine.

This application to register the puppy must contain the breeder's signature, as well as the dog's full breeding information, including:
- Breed, sex, and color of the dog
- Date of birth
- Registered names (and numbers) of the dog's sire and dam
- Breeder's name

The AKC then sends the buyer a registration certificate. It all sounds very official, and it is, of course. But remember that AKC registration does not guarantee the quality of a puppy. And while the AKC can now do DNA testing to help ensure the true parentage of a puppy, that may not mean much if the parents are unsound or unhealthy to begin with.

Most people care about AKC registration because it lets them participate in AKC activities like obedience, field trials, conformation shows, and agility (although some of the events also have non-AKC sponsors). But you can also get a nice

dog from a shelter or a rescue and do many of these activities, especially agility, through other organizations that care nothing about whether your dog has papers or even if he is purebred.

AKC registration allows you to participate in AKC activities like conformation.

Co-Ownership

While many show breeders like to "co-own" dogs with a show buyer, be aware of what you are getting into. The arrangement may include where a dog will reside, showing responsibilities and expenses, and breeding plan details, including who will pay for what. Arrangements should be made in advance for deciding if the dog will spend time with a handler or trainer, and what happens if the dog is not kept in correct show condition. There are no set rules for co-ownership, but various clauses may require you to (a) show the dog until his championship, which may take a long time and may require you to hire a professional handler; (b) if you have bought a female, to pay for some or all of the breeding expenses, while at the same time giving the breeder pick of the litter. This clause may hold good for every litter the female whelps. Unless you really know what you are getting into, I would stay away from this option. It can be complicated and people often are disappointed or surprised by the unexpected results of the contract.

RESCUE OR SHELTER: THE OTHER ETHICAL OPTION

Another wonderful option is to get your dog from a rescue or a shelter. Unfortunately, not all dogs have the good fortune to be born to a responsible breeder. Some got their start in unscrupulous puppy mills or were born to well-meaning but unknowledgeable backyard breeders. Many of these dogs are sold to people who can't care for them properly, and they end up in the shelter or a dog rescue.

Shelters

Most counties are required to operate an animal shelter for impoundment of stray dogs and enforcement of cruelty and neglect laws. Some shelters are run as a private humane society that contracts with the county to provide these services; others are operated by the county itself. There are also private shelters that have no contract with any government agency. These are often small and need to rely heavily upon donations and volunteers. Most private shelters do not euthanize healthy, non-aggressive animals, as public shelters are sometimes forced to do for lack of space. Private shelters are not legally required to accept an animal, so they can generally care for the few they have for long periods while waiting for the right adopter to show up. Many shelters use the name SPCA ("Society for the Prevention of Cruelty of Animals") or "Humane Society." The shelter may or may not have connections to the national organization of the same name. (The national ASPCA is centered in New York City, while the Humane Society makes its headquarters in Washington, D.C.) So when you give to one, you are not necessarily helping to fund the other.

A rescue or shelter is a wonderful option for getting a dog.

Breed Rescues

Another player in the animal shelter sector is the breed rescue. Although there are all-breed and mixed-breed rescues, most rescue groups deal with only one breed, about which the members are experts. Some of these are run by individuals who love the breed, while others are sponsored by local or national breed clubs or rescue networks.

Few breed rescues operate their own kennel or shelter; instead, most use a foster home system. This is a wonderful idea because the foster parents are usually experts on the breed who can carefully evaluate the animal before it is given up for adoption. Some rescues merely operate a referral service, but all can help with problems related to a breed, and most can arrange to remove a dog from a place where he can no longer be cared for.

Pros and Cons of Adoption

Finding a responsible dog rescue as a source for your dog is an honorable and kind thing to do. Many of these dogs simply need a loving home and an open heart. You may not get a show-ring champion, but you'll be doing something even better—you'll be saving a dog's life. Responsible and reputable shelters and rescues do temperament testing and health checks on their dogs, too. Many shelters also offer certificates for spay or neuter discount; some alter or sterilize all dogs before they adopt them out. Some shelters even include microchip identification with every animal.

You seldom know the history of a shelter animal, so you need to rely heavily upon the care and knowledge of the shelter people. You can also

do some of the same tests discussed previously with an older dog. The main problems you want to avoid are aggression and timidity, both of which may be more common with shelter dogs than in the canine population in general.

Don't be afraid to ask questions, especially about the provenance of the animal. Dogs who were turned in by an owner may have been aggressive, had housetraining or behavior problems, or maybe the kids just got bored with the dog.

So, although some dogs may have behavioral or health problems, a good rescue or shelter will evaluate every dog in its care and can give you all the information you'll need to make an informed choice.

Choosing a rescue or shelter dog means saving a life and getting a companion who will be a faithful (and grateful!) friend. Some people, of course, prefer a puppy, but remember that most rescue dogs are

already housetrained, out of the chewing stage, and happy just to tag along on an evening's walk. They are often incredibly

A good rescue evaluates each dog before adopting them out.

loyal and the perfect choice for many people. As Alisa Garbrick, of Basset Rescue of Old Dominion, writes, "I find that the rescued Bassets that I adopted are so grateful that I took them in and gave them a forever home—even more so than the pups I got from breeders."

The great advantage to breed rescue over shelters is that the people running them are truly experts and can offer a wide choice of dogs all from the same breed. Breed rescues can answer all your questions about the breed, and can advise you as to whether or not one of their charges is right for you. They make sure the dogs under their care have veterinary attention. Most spay or neuter their dogs as soon as they come into the system. They interview each would-be adopter carefully and ask many questions. They want to make sure that this placement will be the dog's last home. The breed rescue I work with does house visits and checks with the adopter's veterinarian.

Rescue dogs are seldom free, however, and for very good reasons. The rescue group I work with spent over $40,000 in vet bills last year; we recoup part of that cost by asking for an adoption fee. Older dogs or dogs with health problems may be a little less expensive. There's another reason as well—a psychological one. We have found that if people are not willing to pay a small fee to adopt a dog in the first place—what will they do if a big vet bill arrives?

Some people wrongly assume that if a dog is in rescue it must have severe behavior problems or be sick. This is simply not true. Many wonderful dogs are dumped because people get tired of them, move away, develop an allergy, get a divorce, or simply can't afford to keep a dog anymore. Sometimes owners die. Sometimes the previous owners didn't understand the requirements of the breed in the first place. Some of the more ridiculous things I have heard from these people include:

- "I didn't know Saint Bernards got so big."
- "He doesn't seem to like being home alone 14 hours a day."
- "He seems to want a lot of attention."
- "I didn't know Akitas could be so hard to handle."
- "My Beagle keeps getting lost."
- "My Husky is just shedding everywhere, no matter how much I comb him."
- "This terrier keeps digging holes in the yard."

These owners did not do their research and ended up with the wrong dog for their lifestyle.

3

WHAT BREED IS RIGHT FOR YOU?

While it's easy to acquire a dog, getting the right dog is a different matter. The hardest part about getting the right dog is knowing what is the right dog for you. Sometimes it's really better to ask yourself, "Am I the right person for this breed?" rather than the other way around. Dogs are our best friends. We all know that. So why is it sometimes so darned hard to forge a relationship that should be—well, as natural as apple pie and ice cream? Because just as with apple pie and ice cream, there's a lot more to a dog than meets the eye. The grim fact is that most people spend more time picking the right car than in selecting the right dog, and while the right car will make your life easier, the wrong one won't eat your sofa, bite the kids, or howl all night.

DEVELOPMENT OF THE DOG

A dog is a many-layered thing. This is obvious to anyone who has looked at a Chihuahua and a Saint Bernard, a Papillon and a Great Dane, a Pekingese and a Mastiff. No other animal comes in so many different packages. Yet they all share the same ancestor: the wolf (whether it was one species of wolf or several is a subject of academic debate that doesn't make a whole lot of difference to our current topic, since all species of wolves look and act pretty much alike anyway). Our precious little toy dogs and big, hairy, goofy-looking ones all carry the genetic code for wolf in every cell of their little or big bodies. Many problems we have in dealing with our family pet are due to this

> No other animal comes in so many different packages.

inescapable heritage. There is less mitochondrial DNA difference between wolves and dogs than there is between different racial or ethnic groups of human beings. In fact, taxonomists have recently renamed the domestic dog. It is now *Canis lupus familiaris*—the familiar wolf. So it's important to realize that when we are dealing with dogs, we are dealing with modified wolves.

But that's only half the problem. At least 40,000 years ago, when wolves were domesticated and became dogs, it happened for several reasons, most of which centered directly on food. Sometimes dogs were a food source in themselves, a practice which continues to the present day in many parts of the world. Dogs were enlisted to use their natural heritage to hunt down prey; others were asked to guard food by protecting the livestock or manage food by herding

or driving it. Some people recruited dogs to help prepare food by attaching the animal to a butter churn and compelling it to walk around in a circle; some hauled food around on sledges.

Besides the food connection, dogs were called upon to defend the tribe against intruders, both human and beast. As humans became more "civilized," we drafted dogs to attack or threaten other human beings. Dogs fought in wars and helped put down rebellions. As we became even more "advanced," people thought it would be fun to make dogs fight other animals or even each other. Bull-baiting, bear-baiting, and dog-fighting became a cruel form of mass entertainment. Even small lap dogs began their careers with a serious purpose—to destroy small vermin and, in some cases, to draw fleas from unwashed humans onto themselves.

For thousands and thousands of years, we human beings have worked at domesticating the dog. This means simply that we have tried to develop an animal that is suited to our needs, and who, in some cases, copies our own neurotic behaviors. To this end, we have created a race of beings, all of whom share at least some of the following attributes:

- Total dependence upon humans for their care and keeping;
- Protective instincts that were originally cultivated to save us from attacks by our perceived enemies;
- Powerful territorial senses to warn of the approach of strangers;
- Herding instincts to round up livestock;
- Drafting skills to pull sleds for hundred of miles;
- Powerful prey drives to attack and kill anything that moves;
- Powerful senses of smell that lead to independent hunting.

A Breed's Purpose

The disparity between what dogs *were* and what dogs *are* has produced an enormous amount of debate in the dog world. Although many breeders honor the idea of retaining the original purpose for which the breed was developed, nearly everyone today wants a dog mainly as a pet. Unfortunately, the qualities that make a dog a good pet are not always found in dogs who maintain their original lifestyles. The noble, beautiful, and elegant sighthound may have a prey drive so sharp he will chase down and devour anything in his path. Scenthounds are gentle and companionable animals, but most of them make following their nose a priority. Their main interest in life is following that nose to the next hill, and they will come home when they are good and ready (that is, if they can remember where home is). Terriers were mostly bred to hunt down and kill rats (thankfully, most terrier owners fail to have a rat problem). And while we all admire the fierce intelligence of the Border Collie, his passion to round up contrary sheep does not translate well into suburban living. Most seriously, although many people want a dog to give warning of visitors, most of us of us can do without an attack dog, a highly trained, specialized animal more suited to military installations than a private home. Untrained "attack dogs" end up hurting innocent people and costing their owners wads of money and sometimes time in jail.

So, we are kind of stuck. We have to contend not only with the wolf in our dogs, but also with the sheepdog without sheep, the retriever without a duck, or the hound without a hunter. What this means is that pet owners have to deal with herding, pulling, roaming, aggressive, even phobic behavior that's appropriate for the breed's original purpose but not appropriate for pet-owner relationships today.

BEHAVIORAL TRAITS IN BREED GROUPS

National clubs put the breeds they recognize into groups, usually based on the original function of the dog. Following are some general physical characteristics and personality or behavior traits you might expect from certain breeds, based on American Kennel Club (AKC) groups.

Herding

Most herders have long hair and long ears, and come in a variety of colors. They can have short legs like Corgis (designed to get out of the way quickly while working with cattle) or long ones like Belgian Tervuren, who guard sheep. Size ranges from medium to giant. Colors range from grays and browns generally mixed with white. Breeds include Collies, Australian Shepherds, Australian Cattle Dogs, Border Collies, German Shepherd Dogs, Shetland Sheepdogs, Polish Lowlands, Belgian Sheepdogs, and Old English Sheepdogs.

Herding is a type of modified predatory behavior. Typically, herding dogs nip at the heels of the animals they're herding. In terms of being a family dog, they can get a bit distraught when their herd is not kept together, and will do their best to keep you together when walking as a group. If parents aren't around, herders sometimes step up and herd or nip small children. They are wonderfully intelligent, eager to please, loyal, and affectionate, and they make great pets as long as they get enough exercise.

Hounds

The Hound Group can be broken down into two types: scenthounds and sighthounds.

Scenthounds

These dogs hunt by smell, not sight. Most of these breeds have long drooping ears like Basset Hounds, large nasal cavities, loose wet lips that often drool, and booming voices that can almost wake the dead. They don't have to be fast because they don't keep their prey in sight, but rather follow the scent. They can follow a scent over ground and water even when the scent is several days old. Size ranges from medium to large. Colors are usually brown earth tones. Breeds include Bloodhounds, Beagles, Coonhounds, Dachshunds, Foxhounds, Harriers, Petit Basset Griffons Vendeens, and Otterhounds.

These dogs are pretty stubborn and can be hard to train because of that stubbornness, but they can be quite amusing. Intelligent, they make loyal family pets as long as you're not looking for snap-to obedience. Some drool significantly. Because they were historically bred to hunt together, dogs were selected partially on the basis of non-aggressiveness.

The Nature of Bully-Breeds

Although not an official group, there are breeds that have an infusion of Bulldog, Mastiff, and terrier blood, called "Bully-breeds." They include the American Staffordshire Terrier, Staffordshire Bull Terrier, Bull Terrier, and others. These are formidable dogs who combine the power of Bulldogs and Mastiffs with the quickness and feistiness of terriers. Like terriers, they tend not to like other dogs, but because of their greater power, can be very dangerous if allowed to attack. Although never meant to injure people, it is an undeniable fact that individuals who are poorly bred or from certain suspect lines can cause serious harm. These dogs are best placed with experienced owners who know how to deal with them.

Sighthounds

Sighthounds are dogs who hunt on instinct when they see prey moving and overtake that prey using their speed. Size ranges from toy to giant. Colors are often shades of brown and tan but also white mixed with other colors (parti-color). Breeds include Whippets, Italian Greyhounds, Pharaoh Hounds, Basenjis, Borzois, Irish Wolfhounds, Lurchers, Salukis, and Scottish Deerhounds.

Sighthounds can run far faster than you ever could; the Greyhound is the fastest sighthound and has been clocked at 40 mph (64 kph). They must be fenced for their own safety because they will otherwise take off at the sight of something that looks like prey. Small pocket pets like mice or rats are not usually safe around them. They make great family pets, and train nicely.

Non-Sporting

This group is hard to categorize in that it's somewhat of a catchall. There's a size range of very small (Tibetan Spaniels) on up to very large (Standard Poodle) with every variation in between. There are coated breeds and smooth breeds, "love everyone in the world" types and those that only love their owners.

When it comes to looks, beauty may be in the eye of the beholder for some breeds in this group. The Bulldog's stalwart frame and the Chinese Shar-Pei's wrinkles stand in stark contracts to the sleek lines of the Dalmatian. Colors run the gamut as well, from the tuxedo-like black and white of the Boston Terrier to the large variety of colors in the Lowchen.

Sporting

Sporting dogs are large dogs who make great companions—as long as you like lots of exercise. Spaniels flush birds up into the air, retrievers carry back dead birds and ducks, pointers and setters first "set" (a kind of physical motion like a sit, but not exactly) and then point at game. Most have drop ears. They have a wide range of colors from golden to tan to black to white. Breeds include Labrador Retrievers, Irish Setters, Brittanys, American Water Spaniels, Cocker Spaniels, English Springer Spaniels, and German Shorthaired Pointers.

Sporting dogs make great companions as long as you like lots of exercise. They are noted for being rather vocal. Likeable and fun to be around, they make wonderful family dogs and are affectionate and smart.

Terriers

Terriers generally are small or medium-sized dogs (exceptions include Airedales and Staffordshire Terriers). Prick or dropped ears are generally the norm. Colors are seen in a full range of solid white, blues (a type of gray), browns, and brindles. Some terriers dislike other animals, including dogs. Many terriers have wiry coats, but some have soft, nonshedding coats. Breeds include Cairn Terriers, Irish Terriers, Kerry Blue Terriers, Miniature Schnauzers, Scottish Terriers, Soft Coated Wheaten Terriers, and West Highland White Terriers.

Busy, feisty, and active, many terriers are the canine version of hyperactive children, so they need a lot of exercise. They make excellent watchdogs. Energetic dogs with a real zest for enjoying life, they usually want to be part of everything going on around them. Some—but not all—are fairly aggressive toward other dogs. Some terriers dislike other animals, and most small pocket pets (like rats) are not safe around them. They are smart, affectionate, and they make great—albeit vocal—family dogs.

Toys

A toy dog is defined as being under 20 pounds (9.0 kg), although most of us think of toys as dogs under 10 pounds (4.5 kg). Some breeds are bred down from larger sizes and look like miniatures of the larger breed, such as an Italian Greyhound. Many require professional grooming, and most have hair that does not shed. Breeds include Toy Poodles, Cavalier King Charles Spaniels, Chihuahuas, Havanese, Maltese, Papillons, Pekingese, Pomeranians, Pugs, Shih Tzu, and Yorkshire Terriers.

Delightful companions fit for a lap, many are smart, stubborn, and rule the roost. Some are notoriously difficult to housetrain. They make great watchdogs because their barking alerts you to intruders. They can usually get sufficient exercise indoors and therefore make excellent pets for apartment dwellers or senior citizens. They are affectionate and great lap warmers. They are usually people-oriented and like regular human companionship.

Working

Working dogs guard property, pull sleds, perform military tasks, and save lives with their search-and-rescue abilities (trained or otherwise). They are usually large, strong dogs. Because of their size and strength, they need owners who can train them correctly, but training is easy because of their native intelligence. Colors range from the solid white of the Kuvasc to the solid black of the Newfoundland. Breeds include Boxers,

Sincerely Scenthounds

Members of this group, which include Bassets, Beagles, Black and Tan Coonhounds, and Bloodhounds, are almost universally friendly and amiable and often form close bonds with their owners. They are primarily interested in one thing—the scent of their prey. Don't think you can safely allow your scenthound off leash (ever); he will follow his nose until he can't remember where he is anymore, and he won't come home. You'll have to go looking for him. Scenthounds can learn to live amicably with their natural prey (rabbits and such) but need to be supervised closely.

The sporting dogs (retrievers, setters, pointers, and spaniels) are, by and large, bundles of relentless energy suitable for active families with big yards, time to play, and lots of energy.

Doberman Pinschers, Great Danes, Akitas, Giant and Standard Schnauzers, Rottweilers, and Saint Bernards.

Working dogs were bred to work, so most of them are unhappy without a job of their own. They do not want to spend their lives on the couch. These intelligent dogs train quickly, but many are independent thinkers. They need significant exercise. Because of their size and intelligence, they are not necessarily good family dogs, even though they are very loyal. They generally require experienced owners and a lot of obedience training.

WHAT NATURAL CHARACTERISTICS CAN YOU LIVE WITH?

Now that you know a little bit about the different charactersitcs of each group, you'll need to pick your way carefully through the breeds, deciding which natural characteristics you can live with. For example, as mentioned earlier, hounds are more interested in following a scent than in following you. (After all, you have no idea where the rabbit went. They do and expect *you* to follow *them*.) Most pet owners would prefer to have a dog who stays reliably at their side. The question becomes, do you want a hound badly enough to make sure he is always safe behind a fence or at the end of a leash? Or let's say you adore Australian Cattle Dogs. How much will it bother you that your pet

is likely to nip the heels of every kid on the block until they are herded into a tight, huddled circle? (This recently happened in my neighborhood. The dog wouldn't let the kids get on the school bus.) Maybe you love the idea of a companionable dog like a Siberian Husky; however, can you live with mounds of dog hair choking your every breath? Are you willing to provide him with all the human and canine friendship he needs? Are you willing to hook him up to a sled and let him run for hours in the bitter cold? (If you're not, don't be surprised when he tears your house apart.) You can, of course, give the dog an equal amount of non-sledding exercise, but Siberians were born to pull sleds. That's what they really like, and nothing quite takes the place of it.

All is not lost, however. You *can* find the right dog for your lifestyle if you are willing to adjust and do your homework.

Talking of Terriers

By and large, terriers are a homogenous, closely related lot. If you decide on a terrier, take note that you are getting a bigger dog than will be apparent from size alone. Most terriers are feisty, playful, incredibly loyal, and not crazy about other dogs. While many are playful with children, they may not be tolerant of toddlers. To maintain coats in top terrier condition, they need to be stripped (hand-plucked of dead hair), which is tedious and time-consuming. Most owners of pets elect to have their dogs clipped instead, an operation that softens and discolors the trademark terrier coat. True to their heritage, count on a terrier to bark and dig: If a perfect lawn and an eerie silence are your cup of tea, forget about most members of this group.

Breed Research

Learn everything you can about the breed in which you are interested *before* you go looking at puppies. Read the breed standard, which is a picture-in-writing of the ideal dog of that breed. Some breed clubs also produce an "illustrated standard," although this is a risky business that depends on interpretation of the written standard, which is always the final arbiter. You will find no

photograph of the perfect dog, for the simple reason that there are no perfect dogs, just approximations of that ever-elusive ideal. I suppose someone has already engineered a computerized perfect dog, but again, that would simply be one person's interpretation of the wonderfully vague breed standard.

Learn how much grooming is required for the breed you want and honestly assess your ability to provide it or have it done for you. For instance, I have always wanted an Afghan Hound, but I have enough trouble combing my own hair, let alone something as silky and long and pretty as that! I must be content to admire the breed from afar. An acquaintance of mine was not so wise. He bought an Afghan when they were at their peak of popularity but had neither the time nor the inclination to maintain the coat. As a result, the animal became a pathetic mass of tangled hair and sore skin. Thankfully, the dog was eventually given away to someone who would care for her properly.

Study the history of the breed. This is a wonderful way to learn its original purpose and what qualities went into making it. Find out what health problems are most common in that breed. This will help you ask screening questions of the breeder.

This sounds as if finding the right dog is hard. It is hard, but not terribly hard, which is often better than having it made too simple. Often, someone just "dumps" a dog on us. Sometimes the abandoned animal turns out to be the "best danged dawg I ever had," but more often, the unfortunate creature, not being the right dog for the household, is neglected or improperly treated. Please don't ever accept a dog who is given or dumped on you, unless you truly want the animal and are willing to care for it.

REASONS NOT TO CHOOSE A BREED

Here are three extremely bad criteria to use when trying to decide on the right breed.

Terrific Toys

These cheerful little dogs need less room than their larger counterparts and are often excellent choices for seniors. They can also be lifted easily in case they need to be carried into a car for a trip to the vet. On the other hand, many toy breeds are hard to housetrain, can be excessively noisy, and have a low level of tolerance for children. All are rather fragile and require careful handling.

Popularity

This reasoning goes, "Wow, everyone has one of these. They must be the best dogs!" While it's true that popular dogs often have character traits that makes their popularity well-deserved, it is also true that great popularity may lead to the consequent development of poorly bred strains. Besides, just because a dog is popular with others does not mean he's the best one for you.

Rarity

Some people take the other tack and look for the rarest breed they can find, just to have something "different." The faultiness of this reasoning is obvious. First of all, rare breeds don't stay rare. You may have purchased your Western Colombian Sloth-Hunting Mastiff, confident of being the first on your block to do so, but it won't last. Others will shortly follow, and, pretty soon, you'll just have another trendy dog. Second, there's often a good reason why rare dogs are rare—they are unsuitable pets for some people due to characteristics or unusual physical requirements. In addition, rare breeds have, almost by definition, a smaller gene pool to work with, which may be associated with a higher incidence of hereditary disease.

Nostalgia

Most people start thinking, "Yep, I had a Brittany as a kid on farm. I think I'll get another one. I'm sure he'll be fine in the apartment." Don't kid yourself—the ideal dog of your childhood may not be right for the adult you have become.

4

BREED QUICK-LOOK GUIDE

I've included this handy, dandy "quick-look" guide to help you narrow down your search for the right breed. Each section contains a pertinent question (or questions) about what you are looking for and then lists breeds you might want to consider, and in some cases breeds you should definitely avoid.

EXERCISE NEEDS/ENERGY LEVEL

Q: Do you want a laid-back breed who doesn't need much exercise?

If the answer is yes, Consider:

The Low-Energy Breeds: These breeds win the awards for "Best Couch Potatoes."

- Basset Hound
- Bulldog
- Clumber Spaniel
- Whippet

OR

The Kings of the Lap: These dogs are happiest inside with their owners, snuggling. (They have also been voted "Most Likely to Be Seen in a Purse on Rodeo Drive.")

- Cavalier King Charles Spaniel
- Chihuahua
- English Toy Spaniel
- Japanese Chin
- Maltese
- Pomeranian
- Yorkshire Terrier

Avoid:

The High-Energy Breeds: These breeds must have regular and vigorous exercise. If they don't get it, they can become destructive.

- American Staffordshire Terrier
- Australian Cattle Dog
- Australian Shepherd
- Basenji
- Border Collie
- Dalmatian
- German Shepherd Dog
- German Shorthaired Pointer
- Irish Setter
- Jack Russell Terrier
- Labrador Retriever
- Shetland Sheepdog
- Siberian Husky

Cavalier King Charles Spaniel

GROOMING

Q: Do you have little or no time for grooming?

If the answer is yes, Consider:

The Wash-and-Wear Dogs: Most of the short-haired breeds are considered easy to groom, with just occasional brushing and bathing needed.

- Beagle
- Boxer
- Chihuahua (smooth-coated variety)
- Dalmatian
- Dachshund (smooth-coated variety)
- French Bulldog
- Greyhound
- Miniature Pinscher
- Pug
- Rottweiler

Avoid:

The High-Maintenance Dogs: If you don't like brushing, fussing, and trips to the groomers, the following dogs (and anything similar) may not be for you.

- Afghan Hound
- Bichon Frise
- Briard
- Cocker Spaniel
- Collie (rough-coated variety)
- Komondor
- Maltese
- Old English Sheepdog
- Poodle
- Puli
- Shih Tzu
- Skye Terrier
- Yorkshire Terrier

Q: Will a lot of shedding bother you?

If the answer is yes, Consider:

The Low Shedders: One thing that is surprising is the number of folks looking for a non-shedding "hypoallergenic" dog—they do not exist. All dogs shed, with the exception of hairless breeds like the Xoloitzcuintle. Some dogs shed less than others, little enough so that people with mild (and I mean mild) allergies aren't bothered, but a person with severe allergies to dog hair ought to forget about getting a dog until she gets some medical help for the allergy. The following dogs are as shed-free as it gets.

- Airedale Terrier
- Basenji
- Bedlington Terrier
- Bichon Frise
- Komondor
- Poodle
- Puli

Avoid:

The Sir Sheds A Lot: These breeds shed more than other breeds.

- Akita
- Alaskan Malamute
- Beagle
- Belgian Malinois
- Chow Chow
- Great Dane
- Great Pyrenees
- Kuvasz
- Newfoundland
- Norwegian Elkhound
- Pomeranian
- Rough Collie
- Samoyed
- Siberian Husky

Yorkshire Terrier

HOUSING/LIVING ARRANGEMENTS

Q: Do you live in an apartment?

If the answer is yes, Consider:

The Apartment Dogs: Most toy dogs are great for apartments, but some people want a slightly bigger dog without giving up their urban ways. Here are some small and mid-sized dogs that can manage apartment living.

- American Eskimo Dog
- Basenji
- Basset Hound
- Bulldog
- Chinese Shar-pei
- Cocker Spaniel
- Dachshund
- Keeshond
- Miniature Poodle
- Schipperke
- Smaller Terrier Group Breeds (with the exception of the Jack Russell)
- Sussex Spaniel
- Toy Group Breeds

OR

The Big Apartment Dogs: Okay, you like big dogs and live in a studio apartment. The good news is that some of the very largest breeds have low energy requirements, and if you give them a daily long walk are perfectly suited to urban life. Make sure they have enough room to turn around in, though.

- Anatolian Shepherd
- Borzoi
- Bullmastiff
- Chow Chow
- Doberman Pinscher
- Great Dane
- Greyhound
- Mastiff
- Newfoundland
- Rottweiler
- Saint Bernard
- Samoyed

Avoid:

The "I Need My Space" Breeds: Some breeds just won't do well in a small living area and need lots of room and an outdoor area in order to thrive.

- Border Collie
- Jack Russell Terrier
- Siberian Husky

Q: Do you live very close to other people, and a barking dog will bother the neighbors?

If the answer is yes, Consider:

The Librarians: These dogs tend toward the quiet side.

- Afghan Hound
- Basenji

Basset Hound

- Borzoi
- French Bulldog
- Greyhound
- Newfoundland
- Shiba Inu
- Whippet

Avoid:

The Barkiest Barkers: At some point in their development, these breeds were bred to bark to warn of intruders or move livestock. They have retained this instinct, and although they can be trained to quiet down a little, they will always be more vocal—it's their nature.

- American Eskimo Dog
- Beagle
- Collie
- Dachshund
- English Foxhound
- Finnish Spitz
- Most Terrier Group breeds
- Newfoundland
- Norwegian Elkhound
- Shetland Sheepdog
- Yorkshire Terrier

Sheltie

Q: Will a strong doggy odor bother you?

If yes, Consider:

Dogs Without the Doggy Smell: You know that doggy smell—the one that precedes some breeds before they enter the room. These dogs are relatively odor-free:

- Basenji
- Dachshund
- Finnish Spitz
- Italian Greyhound
- Pharaoh Hound
- Poodle
- Saluki
- Siberian Husky

- Standard Schnauzer
- Whippet

Q: Does the thought of cleaning up dog drool make you down in the dumps?

If the answer is yes, Avoid:

The Wet and the Hairy: These breeds are well-known for their slobbering, drooling, and general all-around salivating.

- Basset Hound
- Bloodhound
- Bulldog
- Gordon Setter
- Irish Setter
- Mastiff
- Neapolitan Mastiff
- Newfoundland
- Saint Bernard

Q: Do you live in a hot climate?

If the answer is yes, Avoid:

The Can't Handle the Heat Hounds: Most dogs do not handle heat as well as humans, but these breeds are particularly vulnerable.

- Alaskan Malamute
- Bernese Mountain Dog
- Bulldog
- French Bulldog
- Keeshond
- Pekingese
- Pomeranian
- Pug
- Samoyed
- Siberian Husky

French Bulldog

SOCIABILITY

Q: Are you (and other family members) away for most of the day?

If the answer is yes, Consider:

The Home Alone Hounds: These breeds can handle being left alone for longer periods than more sociable animals. (But no breed should be left alone for extremely long periods of time.)

- Afghan Hound
- Basenji
- Belgian Sheepdog (all varieties)
- Briard
- Canaan Dog
- Chihuahua
- Chow Chow
- Doberman Pinscher
- Irish Water Spaniel
- Miniature Pinscher
- Pekingese
- Pomeranian
- Puli

Afghan

Avoid:

The Constant Companions: These breeds thrive on human or canine company and need companionship more than some other breeds.

- Bichon Frise
- Border Terrier
- Clumber Spaniel
- Cocker Spaniel (both American and English)
- Fox Terrier (both Smooth and Wire)
- Golden Retriever
- Japanese Chin
- Newfoundland
- Old English Sheepdog
- Otterhound

Q: Do you have children?

If the answer is yes, Consider:

The Tolerant Dogs: These dogs are good with

kids, friendly to strangers, and relaxed in uncertain circumstances. This does not mean that any of these wonderful, stable pets should be subjected to abuse, but it does mean that they are easygoing, tough cookies.

- Basset Hound
- Bloodhound
- Border Terrier
- Bulldog
- English Setter
- Flat-Coated Retriever
- Golden Retriever
- Mastiff
- Newfoundland
- Scottish Deerhound
- Sealyham Terrier

OR

The All-Around Family Dogs: These breeds have a history of fitting in well with many different types of families.

- American Eskimo Dog
- Beagle
- Bichon Frise
- Boston Terrier
- Boxer
- Collie
- Keeshond
- Labrador Retriever
- Miniature Schnauzer
- Newfoundland
- Poodle
- Pug
- Samoyed
- Shih Tzu
- West Highland White Terrier
- Wire Fox Terrier

OR

Pug

Older Children's Playmates: These breeds are not only tolerant, but playful with children. Some are so playful they can knock over a small child, so always supervise.

- Beagle
- Bernese Mountain Dog
- Boxer
- English Setter
- English Springer Spaniel
- Golden Retriever
- Irish Setter
- Labrador Retriever
- Saint Bernard
- Samoyed
- Siberian Husky
- Standard Poodle

Q: Do you have an active social life?

If the answer is yes, Consider:

Friendly Fidos: Some dogs are friendlier to people than others—these breeds never met a person they didn't like.

- Beagle
- English Setter
- Golden Retriever
- Labrador Retriever
- Irish Setter
- Pug

Avoid:

Shy Guys: Many members of these breeds are shy and require consistent, gentle treatment to bring out the best in them.

- Borzoi
- Cavalier King Charles Spaniel
- Chihuahua
- Greyhound
- Italian Greyhound
- Papillon
- Saluki
- Shetland Sheepdog
- Toy Poodle
- Whippet

Golden Retriever

Q: Do you have other dogs?

If the answer is yes, Consider:

The More the Merrier: These breeds not only like you, but they also enjoy your friends, door-to-door salespeople, visiting missionaries, thieves, and especially other dogs.

- Beagle
- Bichon Frise
- Bloodhound
- Cavalier King Charles Spaniel
- Clumber Spaniel
- English Cocker Spaniel
- Foxhound (both varieties)
- Golden Retriever
- Irish Setter
- Old English Sheepdog
- Siberian Husky

SPORTS AND ACTIVITIES

Q: Do you want a jogging partner?

If the answer is yes, Consider:

The Jogging Partners: These dogs are great company on a jog and can physically handle the effort, if conditioned slowly and properly. Mind the weather though; dogs, like people, have problems handling the heat or cold.

- Airedale Terrier
- Border Collie (but this brainy breed needs so much more)
- Dalmatian
- Doberman Pinscher
- Greyhound
- Irish Setter
- Portuguese Water Dog
- Saluki
- Siberian Husky (but not in the heat)
- Standard Schnauzer
- Weimaraner
- Whippet

Q: Do you want to participate in canine sports?

If the answer is yes, Consider:

The Agility Champions: These breeds excel in agility competitions.

- Australian Shepherd
- Belgian Tervuren
- Boston Terrier
- Border Collie
- Corgi
- Jack Russell Terrier
- Shetland Sheepdog
  OR

The Obedience Champions: While all breeds can participate in formal obedience, take a closer look at the following if you want to become a serious competitor.

- Belgian Sheepdog (all varieties)
- Bernese Mountain Dog
- Bichon Frise

Border Collie

- Border Collie
- Collie
- Doberman Pinscher
- English Springer Spaniel
- German Shepherd Dog
- Golden Retriever
- Labrador Retriever
- Poodle (all varieties)
- Welsh Corgi (both varieties)
- West Highland White Terrier

Q: Do you want a winning show dog?

If the answer is yes, Consider:

The Westminster Winners: Do you have a passion to take it all at Westminster? Don't get an English Foxhound or a Labrador. If you go by the principle "Do what works," choose a breed whose winning ways have captured the judges' eyes and hearts for over a century. With history as our guide, here are your Best Bets.

- Boxer
- English Setter
- English Springer Spaniel
- Miniature Poodle
- Pekingese
- Scottish Terrier
- Smooth Fox Terrier
- Standard Poodle
- Toy Poodle
- Wire Fox Terrier

Q: Do you live near water?

If the answer is yes, Consider:

The Water Dogs: If you live near the water, treat yourself to a breed that can take full advantage of the opportunity to swim.

- American Water Spaniel
- Chesapeake Bay Retriever
- Curly-Coated Retriever
- Flat-Coated Retriever
- Golden Retriever
- Irish Water Spaniel
- Labrador Retriever
- Newfoundland
- Poodle
- Portuguese Water Dog

Collie

TRAINING

Q: Do you have little or no experience training a dog?

If the answer is yes, Consider:

The First-Timers: These dogs are great for first-time owners due to their even temperament and trainability.

- Cavalier King Charles Spaniel
- Golden Retriever
- Labrador Retriever
- Whippet

Avoid:

The Challenging Breeds: These dogs may attempt to wrest control and are only for the most experienced, strong owners. These breeds are all formidable. Some smaller breeds may also attempt to rule the roost but can be more easily controlled.

- Akita
- American Staffordshire Terrier
- Anatolian Shepherd
- Bouvier Des Flandres
- Briard
- Bull Terrier
- Bullmastiff
- Chesapeake Bay Retriever
- Chow Chow
- Doberman Pinscher
- German Shepherd Dog
- Giant Schnauzer
- Komondor

Labrador Retriever

- Kuvasz
- Rhodesian Ridgeback
- Rottweiler
- Saint Bernard
- Standard Schnauzer

OR

The Excitable Breeds: These highly excitable dogs need owners who are patient, relaxed, and can keep their cool during training! They have enough problems with their nerves without having to deal with yours, too.

- Black and Tan Coonhound
- Boxer
- English Toy Spaniel
- Fox Terrier (wire and smooth)
- German Shorthaired Pointer
- Irish Setter
- Norwegian Elkhounds
- Puli
- Vizsla
- Weimaraner

Rottweiler

Puli

PART TWO

THE BREEDS

5

BREED PROFILES

The profiles in this section consist of 173 American Kennel Club (AKC) recognized breeds.

USING THE PROFILES TO CHOOSE YOUR BREED

Every dog is an individual and can defy breed "generalities." What I list in the dog profiles are tendencies, not certainties. There are lethargic Dalmatians and over-excitable Bulldogs. There are aggressive Labradors and pussy-cat Komondorok. In this book we can only generalize, keeping in mind the attendant and necessary evils thereof.

Obviously I did not rely solely upon my own experience in developing these profiles. I have owned dogs all my life, mostly hounds and sporting breeds, with a few toy dogs as well. However, no one person is learned enough to qualify as expert on all breeds. So I have had to rely a good deal on the opinions of people I respect. Of course, my consultants may also be biased. It is an incontrovertible fact that the people who know the most about each individual breed are breeders. But breeders may also be prejudiced not only in favor of their breed over others, but also in favor of certain characteristics they try to produce in their breed. This can account for varying descriptions of character. This is one reason why I did not rely upon breeders only as consultants, but also surveyed experienced pet owners, including people who have no particular attachment to any one breed. They proved to have the most interesting opinions of all. To get an insider's view of the possible problems with a particular breed, examine the breed standard and read between the lines. If the standard says that the breed should never be timid, for example, you can bet that excessive timidity is a problem the breeders are trying to correct.

Personality traits, for example, were assembled from both my own knowledge and with the suggestions of long-time breeders and owners, many of whom quailed at the thought of saying something "negative" about their beloved breed but who bravely did so anyway. No breed is perfect, and no breed is perfect for every family. Skillful training and individual genetic quirks can make important differences in how each dog may react. That being said, the following profiles feature some important considerations you need to make in choosing your dog.

Origin

This refers to the area or region where it is commonly believed the breed originated. Sometimes this is nothing more than a guess, because we simply aren't sure where a breed got its start. For very old breeds, the problem is more complex, because ancient people used different standards to determine what a breed was. For them, a breed was a particular group of dogs that were accomplished at an assigned task. Various members of a herding "breed" might look quite different, something that we still see to some extent in working Border Collies, who often bear scant resemblance to their show counterparts—or even to each other.

Original Purpose

While we are pretty sure of the primary function of many breeds, we do well to remember that many of them had more than one purpose.

Personality

To my mind, nothing is more important than the personality, or character, of the dog you choose. Remember, personality is mostly inherited and thus closely related to breeding. Training can modify, but not alter, the basic character of any dog. Of course, not every person wants the same character in her pet. Some people prefer an adoring lapdog, others an independent partner in play.

Personality is bred into dogs in the same way that instinctive ability is. In fact, ability is largely a function of personality, rather than any special combination of muscles. Gordon Setters have the physical ability to herd sheep—they're just not interested. The personality traits associated with herding ability remain with the herding dog whether there are any sheep around or not.

For an interesting sidelight on the possible defects of your breed's personality, read the breed

Intelligence means different things under different circumstances.

aficionados of each breed always claim that their breed is brilliant.

Sometimes you will note apparently opposite characteristics being assigned to the same breed. There are two possible reasons. One reason may be that there is a wider than usual divergence among individual members of the breed; some, for example, being very serious, others carefree, so I might use both adjectives. In other cases, I received enough contradictory descriptions from my consultants that I decided to play it safe and put down both characteristics.

One problem in trying to ascertain a dog's personality is trying to find out exactly what that character is. There are not only differences between individual dogs, which we expect, and disputes among experts, which we also expect, but there are frequently internal contradictions within sources. In researching this book, I have come upon this phenomenon over and over. In one obviously hypothetical example, the writer asserts that the Northern Flatland Retrieving Moosedog is just jim-dandy with kids; ten pages later, he solemnly warns you against owning one if you have any children under 12 because the Northern Flatland Retrieving Moosedog is unreliable, irritable, aggressive, and very large.

Breed Traits

Under this category, I list many of the important traits a breed may exhibit that could impact an owner's lifestyle. These traits include energy level inside the home, guarding or protection tendencies, watchdog potential, territoriality, weather tolerance, strong doggy odor, and whether they drool or snore.

standard. If the standard says something like, "Should never be shy," it means that shyness is a problem in the breed. The German Shepherd standard informs us that dogs who bite the judge will be disqualified from the show ring. Actually, any dog of any breed who bites the judge is disqualified, but when a standard goes out of its way to mention the possibility, one has to wonder.

I should also state the obvious: Dogs are individuals, and while a certain personality trait may be true of the breed as a whole, it may not apply to a particular dog. With this caveat clearly in mind, it is safe and prudent to generalize about breeds. It would not serve you well to merely remark that every dog is different and that you are basically on your own trying to find a dog whose temperament you can manage.

For the most part, I have left off "intelligent" under personality. All dogs are about as smart as they want to be, and intelligence means different things under different circumstances. While a Bloodhound is unlikely to be an Obedience Trial Champion, he is hard to beat at tracking. Besides,

I have noted cases where dogs are notorious barkers or diggers. While some people want their dogs to warn of visitors, the dogs I have listed as barkers may bark to the point of annoyance. Digging is also usually frowned upon, but many breeds such as terriers and Siberian Huskies dig by nature. (Most dogs dig just for the fun of it, but others do use it as an escape tool). If dogs would only bark when they were digging, of course, owners would be alerted to their nefarious activity and go out to stop it. Sadly, most dogs, even barky ones, are ominously quiet when they dig. I have also occasionally indicated in this section whether members of this breed should be trusted off-leash.

Lastly, in certain cases I note if a particular breed is appropriate for a first-time owner or is best with someone with experience.

Physical Attributes

The physical appearance of a dog is the first thing we see, and, for many people, it's a determining factor. It shouldn't be—at least it shouldn't be a determining factor in favor of a dog, although it could conceivably be the single most important criterion in deciding against a certain breed. Even the dog that looks just right may be all wrong for you.

Size

I give the minimum and maximum average height at the withers for each breed, as well as minimum and maximum acceptable weight. My listing does not always correspond to any particular breed standard, since in some breeds, animals routinely run larger or smaller than this standard. In many breeds, it is very common for show dogs to be larger than field dogs and for pets to be bigger than either.

In most breeds (but not all), males are larger than females. In a few cases, the difference is considerable. (This is called sexual dimorphism and is characteristic of human beings as

Size is just one determining factor in choosing a breed.

well.) If you are buying a puppy and size is critical, ask the breeder if the males are likely to be much larger or heavier than the females.

While most people have a prejudice in favor of a certain-sized dog, we shouldn't let our biases be the sole determinant. For example, many big dogs are not right for small apartments, older people, timid, easily intimated people, or couples with toddlers. Toy breeds carry their own risk factors; many are easily knocked over or dropped by rambunctious youngsters, and a frail elderly person could get hurt tripping over a Basset Hound. There are many exceptions, of course, but common sense tells us to choose a dog of the right size for our needs and ability to handle safely.

Color

I have included all the acceptable colors of each breed. If a breeder tries to sell you a different color from one listed, that color is non-standard and probably not acceptable. If any particular color is preferred, I have so stated. For example, Scottish Terriers come in several colors, although we usually think of them as black. There are, of course, some unconfessed preferences. For example, many show judges prefer a red Chow Chow to a black one, merely because they can see his features more clearly. Other judges have personal preferences. Dappled Dachshunds, for example, were rarely seen because judges did not prefer them. Now they're showing up in the ring again. A lot of show judges seem to like a lemon-and-white or red-and-white Beagle over an equally nice tricolor. You just have to decide what is important to you.

Coat Type and Grooming

I describe the coat type for each breed, including length, double or single coat, and other important descriptors.

The level of grooming maintenance ranges from low/minimal, to moderate, to high. Some people actually enjoy grooming dogs, while other people (like me) would rather be doing something else. Don't select a breed whose grooming requirements are more than you can realistically handle. Some breeds, like terriers, Cocker Spaniels, and Poodles, require regular professional trims to look their best, while others, like Weimaraners and Pointers, are basically wash-and-wear dogs. Of course, if you are planning on showing a dog, the grooming commitment rises exponentially. This is especially true with some breeds whose elaborate coats require hours of professional skill. For example, a show terrier's coat needs to plucked or stripped in a time-consuming process; pet terriers can simply be clipped. Show Yorkies, Old English Sheepdogs, and Maltese have incredibly long and spectacular coats; your lucky pet, however, can get away with a quick trim.

Professional Grooming

Obviously it doesn't hurt to have any dog professionally groomed, especially if he rolls in something horrible. It's also true that no dog really *needs* to be professionally groomed, especially if you yourself are handy with the clippers. For general purposes, however, and assuming that you're like me (not knowing left-handed scissors from right-handed ones), I list those breeds that are commonly taken to the groomers for shaping and trimming.

Shedding

Don't get easy grooming mixed up with allergy potential. People allergic to dog hair often find that terriers and Poodles shed very little, while a Dalmatian or Siberian Husky seems to float in an eternal aura of loose hair. What is shed most often is the undercoat, and dogs with little or no undercoat tend to shed less than dogs with a lot of undercoat. White dogs seem to shed more than dark ones; northern breeds with heavy double coats are supposed to shed only twice a year, but because they no longer live in arctic conditions, they may shed at any time or all the time. Dogs with longer hair, like setters or Afghans, have a longer shed cycle than shorter-haired dogs, so they actually shed less. While I have listed the shedding potential of each breed (from light/minimal, to moderate, to heavy), it's important to remember that shedding is variable within breeds, at least to some degree. Regular grooming and proper nutrition keeps shedding down to its natural minimum.

Health Concerns

Each breed has specific health issues. Many of these diseases are heritable and have developed, almost of necessity, with the rise of specific breeds. Only wild, randomly bred animals are mostly free of dangerous genetic diseases. Responsible breeders are doing their best to eliminate serious genetic problems in their breed, but because many are working with a small gene pool to begin with (a problem that can be exacerbated with so-called line-breeding or inbreeding), it is hard to eradicate all problems. You can do your part by finding out what diseases are in the breed and line you are looking at. Luckily for adopters (as opposed to puppy buyers), many genetic problems show up in very young dogs, and they are not bred. In this section, I have listed the most common health ailments, some by their abbreviations, which can be found in the glossary in the back of this book.

Certain orthopedic problems, like hip and elbow dysplasia, threaten many larger breeds, while toy breeds have a predilection for patellar luxation (loose kneecaps). Eye problems, allergies and skin diseases, and von Willebrand's disease (a bleeding disorder) can be inherited and affect many breeds. Short-snouted or snub-faced dogs are prone to breathing difficulties and respiratory ailments, some of which are so bad that airlines won't permit them to fly. (They snore, too.) Many sighthounds, like Greyhounds and Salukis, are sensitive to anesthesia. As a rule, the heaviest and largest breeds tend to live shorter lives than their smaller cousins. In this section, I list some problems that may affect your breed more commonly. However, most of these problems are fairly rare.

Before being bred, the hips or elbows of breeds vulnerable to dysplasia should be x-rayed and the radiographs examined by the Orthopedic Foundation for Animals (OFA) or PennHip™. OFA makes preliminary readings before the dog reaches two years of age and permanent readings after two years of age. PennHip™, which some veterinarians consider more practical, takes three separate radiographs to check hip joint flexibility.

Eye tests are performed by veterinary ophthalmologists and sent to the Canine Eye Registration Foundation (CERF) for certification. Eye tests must be repeated annually; however, hip x-rays must only be done once unless the breeder chooses to do a preliminary check on a young dog. Tests for many bleeding disorders, including von Willebrand's, can also be performed and affected animals eliminated from the breeding stock.

However, don't let this litany of potential health problems frighten you. Your dog probably will not get any of the diseases listed. The list simply means that these diseases are more common in that breed than in others. In cases where there is genetic predisposition, your dog or his parents should be screened if possible.

Exercise

Exercise needs for each breed are rated as low, moderate, or high. Before you choose a dog, realistically assess how much time you can give to your dog's exercise needs. Any dog who does not get sufficient exercise is likely to develop behavior problems. Energy level can be linked directly to metabolism, which is partly a function of breed. Diet also plays a role, as does climate. The size of the dog is only indirectly linked to exercise needs. Many small dogs need proportionally much more exercise than larger ones, but the toy breeds can usually satisfy their requirements by tearing around your apartment. Some very large breeds, like Saint Bernards and Great Danes, actually do not require nearly as much exercise as you might think. They can even be kept in an apartment, as long as they get a good walk twice a day. On the other hand, setters and pointers need acres of free-range exercise to be kept at their happiest; if given enough room, most of them will self-exercise. Sighthounds, like Deerhounds, Rhodesian Ridgebacks, and Greyhounds, although they need a lot of exercise to keep trim, need stimuli to get

it. They won't just take off on their own around the field. This is true of many other individual dogs as well. Just because you have a fenced-in yard does not mean automatically that your dog will use it to exercise. Many apartment dogs who are walked daily get much more exercise than a perpetually fenced suburban dog.

Housing

Here I indicate whether or not a dog is suited to live an urban lifestyle. Nearly all dogs are fine for the country or suburban home, as long as they are not left outside at night. As a rule, of course, small dogs are better suited to apartments than are large ones. But this is a rule with many exceptions. Certain large dogs are phlegmatic and unflappable enough to thrive in the city, while some small dogs are too energetic or noisy to be ideal urban pets.

Sociability

In this section I note if a certain breed tends to be a one-person dog or bonds to the entire family.

I also note how well the average member of the breed behaves with children. (I am referring to the family's children here. Other children can be classed as strangers.) A dog who is "good with children" means that he is not likely to challenge them for dominance, and that the breed tends to be tolerant. Of course, there are limits to tolerance, and the most even-tempered of dogs can be provoked. Not all breeds that are good with kids are playful or make good companion dogs in the sense that they will play fetch for hours or are safe off a leash. Those qualities are listed elsewhere.

On the other hand, just because I have a breed listed as "not good with children" doesn't mean your family can't own such a dog. It means you have to be careful and be fully committed to socializing your child and your dog. Be prepared to work hard and keep an eye on child-dog interactions until you know for certain they are firm friends.

Interaction with "strangers" is a little different. A stranger is not necessarily a serial killer skulking around the bushes outside your house. A stranger is someone your dog does not know, even if you do. The category includes strange children, so be careful if yours is a breed that doesn't cotton to strangers.

Lastly, I note if the breed is good with other pets, including dogs, cats, and small animals.

Trainability

I categorize trainability as low, average, or high. Trainability has very little to do with intelligence, although the two are often confused. People tend to think that the smartest dogs are the ones who do what we want. These breeds include retrievers and herding dogs who were brought up to follow specific directions and to work closely with humans. However, some dogs were bred to be

Some breeds are very sociable with other dogs.

leaders. They expect you to follow them, not the other way around. In consequence, these independent, highly intelligent animals are sometimes labeled "dumb" because they obey their own instincts rather than your orders. This doesn't mean these breeds can't be trained; however, it often requires more patience and different methods.

Activities

This category contains some important structured activities you might wish to participate in with your dog. Activities include both dog sports and dogs at work. Dogs sports include agility, canine freestyle, carting, coonhound events, earthdog trials, flyball, flying disc events, foxhound events, herding, lure coursing, obedience trials, pointer tests and trials, rabbit hound events, retriever tests and trials, Schutzhund competition, sled dog racing, tracking, and weight pulling, all of which are defined in the glossary at the back of this book. A working dog's activities include acting as assistance dogs, guide dogs, guard dogs, herders and livestock protection dogs, military and police dogs, bomb, drug, and accelerant sniffers, search and rescue dogs, sled dogs, and therapy dogs.

One favorite canine-human occupation of mine is therapy work. Your dog doesn't have to be purebred to participate or have any particular talents beyond controllability, calmness, and quiet friendliness. Most nursing homes, hospitals, and rehabilitation places will welcome your visits, although some require certification from a recognized program like Therapy Dogs International or the Delta Society. Certification programs vary, but many require that your dog complete a full obedience course and a health screen, and be of a certain age (usually one year) and well-groomed and clean. To find out what programs may be available in your area, contact a local nursing home or hospital.

Many breeds are smart enough for obedience but just don't seem to enjoy it. Some get bored by the mindless repetition; others are just too stubborn to find obedience a thrill. That doesn't mean you can't take your Bulldog to obedience trials if you want; in fact, you should. Those events need more fun injected into them, and your charming Bulldog pitted against those serious Labradors, Golden Retrievers, and Border Collies would be a welcome change. The AKC and various breed clubs can offer more information about many of these programs.

All dogs, whether they "do" anything or not, of course, can be great companions. If you're like me, you may want nothing more from your pet than to be a walking companion, good listener, snugglebug, and source of joy. Other people want more. For each breed I have included some activities for which the breed is famous.

Each breed is color coded by its AKC-assigned group.

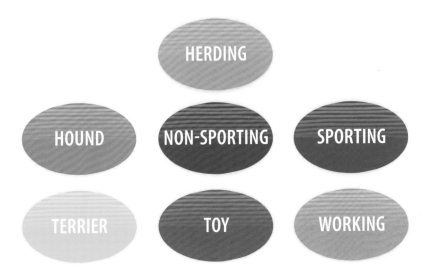

AFFENPINSCHER

Origin: Germany or Eastern Europe, 1600s.
Original Purpose: Killing small vermin; lapdogs.
Personality: Obstinate, loyal, playful, game, lively, busy.
Breed Traits: Alert; a barker. Needs constant companionship. Likes to play. Able to climb. Cannot handle cold. Probably does best with an experienced dog owner.
Physical Attributes: 9 to 12 in (23 to 30.5 cm); 7 to 11 lb (3 to 5 kg). Colors are black, gray, silver, red, beige, black-and-tan.
Coat Type and Grooming: Harsh, dense outercoat. Fairly high maintenance; must be brushed several times a week (even then he looks scruffy, which is part of the charm). He should be professionally shaped and trimmed every three months. Show dogs need to be stripped; pets can be clipped. Slight shedding.

Life Span: 12 to 14 years.
Health Concerns: Hip dysplasia, Legg-Perthes disease, patellar luxation.
Exercise: Moderate to high; small enough to have his exercise needs met easily with daily walks.
Housing: Ideal for apartment life.
Sociability: Tends to bond with one person. Must be carefully supervised with infants and toddlers; gets along fine with gentle, older children. Good with other pets if socialized early.
Trainability: Average; needs consistent training. Can be difficult to housetrain.
Activities: Obedience, agility.

5 Facts

Needs company
Professional grooming
Ideal for apartment life
Bonds with one person
Can be barky

AFGHAN HOUND

Origin: Afghanistan; has been depicted in 4,000-year-old drawings.

Original Purpose: Hunting gazelle, antelope, deer, leopards, and hares; protecting sheep.

Personality: Aloof, pleasant, independent, spirited, dignified (but with a silly streak), gentle if well socialized.

Breed Traits: Tall, elegant, refined, and aristocratic on the outside, but tough and agile on the inside. Despite independent nature, needs human companionship. When bored, can become destructive. Given sufficient running time are usually quite calm, especially as they mature. Can handle cold, wet, or windy weather without difficulty. Great jumpers and can easily leap over boundary fences. Not recommended for first-time owners.

Physical Attributes: 25 to 28 in (63.5 to 71 cm); 50 to 65 lb (22.5 to 29.5 kg); famous for the elegance of his movement. Any color or mixture of colors from pale cream and fawn to deep black.

Coat Type and Grooming: Long, thick, silky; has accurately been described as a "mane." Very high maintenance, including several hours a week of thorough brushing to prevent mats, which form easily and daily. Should not be clipped or trimmed. Older pets are sometimes shaved for their comfort. Professional grooming is highly desirable. Moderate shedding. Adolescent Afghans (12 to 18 months) who are shedding their soft puppy coat and growing in an adult coat need special care.

Life Span: 10 to 12 years.

Health Concerns: Eye problems such as cataracts, allergic dermatitis, cardiomyopathy, hip dysplasia, hypothyroidism. Like other sighthounds, sensitive to anesthesia.

Exercise: High; needs a great amount of exercise in a fenced area.

Housing: Adaptable to apartment life if given sufficient exercise.

Sociability: May bond to one person or remain aloof even to family members. Usually rather fond of the older children in the family. Reserved with strangers. Good with other dogs, especially other Afghans. They have a strong prey drive, and most need to be watched around cats and other small pets.

Trainability: Low to average; can be obstinate; only gentle training methods work with this dog. Early socialization required.

Activities: Lure-coursing, obedience, agility, therapy.

5 Facts

High-maintenance coat
Adaptable to apartment life
Reserved toward strangers
Needs gentle training
Independent

AIREDALE TERRIER

Origin: Yorkshire, England (specifically the river valley of Aire), 1800; Welsh Terrier, Border Collie, and Otterhound possibly in the background.

Original Purpose: Badger, fox, and otter hunting; messenger and ambulance dogs during World War I. (Despite his vaunted loyalty, the Airedale served both the British and the Germans.)

Personality: Protective, good-natured, loyal, independent, brave, people-oriented.

Breed Traits: Fine guard dog. Some individuals can be dominant. Requires a lot of owner interaction. Great swimmers and good trackers, probably due to an early infusion of Otterhound. Not for a timid owner

Physical Attributes: 22 to 24 in (56 to 61 cm); 43 to 60 lb (19.5 to 27 kg); rather square shaped. The tallest and newest of the terrier breeds, he is

often called the "King of Terriers." Colors are black-and-tan or reddish tan with a black or grizzle saddle.

Coat Type and Grooming: Thick, hard, wiry double coat. Moderate to high maintenance. Professional grooming is necessary, especially for a show coat. Most pet owners just clip the coat. Slight shedding.

Life Span: 10 to 14 years.

Health Concerns: Skin allergies (like many terriers), hip dysplasia, von Willebrand's disease and other bleeding disorders, gastritis, retinal dysplasia, low thyroid function.

Exercise: Moderate to high. Sufficient leash walking is enough, but if not given enough exercise becomes extremely restless.

Housing: Apartment life is not ideal, but he is adaptable if given sufficient exercise.

Sociability: Good family dog. Tolerant with kids but needs to be supervised with small children because of his enthusiasm. Will try to dominate other pets; however, with early exposure and socialization, he can learn to get along.

Trainability: Average; needs consistent strong training.

Activities: Hunting, obedience (perhaps the very best in the whole Terrier Group), agility, therapy dog, search and rescue, guard dog, tracking, herding.

5 Facts

Strong minded
Professional grooming
Tolerant with kids
Consistent training
Protective

AKITA

Origin: Japan, 1600s. Was rendered almost extinct during World War II and survived because defiant owners, instead of selling them for meat as was ordered, released them into the mountains, where enough of this tough, hardy breed survived.

Original Purpose: Hunting large game, including wild boar; dog fighting.

Personality: Loyal, stubborn, bold, affectionate, courageous, fearless.

Breed Traits: Powerful, large, graceful. Fiercely protective. Territorial. A superb watchdog who barks only when he suspects something is really wrong. Usually quiet in the house. Can withstand bitter cold, but has a very low heat tolerance. Needs a high fenced-in yard. Should be owned only by a very experienced person; definitely not for first-time dog owners.

Physical Attributes: Females at least 23 in (58.5 cm), usually 24 in (61 cm); males at least 25 in (63.5 cm), up to 28 in (71 cm); 75 to 115 lb (34 to 52 kg). Any color including white, brindle, gray, red, and pinto; usually white underneath.

Coat Type and Grooming: Double coat, a soft inner and coarse, harsh outer coat. High maintenance; daily brushing with a pin brush; no trimming. Professional grooming is optional. They shed profusely twice a year.

Life Span: 10 to 12 and more years.

Health Concerns: Eye problems (PRA, retinal dysplasia), hip dysplasia, OCD, patellar luxation, autoimmune problems.

Exercise: Moderate.

Housing: Best in rural or suburban homes.

Sociability: Very tolerant of the family. Can be intolerant of other children and can show aggression by overprotecting "his" children. Aloof and standoffish with strangers. Aggressive around strange dogs and often aggressive to small animals.

Trainability: Average. Although quick learners, they do have minds of their own, and do not, as a rule, make good obedience dogs. Must be carefully socialized.

Activities: Guard dog, tracking.

5 Facts

**High guarding instinct
Not for beginners
Aloof with strangers
Daily brushing
Quiet in house**

ALASKAN MALAMUTE

Origin: United States; one of the most ancient breeds believed to originate in Alaska.

Original Purpose: Sled dog; hunter of polar bear.

Personality: Affectionate, social, loyal, dominant, tenacious, strong-willed.

Breed Traits: Largest of the sled dogs and really enjoys pulling. Very powerful. Generally well-mannered in the home if properly exercised. Good sense of smell. Can withstand an immense amount of cold, but has very little heat tolerance. Like many northern breeds, he has a wonderful smile. A roamer who should not be let off a leash in an unfenced area. Best with an experienced owner.

Physical Attributes: Typically 23 to 25 in (58.5 to 63.5) and 75 to 85 lb (34 to 38.5 kg); a definite wolf-like appearance. Colors are shades of gray, cinnamon, black with white markings, more rarely pure white.

Coat Type and Grooming: Medium-long, harsh, dense outercoat; soft, oily undercoat. Some come in a "woolly" variety, which, while unacceptable for show dogs, has a certain charm. High maintenance; needs daily brushing, especially when shedding, which is seasonally very heavy. Professional grooming is optional.

Life Span: 11 to 14 years.

Health Concerns: Glaucoma, hip dysplasia, zinc-deficiency skin disorders, chondrodysplasia (dwarfism).

Exercise: High; must have vigorous daily exercise; without exercise, can be hyperactive or destructive or become overweight. Lack of exercise can contribute to problem behaviors like digging and barking.

Housing: Not suited for apartment life; needs a fenced-in yard.

Sociability: Not a one-person dog. Good with older kids, but should be supervised; not good with young children. Very friendly to people, and does not make a good watchdog. Can be quite aggressive toward other dogs, at least until the hierarchy is established; will not like your cat or other small pets.

Trainability: Low to average; does best with a strong, experienced, patient trainer. Will try to dominate his owner unless trained well and early; does not make a good obedience dog; .

Activities: Sledding, skijoring, weight-pulling.

5 Facts

Largest of the sled dogs
Little heat tolerance
Needs plenty of exercise
For experienced trainer
Daily brushing

AMERICAN ENGLISH COONHOUND

Origin: United States, 1900s.
Original Purpose: Coon hunting.
Personality: Outgoing, sociable, confident, pleasant, stubborn.
Breed Traits: Fast. Lives for the hunt. Loves to bark.
Physical Attributes: 21 to 27 in (53.5 to 63.5 cm); 40 to 65 lb (18 to 29.5 kg). Colors are blue and white ticked, red-and-white ticked, tricolor ticked, red-and-white, and white-and-black.
Coat Type and Grooming: Hard, protective, medium length. Minimal care; wash-and-wear coat.
Life Span: 11 to 12 years.
Health Concerns: Hip dysplasia.

Exercise: High; the best exercise for this breed is letting him do what he loves—hunting.
Housing: Best in country where he has room to hunt.
Sociability: Gets along well with others. Pleasant family companion. Gets along well with other dogs.
Trainability: Low to average. Only has interest in hunting, at which he excels.
Activities: Hunting.

5 Facts

Good for apartment life
Loyal
Reserved toward strangers
Needs training
May bark

AMERICAN ESKIMO DOG

Origin: United States, early 1900s; a member of the Northern spitz family of dogs.

Original Purpose: Companion; watch dog; performing artist.

Personality: Loyal, independent, alert, loving, protective, lively.

Breed Traits: Good in cold weather but no heat tolerance. Many are extremely vocal, which means they are barkers. Some individuals can be timid. A good dog for a first-time owner.

Physical Attributes: The breed comes in three accepted sizes: 9 to 12 in (23 to 30.5 cm), 6 to 10 lb (2.5 to 4.5 kg) for Toys; 12 to 15 in (30.5 to 38 cm), 11 to 20 lb (5 to 9 kg) for Miniatures; and 15 to 19 in (38 to 48.5 cm), 20 to 40 lb (9 to 18 kg) for Standards. There is no official weight standard. Snowy white color is preferred; cream or biscuit with white acceptable.

Coat Type and Grooming: Undercoat soft, thick, fairly soft; outercoat mostly longer guard hairs. High maintenance; requires two or three thorough brushings a week. Shed profusely once a year when they "blow their coat." Professional grooming is optional.

Life Span: 14 to 15 years.

Health Concerns: Fleabite dermatitis, urinary tract stones, PRA, seizures, hip dysplasia.

Exercise: High. If he does not get sufficient exercise, this breed can be destructive in the home.

Housing: Adaptable to almost any living situation.

Sociability: Devoted to his family. Generally good with kids. Very reserved around strangers. Usually good with other pets.

Trainability: High; very easily trained.

Activities: Obedience, agility.

5 Facts

Easily trained
Adaptable
Good for first-time owner
Devoted to family
May bark

AMERICAN FOXHOUND

Origin: United States, 1600s. (Of course, there was no United States in the 1600s, so let's just say "the colonies.")

Original Purpose: The American Foxhound is bred for hunting, like his English cousin. However, the American version is more streamlined and faster, because hunters in the Kentucky and Tennessee mountains were looking for a fast dog who could work alone if necessary and startle, chase, and even kill a deer.

Personality: Independent, free-spirited, tough, kind, gentle.

Breed Traits: Fast. Active. Not protective but make excellent watchdogs. Well behaved in the house, even though they were traditionally kept outside in a kennel with other Foxhounds. Possess a great sense of smell. Has a beautiful voice and uses it.

Physical Attributes: 21 to 25 in (53.5 to 63.5 cm); 60 to 70 lb (27 to 31.5 kg). Color is any hound color, which in this case almost always means a tricolor (black, brown, and white). The black is often confined to "saddle" over the back, and the legs and tail tip are usually white.

Coat Type and Grooming: Hard and short coat. Minimal care. Average shedding.

Life Span: 10 to 12 years.

Health Concerns: Hip dysplasia, deafness.

Exercise: High. Needs enormous amounts of exercise in a safe, fenced area.

Housing: Too active to adapt to city life; not suitable for apartment life.

Sociability: Tolerant and loving with children. Reserved with strangers. Like most pack dogs, he is superb around other dogs, as well as most other pets.

Trainability: Average. Easily trained for what he was bred to do; more difficult for obedience work. (In this, he resembles most hounds.)

Activities: Fox hunting, field trials, tracking.

5 Facts

Reserved with strangers
Not good for apartment life
Needs tons of exercise
Good with kids
Independent

AMERICAN STAFFORDSHIRE TERRIER

Origin: United States, 1800s; ancestors, along with the Bulldog, Bull Terrier, and Staffordshire Bull Terrier, came from England.

Original Purpose: Dog fighting; bull-baiting.

Personality: Tenacious, stubborn, happy, affectionate, docile (in the family setting), protective, territorial.

Breed Traits: Excellent watch and guard dog. Can be protective. Some individuals are able to climb almost as well as a cat. Less noisy than many other terriers. If carefully bred and correctly trained, this loyal dog is a wonderful pet; however, he is not for novice or timid owners.

Physical Attributes: 17 to 19 in (43 to 48.5 cm); 40 to 75 lb (18 to 34 kg). Stocky and heavy-boned, with immensely powerful jaws. This breed comes in an amazing assortment of colors, including solid, parti, and brindled.

Coat Type and Grooming: Short, glossy, stiff. Minimal care; a quick brush up with a currycomb will do it. Light to moderate shedding.

Life Span: 12 to 15 years.

Health Concerns: Cataracts, CMO, hypothyroidism, hip dysplasia, thyroid and heart problems.

Exercise: Moderately high; enjoys long walks; will become restless if not given sufficient exercise.

Housing: Can live equally well in town or country.

Sociability: Tends to bond with one person. Usually good with family children (despite his fearsome reputation) if socialized properly. If aroused, however, this breed can be dangerous and should not be around strange children. Protective of family but friendly to strangers if introduced by the owner. Will fight with other dogs; not good with other pets in general.

Trainability: Moderate to high. This breed may challenge his owner for dominance; needs very firm training beginning from the instant you bring him home. Socialization must begin very early.

Activities: Tracking, agility, search and rescue.

5 Facts
Tenacious
Minimal grooming
Bonds to one person
Not good with other pets
Adaptable

AMERICAN WATER SPANIEL

Origin: United States, 1800s; some say the dog's ancestors came to the United States with the Pilgrims.

Original Purpose: An all-purpose hunting dog who can retrieve from both land and water. This is one of the only two sporting breeds developed in the United States.

Personality: Tractable, friendly, sensitive.

Breed Traits: Makes a good watchdog and guard dog. Some can be shy. Some seem to have a strong odor. Must be able to swim to be completely happy.

Physical Attributes: 15 to 18 in (38 to 45.5 cm); 25 to 50 lb (11.5 to 22.5 kg). Colors are solid brown, chocolate, or liver.

Coat Type and Grooming: Close curls. The almost-waterproof coat needs regular care; the tight curls respond better to combing than brushing. Professional grooming is preferable; some trimming required; some shedding.

Life Span: 10 to 15 years.

Health Concerns: Patellar luxation, PRA, detached retina.

Exercise: Moderate. Needs outdoor exercise; much more when young.

Housing: Only adaptable to apartment life with plenty of exercise.

Sociability: Excellent with most people as a rule. Some individuals are not child-friendly; early socialization is important. Usually okay with other pets, although some can be aggressive with strange animals.

Trainability: High. Benefits from basic obedience training.

Activities: Hunting, tracking, obedience.

5 Facts

Loves to swim
Regular coat care required
Needs outdoor exercise
Not for apartment life
Friendly

ANATOLIAN SHEPHERD DOG

Origin: Turkey.

Original Purpose: Flock guarding; wolf hunting; combat dog.

Personality: Serious, laid-back, alert, bold, independent.

Breed Traits: Makes an excellent watchdog and guard dog. Highly territorial. Rather low energy level. A strong, highly experienced owner is essential.

Physical Attributes: 27 in (68.5 cm) minimum for females; 29 in (73.5 cm) minimum for males; 110 to 150 lb (50 to 68 kg). Colors are fawn-and-black; also cream, off-white, brindle, and pinto.

Coat Type and Grooming: Outercoat variable from short and straight to long and wavy; undercoat dense and short. Moderate maintenance; needs brushing once a week. Average shedding.

Life Span: 13 to 14 years.

Health Concerns: Hip and elbow dysplasia, thyroid disease.

Exercise: Average; needs daily exercise.

Housing: Adaptable to most living situations.

Sociability: Good with children; patient but not playful. Extremely suspicious of strangers. Good but dominant with family pets; not always good with strange animals.

Trainability: Low. Because of his propensity to guard, needs early, consistent training.

Activities: Shepherd's dog, guard dog.

5 Facts

High guarding instinct
Moderate coat maintenance
Not for beginners
Low energy
Independent

AUSTRALIAN CATTLE DOG

Origin: Australia, 1800s. Ancestry may include blue-merle Collies, black-and-tan Kelpies, dingoes, and perhaps Dalmatians.

Original Purpose: Cattle herding.

Personality: Hardworking, independent, energetic, alert, courageous.

Breed Traits: Playful but can be nippy, a quality needed to herd cattle. Happiest when working or training. Strong independent character means he is best with experienced owners.

Physical Attributes: 17 to 20 in (43 to 51 cm), 35 to 45 lb (16 to 20.5 kg). Colors are red speckled, blue or blue-mottled; puppies are born white.

Coat Type and Grooming: Straight outercoat, short dense undercoat. Minimal care; a good brushing once a week is sufficient. Moderate shedding.

Life Span: 10 to 13 years.

Health Concerns: Eye problems (PRA, cataracts), deafness, hip dysplasia.

Exercise: Very high; a tireless working dog.

Housing: Would not do well in an apartment; needs lots of space to meet his high exercise needs.

Sociability: Needs to be supervised with children. Suspicious of strangers. Suspicious of and dominant to other dogs; will chase cats.

Trainability: Extremely high; positive reinforcement works best with this energetic breed.

Activities: Cattle herding, herding trials.

5 Facts

Hardworking
Not for apartments
Minimal grooming
Suspicious of strangers
Tireless

AUSTRALIAN SHEPHERD

Origin: United States, 1800s. Despite the name, these are American dogs.

Original Purpose: Herding livestock.

Personality: Enthusiastic, good-natured, loving, hardworking, even-tempered.

Breed Traits: Active and agile. Needs a job to do. Can be hyperactive in the house. Experienced owner recommended.

Physical Attributes: 18 to 23 in (45.5 to 58.5 cm); 40 to 65 lb (18 to 29.5 kg). Comes in a wide array of exciting colors, including an overall coloration of black, red, blue or red merle; may have a white blaze and white markings on the chest, neck, and legs. Copper markings on face and legs are permitted.

Coat Type and Grooming: Medium-length double coat; can be straight or wavy. High maintenance; needs daily grooming. Heavy shedding.

Life Span: 12 to 14 years.

Health Concerns: Hip dysplasia, eye problems (cataracts, PRA, Collie eye anomaly), deafness, von Willebrand's, thyroid disease.

Exercise: Very high. (They were bred to handle an entire herd of sheep, after all.)

Housing: Does not do well in an apartment; needs lots of space to meets his high exercise needs.

Sociability: Bonds to whole family. Good with children, although some dogs may try to herd them by nipping. Aloof with strangers. Good with other dogs; needs socialization with smaller pets.

Trainability: High; happiest when working or training.

Activities: Herding, agility, obedience.

5 Facts

High exercise needs
Not for apartments
High-maintenance coat
Bonds to whole family
Needs a job to do

AUSTRALIAN TERRIER

Origin: Australia, 1900s. Background includes Dandie Dinmont, Irish, and Yorkshire Terriers.

Original Purpose: Hunting mice and rats; tending sheep.

Personality: Plucky, extroverted, alert, brave, sensible, adaptable.

Breed Traits: Energetic and active. Good watchdog, although not protective. More dependent than some other terriers. Quiet (for a terrier) but has a loud bark. Likes to dig.

Physical Attributes: 10 to 11 in (25.5 to 28 cm); 12 to 18 lb (5.5 to 8 kg); one of the smallest terriers; has a spotted tongue. Colors are blue saddle and tan body, blue black, or silver black with tan, sand, or red markings.

Coat Type and Grooming: Harsh, long double; soft topknot. Medium to high maintenance; needs brushing two or three times a week; hair in eyes may need to be plucked; frequent bathing is recommended. Professional grooming is recommended, including monthly trimming and stripping for show dogs. Light shedding.

Life Span: 13 to 14 years.

Health Concerns: Legg-Perthes.

Exercise: Moderate to high.

Housing: Adapts well to apartment life if given enough exercise.

Sociability: Tends to bond to one person. Good with children if socialized with them; however, can be snappy when irritated. Reserved with strangers. Does well with other pets if raised with them; may be same-sex aggressive.

Trainability: Average to high; needs firm obedience training.

Activities: Earthdog trials, agility.

5 Facts

Energetic
Reserved with strangers
Good watchdog
Bonds to one person
Adaptable

BASENJI

Origin: Central Africa (Congo).

Original Purpose: Vermin hunter; driving game into a net.

Personality: Cheerful, self-reliant, affectionate, playful, curious, obedient.

Breed Traits: Alert; makes a very good watchdog, although not protective. Some poorly bred individuals are aggressive. Can be hyperactive in the house. Needs to stay on a leash when not in a secure fenced area. Although known as a "barkless" dog, he does make noises, including wails, chortles, and yodels. No cold tolerance. Considered both a sighthound and a scenthound, making him unique among dogs. Not ideal for novice owners.

Physical Attributes: 16 to 20 in (40.5 to 51 cm); 22 to 25 lb (10 to 11.5 kg). Noted for his unique ringtail. Expression looks either worried or quizzical, depending on your viewpoint. Chestnut red is by far the most common color, but can also come in black, black-and-tan, and brindle. All colors should have white feet, chest, and tail-tip.

Coat Type and Grooming: Short, silky. Minimal care needed; a quick brushing once a week will suffice. These dogs are very clean, often grooming themselves like a cat. Very light shedding.

Life Span: 10 to 13 years.

Health Concerns: Eye problems (PRA), hernias, Basenji enteropathy, anemia, kidney problems (Fanconi syndrome, peculiar to Basenjis and people).

Exercise: Medium to high; can be destructive if not given sufficient exercise.

Housing: Most are not suited for apartment living, unless given frequent long walks.

Sociability: Loves kids; however, not always good with very young children and should be supervised (only because he can be almost too playful). Aloof with strangers. May try to dominate other pets.

Trainability: Low; although responsive when properly motivated, his attention is bound to lag with repetitive training. Needs early socialization.

Activities: Lure-coursing, agility.

5 Facts

Clean
Reserved toward strangers
Low trainability
Not for novice owner
"Barkless"

BASSET HOUND

Origin: France, mid-1500s. Bred down from the Bloodhound.

Original Purpose: Hunting hares and rabbits. Bred to accompany pedestrian (as opposed to mounted) hunters.

Personality: Friendly, calm, placid, devoted, stubborn, mild.

Breed Traits: A fine watchdog but not protective. Well suited to a family with a sense of humor. Low energy. Second only to their ancestor the Bloodhound in their ability to scent; despite (or because of) this trait, they enjoy rolling in foul-smelling messes. Drool a lot and howl delightfully, although are usually quiet in the house. Cannot be trusted off leash. Typical hound smell.

Physical Attributes: 13 to 15 in (33 to 38 cm); 40 to 80 lb (18 to 36.5 kg); sturdy, with ears extending beyond tip of nose. Any hound color: red and white, tricolor, lemon-and-white.

Coat Type and Grooming: Medium-short but very dense. Moderate to high maintenance; weekly brushing important. Eyes and ears need extra care; people who don't like the houndy smell should bathe their Bassets regularly. Average shedding.

Life Span: 12 to 13 years, but some much longer.

Health Concerns: Eye ailments (glaucoma, PRA), bleeding disorders (thrombopathia, von Willebrand's), thyroid problems, allergies, orthopedic problems (elbow dysplasia, herniated disk, OCD, panosteitis), obesity.

Exercise: Moderate; if not given enough, the Basset gains weight rapidly; has more endurance than you might think.

Housing: Can adapt to apartment life if walked regularly.

Sociability: Loves everyone. Excellent with children, although not very playful. Good with all other pets.

Trainability: Low; responds best to food rewards. Like many other hounds, Bassets can be stubborn and slow to housetrain, so it is important to begin housetraining early.

Activities: Tracking, field trials, rabbit hunting.

5 Facts

Adaptable
Typical hound smell
Low energy
Loves everyone
Stubborn

BEAGLE

Origin: England, 1000–1300s. Some people trace the Beagle's ancestry to Egypt; others to Greece. More commonly it is believed that Beagle ancestors came to England with William the Conqueror and were probably bred down from the Foxhound.

Original Purpose: Rabbit trailing.

Personality: Independent, merry, gentle, willful, energetic, stubborn.

Breed Traits: Sturdy, athletic, and highly energetic. Some individuals are excessively shy. If given company and exercise, they can be quiet in the house. Not a good breed to leave home alone all day; they are pack (both human and animal) dogs and can suffer severe separation anxiety if left alone. Not territorial, but they bark at everything. Can escape yards by digging under fences. Can never be let off leash outside a fenced area—they will just follow their excellent noses and run off. Fine howlers.

Physical Attributes: Two sizes (for show purposes): 13 in (33 cm) and 15 in (38 cm); 17 to 35 lb (7.5 to 16 kg); this division has been in place since 1890. The smallest of the scenthounds. Any true hound color allowed, such as black-and-tan, red-and-white, or lemon-and-white; white tip on tail preferred.

Coat Type and Grooming: Short and hard. Minimal care. Ears need special attention. Year-round shedding, with extra in spring.

Life Span: 12 to 16 years.

Health Concerns: Eye problems (glaucoma, PRA, cataracts, ectropion), heart disease (pulmonic stenosis), allergies, ear infections, disc problems, cancer, gastritis, epilepsy, deafness, anemia, obesity.

Exercise: Average to high, depending partly on whether or not they come from show stock. Field trial and show Beagles are much more laid back than hunting stock. Beagles who don't get their exercise needs met become hyperactive in the house.

Housing: Not really suitable for apartment living, but it is possible if given generous amounts of exercise.

Sociability: Sociable to everyone. One of the best dogs with children, especially if exposed when young. Excellent with other pets; in fact, they do much better with other dogs as companions.

Trainability: Average. They can be difficult to train; however, they are strongly food-motivated, so positive reinforcement using treats can work well. They do best with obedience training. They take a long time to housetrain.

Activities: Hunting (rabbits, pheasant), tracking, flyball, agility, field trials.

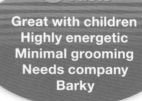

5 Facts

Great with children
Highly energetic
Minimal grooming
Needs company
Barky

BEARDED COLLIE

Origin: Scotland, 1800s. Closely related to the Old English Sheepdog and Border Collie.

Original Purpose: Sheepherder.

Personality: Friendly, lively, sweet-natured, cheerful, joyful, exuberant.

Breed Traits: Needs close human companionship. Has a sense of humor.

Physical Attributes: 20 to 22 in (51 to 56 cm); 45 to 55 lb (20.5 to 25 kg). They seem to bounce when they run. One source I consulted claimed that one of the Beardie's most attractive features was his keen, observant eyes—this may be so; unfortunately, they are usually covered up by hair. Colors are any shade of gray or chocolate; may have white chest, blaze, and tail tip. Some individuals have tan markings.

Coat Type and Grooming: Thick double coat with flat, harsh, shaggy outercoat and a soft furry undercoat. High maintenance; needs very thorough brushing twice a week to keep coat from matting. Professional grooming is recommended, but pet dogs can be clipped down. Heavy shedding.

Life Span: 12 to 15 years.

Health Concerns: This is a healthy breed on the whole; some problems with hip dysplasia, epilepsy, intestinal disease.

Exercise: Moderate to high; tend to slow down as they mature.

Housing: Apartments are not ideal. They do best with a lot of running room, especially when young.

Sociability: Good with children but may try to herd them; may be a bit rambunctious for toddlers. Friendly to strangers. Good with other pets, especially with their own breed; may try to chase small animals.

Trainability: Moderate.

Activities: Herding, agility.

5 Facts

Exuberant
Needs room to run
High-maintenance coat
Good with children
Friendly

BEAUCERON

Origin: France, 1500s.

Original Purpose: Herding sheep and cattle; guard dog.

Personality: Strong, courageous, resilient, even-tempered, clever, versatile, watchful, affectionate, loyal, spirited.

Breed Traits: Active. Serious working dog. Outstanding guard dog. Not for novice owners.

Physical Attributes: 24 to 28 in (61 to 71 cm); up to 110 lb (50 kg). Colors are black-and-tan, harlequin (gray, black, tan).

Coat Type and Grooming: Coarse, dense, close-lying outercoat and short, fine, dense, downy undercoat. Minimal care; his coat is naturally weather-proof. Heavy shedding of the undercoat.

Life Span: 10 to 12 years.

Health Concerns: Bloat and hip dysplasia.

Exercise: High; active and athletic, they need a challenging physical regimen.

Housing: Best in rural or suburban; these dogs need lots of space.

Sociability: Very loyal family dog. Great with children if socialized early. Reserved with strangers. May be aggressive with other dogs.

Trainability: High, but not a dog for a novice trainer. Trainers often find that they need to keep up with him and not the other way around.

Activities: Police work, tracking, herding trials.

5 Facts

Loyal
Not for apartments
Serious working dog
Not for novice owners
Minimal grooming

BEDLINGTON TERRIER

Origin: Northumbria, 1800s. The breed takes its name from its English town of origin.

Original Purpose: Created by miners to help kill rabbits, foxes, and weasels.

Personality: Companionable, mild, stubborn.

Breed Traits: Much more mellow than other terriers, although still energetic. Makes a good watchdog but is not protective. Calm in the house if properly exercised. Some are barky.

Physical Attributes: 15 to 17 in (38 to 43 cm); 17 to 23 lb (7.5 to 10.5 kg); graceful, with a Whippet-like arched topline. Colors are blue, liver, or sandy—although Bedlingtons look basically off-white. Born black or dark brown.

Coat Type and Grooming: Short, "linty," and curly. High maintenance; requires daily brushing. Professional grooming is required, especially for show dogs, and every couple of months to shape the coat. Almost no shedding.

Life Span: 15 to 16 years.

Health Concerns: Copper toxicosis, PRA, cataracts.

Exercise: Moderate; able to self-exercise.

Housing: Suited to urban life but is adaptable to any living situation.

Sociability: Tends to bond with one person. Fairly good with children if socialized early. May be tolerant when socialized to other pets but aggressive to strange dogs.

Trainability: Low to moderate.

Activities: Earthdog trials, obedience.

5 Facts

Companionable
Mellower than other terriers
Professional grooming
Bonds to one person
Adaptable

BELGIAN MALINOIS

Origin: Belgium, 1800s.
Original Purpose: Stock herding.
Personality: Protective, serious, energetic, confident, devoted, alert.
Breed Traits: Hardy, active. Needs a strong, experienced owner to avoid becoming aggressive.
Physical Attributes: 22 to 26 in (56 to 66 cm); 60 to 80 lb (27 to 36.5 kg). Colors are rich fawn to mahogany with black tips on hairs; black mask and ears.
Coat Type and Grooming: Hard, straight coat somewhat shorter than that of the German Shepherd; dense undercoat. Average maintenance. Weekly brushing required; professional grooming is not needed. Heavy shedding once a year.
Life Span: 10 to 12 years.

Health Concerns: Cancer, skin diseases, hip and elbow dysplasia, PRA, epilepsy.
Exercise: High; needs lots of exercise and mental stimulation.
Housing: Not suited to apartment life; needs room to exercise.
Sociability: Good with gentle children. Usually friendly to strangers, although some are shy or reserved. Not always good with other pets; has a strong prey drive and should be socialized early with cats.
Trainability: Extremely high.
Activities: Police work, herding, search and rescue, tracking, protection, service dog, obedience, jogging companion, Schutzhund.

5 Facts

For experienced owners
Not for apartments
Needs mental stimulation
Highly trainable
Active

BELGIAN SHEEPDOG

Origin: Belgium, 1800s.
Original Purpose: Herding.
Personality: Protective, devoted, playful, biddable, reserved, versatile.
Breed Traits: Active. Needs plenty of attention and a job to do. Not for beginners.
Physical Attributes: 22 to 26 in (56 to 66 cm); 60 to 65 lb (27 to 29.5 kg). Color is black with or without white markings.
Coat Type and Grooming: Long, dense, with an extremely dense undercoat. High maintenance; brushing required at least three times a week. Professional grooming is optional. Heavy shedding once a year.

Life Span: 10 to 12 years.
Health Concerns: Seizures, eye problems.
Exercise: High; this dog needs a lot to do.
Housing: Not suited to apartment life; needs room to exercise.
Sociability: Good with gentle children. Aloof with strangers. May not be good with small pets.
Trainability: Extremely high.
Activities: Herding, guard dog, obedience, sledding, agility, tracking, Schutzhund.

5 Facts

Highly trainable
Not for apartments
High-maintenance coat
Not for novice owners
Needs a job to do

BELGIAN TERVUREN

Origin: Belgium, 1800s.

Original Purpose: Stock herding.

Personality: Alert, protective, energetic, self-assured, loyal, honest.

Breed Traits: Watchful and protective of his family. Requires a lot to do and a lot of companionship. Not recommended for novice owners.

Physical Attributes: 22 to 26 in (56 to 66 cm); 60 to 65 lb (27 to 29.5 kg). Colors are shades of red, mahogany, fawn, gray with black overlay (tip of each hair black), and a black mask.

Coat Type and Grooming: Dense double coat longer than that of the Malinois. Moderate to high maintenance. Professional grooming is optional. Heavy shedding once a year.

Life Span: 10 to 12 years.

Health Concerns: Epilepsy.

Exercise: High.

Housing: Not suited to apartment life; needs room to exercise.

Sociability: May be a one-person dog. Playful with children but may try to herd them. Tends to be suspicious of strangers.

Trainability: Very high; needs firm (but not harsh) handling, as well as early socialization.

Activities: Police dog, search and rescue, herding trials, Schutzhund.

5 Facts

Highly trainable
Not for apartments
High-maintenance coat
Not for novice owners
Protective

BERNESE MOUNTAIN DOG

Origin: The Bern canton of Switzerland. This is still the most popular dog in Switzerland—you see them everywhere, wearing their famous "cow" collars.

Original Purpose: Cart-pulling; guard dog; cattle and sheep drover.

Personality: Good-natured, cheerful, easygoing, kind, sweet, devoted.

Breed Traits: Excellent watchdog but not protective. Exceptionally tolerant of cold. Suffer in hot weather; not well suited to a warm climate. This is a slow-maturing breed.

Physical Attributes: 23 to 27 in (58.5 to 68.5 cm); 75 to 120 lb (34 to 54.5 kg). Tricolor; white on chest, paws, and tail.

Coat Type and Grooming: Soft, silky, wavy; medium long. High maintenance; daily grooming required. Ears and nails need special care. Average shedding; the Berner "blows his coat" twice a year.

Life Span: 8 to 10 years.

Health Concerns: Orthopedic problems (hip and elbow dysplasia, OCD), histiocytosis, cancer, aortic stenosis.

Exercise: Low to moderate.

Housing: Adaptable to apartment living with adequate exercise.

Sociability: Enjoys the whole family but often forms a special attachment to just one family member. Excellent with children but can topple a toddler, so must be supervised. Usually very good with people, but some individuals are shy and reserved with strangers. Generally very good with other dogs and pets.

Trainability: Very high; this is a sensitive, quick-to-learn breed.

Activities: Therapy dog, drafting.

5 Facts

Easygoing
Good with other pets
Daily grooming
Devoted to children
Learns quickly

BICHON FRISE

Origin: France or Tennarife (Canary Islands of Spain), 1300s.

Original Purpose: Companion (the word "bichon" is French for "lapdog"); performing dogs.

Personality: Playful, perky, friendly, cheerful, happy-go-lucky, affectionate.

Breed Traits: Craves human companionship and should not spend long hours alone; requires a lot of attention. Sturdy. Can be active in the house.

Physical Attributes: 9 to 11 in (23 to 28 cm); 7 to 12 lb (3 to 5.5 kg). Adult Bichons are always white, but puppies up to 18 months old can have traces of buff, cream, or apricot.

Coat Type and Grooming: Fluffy, fine, and somewhat silkier than a Poodle's, although it has Poodle-like curls that are best groomed with a slicker brush; outercoat coarser and curlier. Very high maintenance; requires grooming every day, even for a pet coat. Frequent bathing is important, and eyes need special care. Professional grooming is recommended every month for a show coat. Does not shed, but dead hair from undercoat must be combed out to prevent mats and hot spots.

Life Span: 13 to 15 years.

Health Concerns: Skin problems (allergies), ear infections, eye problems, bladder stones, patellar luxation. The breed also benefits from a different vaccination protocol than is common for most breeds.

Exercise: Low. Gets along on only a little exercise but can be active in the house.

Housing: Ideal in any situation; especially suited for apartment life.

Sociability: Excellent with older kids, but a few are too sensitive for toddlers. Friendly to strangers. Very good with all other pets.

Trainability: High; this breed is excellent at picking up tricks. Some have housetraining problems.

Activities: Obedience, agility, therapy dog.

5 Facts

Craves companionship
Good with other pets
No shedding
Playful
Low exercise

BLACK AND TAN COONHOUND

Origin: United States, 1700s.

Original Purpose: Hunting raccoon, opossum, and other climbing game, as well as deer.

Personality: Amiable, stubborn, fearless, gentle, eager, loyal.

Breed Traits: Strong, alert, agile. Some are protective. Powerful hunting instinct. Tendency to bay or howl. Quiet in the house if well exercised. Like other hounds not reliable off leash, and will leave you to go hunting if left outside a fenced area.

Physical Attributes: 23 to 27 in (58.5 to 68.5 cm); 50 to 80 lb (22.5 to 36.5 kg). Color is black with tan markings above the eyes, muzzle, chest, and legs.

Coat Type and Grooming: Short and dense. Minimal care, but need their ears cleaned regularly. Average shedding.

Life Span: 10 to 12 years.

Health Concerns: Hip dysplasia, eye problems (PRA, juvenile cataracts, entropion).

Exercise: Moderate to high.

Housing: Not suited for apartment life; enjoys the outdoors.

Sociability: Very gentle but basically not interactive with children. Reserved or suspicious with strangers. Good with other dogs; some can be testy, especially with cats.

Trainability: Low to medium, depending on what you are trying to train him to do. If it's hunting raccoons, it's easy; if it's obedience work, it's not.

Activities: Hunting, coonhound trials.

5 Facts

Not for apartments
Minimal grooming
Powerful hunting instinct
Gentle with children
May howl or bay

BLACK RUSSIAN TERRIER

Origin: Russia, 1900s.

Original Purpose: Military security; protection.

Personality: Protective, balanced, calm, confident, loyal, highly intelligent, sensitive, enthusiastic.

Breed Traits: Large, agile, tough, athletic. Boisterous outdoors, he is calmer inside the home when given enough exercise. Loves the snow; his weatherproof coat can withstand a variety of environments. Strong guarding instincts. Not recommended for novice owners.

Physical Attributes: 25 to 30.5 in (64 to 77 cm); 80 to 143 lb (36.5 to 65 kg). Colors are black, black with gray hairs.

Coat Type and Grooming: Hard, rough, ample, broken outercoat and thick, soft undercoat; rough, brushy mustache and beard. High maintenance. The distinctive mop of hair over his eyes and under his chin (the beard) needs to be brushed, and the coarse fur on the body is typically hand-stripped. Professional grooming is desirable.

Life Span: 10 to 12 years.

Health Concerns: Bloat and hip dysplasia.

Exercise: High; this large, athletic dog needs several daily jaunts to stay in shape.

Housing: Can do well in an apartment if properly exercised.

Sociability: Loyal to their families. They love children. Aloof with strangers. Amenable to most other animals so long as they are socialized to them from an early age.

Trainability: High, but not a dog for beginners. Training must be undertaken with a loving, but firm, hand. Obedience training and early socialization are necessary to help curb any overly protective instincts.

Activities: Agility, obedience, rally, tracking, police dog.

5 Facts

High grooming
Strong guarding instincts
Needs experienced trainer
Devoted to children
Loves the snow

BLOODHOUND

Origin: Belgium, 700s, and later the rest of Europe and England, although this breed's ancestors can be traced back more than 2,000 years. Once called St. Hubert's Hound, it was a favorite of French royalty.

Original Purpose: Hunting and trailing.

Personality: Gentle, solemn, sensitive, dignified, affectionate, kind.

Breed Traits: Deep, frightening bark may scare away strangers. In certain circumstances, can be protective, although he must be exceedingly provoked. Some are shy. Lots of drool, lots of slobber. This largest and strongest of all scenthounds is tireless but quiet, even lazy, in the house if given enough exercise; older dogs especially are quite calm. Has the best sense of smell of any dog. Can never be let off a leash outside a secure fenced area; once on a trail, they can't be called off. Best with an experienced owner.

Physical Attributes: 23 to 27 in (58.5 to 68.5 cm); 80 to 110 lb (36.5 to 50 kg). Colors are black and tan, red and tan, tawny.

Coat Type and Grooming: Short, thin, and smooth. Minimal care; however, they need their faces and ears cleaned regularly. Moderate shedding, mostly seasonal.

Life Span: 7 to 10 years.

Health Concerns: Bloat, hip and elbow dysplasia, OCD, eyelid problems, ear infections, skin infections.

Exercise: Moderate to high; these active dogs need plenty of outdoor exercise.

Housing: Not suited for apartment life; enjoys the outdoors.

Sociability: Very sociable in the family. Quite tolerant of children but are not playful; they may be too big for toddlers. Enjoy meeting new people but are not always demonstrative. Very good with other pets, although a few may chase small animals.

Trainability: Low to moderate; they take naturally to their ancestral task of man-trailing but are difficult to train in obedience work. They need careful training and are best with only the most savvy of dog owners.

Activities: Police work, tracking, search and rescue.

5 Facts

Needs outdoor exercise
Good with other pets
Minimal grooming
Great scenting ability
Drools

BLUETICK COONHOUND

Origin: United States, 1900s.

Original Purpose: Hunting raccoons.

Personality: Devoted, intelligent, easygoing, charming, loyal, hardworking.

Breed Traits: Cannot be trusted off leash in an open area. Quiet in the house if well-exercised.

Physical Attributes: 21 to 30 in (53 to 76 cm); 45 to 100 lb (20.5 to 45.5 kg). Color is dark blue, thickly mottled with black spots.

Coat Type and Grooming: Smooth, glossy, fairly coarse, lying close to the body. Minimal care, but their ears need to be regularly checked for infection. Moderate shedding.

Life Span: 10 to 12 years.

Health Concerns: Ear infections.

Exercise: High; vigorous daily exercise and the opportunity to hunt are needed.

Housing: Not suited for apartment life.

Sociability: Fine family dog. Friendly with children. Thrives in the company of other dogs; cannot be trusted around small pets.

Trainability: Low to average. A natural for the hunt but has tendency toward stubbornness when not in the field.

Activities: Hunting, coonhound trials.

5 Facts

High exercise
Good with other dogs
Minimal grooming
Not for apartment living
Hardworking

BORDER COLLIE

Origin: Great Britain.

Original Purpose: Shepherding.

Personality: Workaholic, excitable, quick thinking, dependable, alert, intuitive.

Breed Traits: Hardy, extremely agile. While I promised not to evaluate the intelligence of dogs, no one denies that the Border Collie is one of the most brilliant of all breeds. (That's one reason I don't own one. I make it a firm policy not to own a dog smarter than I am.) Requires a very experienced owner.

Physical Attributes: 19 to 22 in (48.5 to 56 cm); 32 to 50 lb (14.5 to 22.5 kg). Colors are black-and-white, brown, sable, and merle; most have a white blaze; many have tan markings.

Coat Type and Grooming: Two types: Both are double and dense. One type has moderately long outercoat and the other has shorter hair. Fairly high maintenance; needs frequent hard brushing to remove dead hair. Professional grooming is optional. Average shedding.

Life Span: 11 to 14 years.

Health Concerns: Eye problems (PRA, Collie eye), seizures, deafness, hip dysplasia.

Exercise: Extraordinary; requires an athletic, motivated owner. Don't even consider this breed unless you are training for the Olympics, are an obedience or agility aficionado, or have a large herd of sheep that need regular rounding up; otherwise, you will end up with a neurotic dog. It is not enough for the Border Collie to just move around; he has to think and solve problems in order to be happy.

Housing: Under no circumstances should this breed be kept in an apartment—he really needs to live where there is plenty of room to run.

Sociability: Good with children but may try to herd small ones and nip them in the process. Very reserved toward strangers. Gets along with other dogs but may try to herd small animals.

Trainability: Highly trainable but needs strong, early socialization to prevent dominance or shyness.

Activities: Herding trials, agility, obedience, tracking, flying disc, flyball.

5 Facts

Quick thinking
High exercise requirements
Frequent brushing
Not suited for apartments
Workaholic

BORDER TERRIER

Origin: Border region (Cheviot Hills) between England and Scotland, 1700s; related to the Dandie Dinmont.

Original Purpose: Catching foxes and later other small game.

Personality: Loyal, alert, affectionate, inquisitive, friendly, assertive.

Breed Traits: Rugged, racy, very active. Not protective, but a good watchdog. Some individuals are timid. Many are barky and tend to be diggers.

Physical Attributes: 11 to 15 in (28 to 38 cm); 11 to 16 lb (5 to 7.5 kg). Colors are red, tan, wheaten, grizzle-and-tan, blue-and-tan; dark muzzle.

Coat Type and Grooming: Wiry flat outercoat, short dense undercoat. Fairly high maintenance; once-a-week brushing, some trimming on the head, legs, neck, and tip of tail. Show dogs need to be handstripped every 6 months; clipping is acceptable for pets. Light to moderate shedding.

Life Span: 12 to 15 years.

Health Concerns: Legg-Perthes, patellar luxation, eye problems (cataracts, PRA), hip dysplasia.

Exercise: Moderate to high.

Housing: Adaptable to apartment life but prefers the country.

Sociability: Very attached to his owner. Excellent with children if well socialized. Good all-around family dog; enjoys being around people. Usually good with other dogs of the opposite sex, also good with family cats if conditioned early; may chase small or unknown animals.

Trainability: High; obedience classes are very important for this breed. They are easy to housetrain.

Activities: Earthdog trials, hunting, tracking, agility.

5 Facts

Rugged
Attached to family
Above-average grooming
Adaptable
May bark

BORZOI

Origin: Russia, Middle Ages.

Original Purpose: Hunting of wolves and hares; often hunted in packs.

Personality: Docile, calm, gentle, aloof, independent, courageous.

Breed Traits: Elegant, graceful. Quiet in the house. They handle cold very well. An escape artist, so needs a fenced-in yard. There is a rare but definite propensity to fierceness against enemies. Not ideal for a first-time owner.

Physical Attributes: 26 to 34 in (66 to 86.5 cm); 60 to 110 lb (27 to 50 kg). Males are considerably larger than females. The topline curves upward; this is to provide for the double-suspension gallop characteristic of Borzoi and other sighthounds— it's what makes them so fast. All colors and patterns, but white with spots is most common.

Coat Type and Grooming: Silky, shiny with feathering; either flat or wavy. Fairly high maintenance; twice a week brushing to prevent mats. The male has a longer, thicker coat than the female and needs more attention. Professional grooming is optional; some trimming is required. Moderate shedding; females may shed more than males.

Life Span: 8 to 13 years.

Health Concerns: Bloat, bone cancer, dental problems, allergic dermatitis, PRA, cataracts, retinopathy, heart disease. This dog is sensitive to anesthesia, like most sighthounds.

Exercise: High; loves the outdoors and needs room to run.

Housing: Surprisingly good in apartments with frequent exercise.

Sociability: Tolerant of gentle older children but not playful; may be too big for toddlers. Some are reserved or timid with strangers. Very good with other dogs and prefers other sighthounds most of all. In fact, it is recommended that Borzoi not be the home's only dog. However, Borzoi are distinctly not good with small, fluffy dogs or cats that may remind them of game.

Trainability: Low; they are easily bored. Requires an experienced handler, and obedience classes are a must with this dog; they require gentle, consistent training.

Activities: Therapy dog, lure-coursing.

5 Facts

Graceful
Not for novice owner
Above-average grooming
Easily bored with training
Quiet

BOSTON TERRIER

Origin: Boston, 1870s. English Bulldog and English White Terriers are in the background. The first Boston Terriers were larger than the ones seen today.

Original Purpose: Companion, although they did not object to chasing the occasional rat or two.

Personality: Affectionate, playful, lively, devoted, friendly, strong-willed.

Breed Traits: Despite the name "terrier," he was not bred to chase vermin but to be a companion animal. Makes a good watchdog. Generally well-mannered; adult dogs are especially laid-back. Cannot handle extremes of heat or cold.

Physical Attributes: 12 to 17 in (30.5 to 43 cm); 11 to 25 lb (5 to 11.5 kg). Short snout and muzzle. Colors are black, brindle, or seal with white markings including a muzzle band, blaze, and forechest. A white collar and white markings on the legs are also desirable.

Coat Type and Grooming: Short, shiny. Minimal care; once-a-week brushing. Minimal shedding.

Life Span: 10 to 15 or more years.

Health Concerns: Bloat, respiratory problems, tumors, Cushing's disease, thyroid disease, deafness, heart problems, skin problems (allergies), cataracts, cancer.

Exercise: Low to medium.

Housing: Ideal for apartment life.

Sociability: Very good with most kids; a few not tolerant of young children. Generally good with other pets; some males can be somewhat aggressive to other male dogs.

Trainability: High, although the breed can be stubborn.

Activities: Obedience, agility.

5 Facts

Well mannered
Minimal grooming
Ideal for apartments
Good with children
Devoted

BOUVIER DES FLANDRES

Origin: Belgium and France, 1600s.

Original Purpose: Herding cows, police work, farm work, cart-pulling.

Personality: Stable, protective, steady, loyal, fearless, calm.

Breed Traits: Powerful, compact, big, strong. Slow to mature. An excellent watchdog. Not a good dog for novice owners; he may try to dominate.

Physical Attributes: 23 to 27 in (58.5 to 68.5 cm); 90 to 110 lb (41 to 50 kg). Colors are fawn to black, salt and pepper, brindle, gray.

Coat Type and Grooming: Rough, thick, wiry, medium-length outercoat; soft dense undercoat. High maintenance; requires a thorough brushing every day. Professional grooming is highly desirable. Moderate to high shedding.

Life Span: 10 to 12 years.

Health Concerns: Hip dysplasia, OCD.

Exercise: High; needs plenty of exercise.

Housing: Likes the outdoors; best living in the country or with plenty of room to run.

Sociability: Bonds to one person. Particularly fond of children. Good with other pets if socialized very early; can be bad with cats.

Trainability: High but needs an experienced trainer; can be domineering. Obedience classes are a must.

Activities: Herding trials, security, agility, therapy dog, police and guide dog, cattle drover.

5 Facts

Good watchdog
Not for first-time owners
Professional grooming
Bonds to one person
Likes the outdoors

BOXER

Origin: Germany, 1800s; a German descendant of the Mastiff.

Original Purpose: Police work; pit fighting; bull and bear baiting; boar hunting.

Personality: Exuberant, courageous, alert, playful, affectionate, biddable.

Breed Traits: An excellent watch and guard dog. They need a lot of human interaction. Sturdy, agile, athletic, strong. Some are hyperactive. They can be escape artists. Have very little tolerance for heat and they snore due to the shortened muzzle.

Physical Attributes: 21 to 25 in (53.5 to 63.5 cm); 55 to 80 lb (25 to 36.5 kg). Colors are fawn and brindle, usually with white markings.

Coat Type and Grooming: Smooth, short. Low maintenance; a quick once-a-week brushing will suffice. Average, seasonal shedder.

Life Span: 8 to 12 years.

Health Concerns: Various cancers (osteosarcoma), PRA, orthopedic problems (arthritis, hip dysplasia), heart disease (cardiomyopathy, SAS), dental problems, allergies, bloat, digestive difficulties (soy intolerance), obesity, enteritis, corneal ulcer. White Boxers are often blind or deaf.

Exercise: High, especially when young.

Housing: Can manage in a large apartment if given a chance to run every day.

Sociability: Excellent with the whole family, including children, although they can be too rambunctious for very small children. They like friendly strangers also, if properly introduced, but are suspicious of unannounced visitors. Males may be aggressive with dogs they do not know.

Trainability: High, but these dogs can be stubborn and need early obedience training. Best with an experienced trainer.

Activities: Obedience, agility, therapy dog, police work.

5 Facts

Exuberant
Low-maintenance coat
Needs a lot of interaction
Devoted to family
Good watchdog

BOYKIN SPANIEL

Origin: United States, 1900s.
Original Purpose: Hunting; waterfowl retriever.
Personality: Docile, pleasant, obedient, friendly, affectionate, versatile.
Breed Traits: Makes an excellent hunting and family dog.
Physical Attributes: 14 to 18 in (35.5 to 45.5 cm); 25 to 40 lb (11 to 18 kg). Colors are dark chocolate, liver.
Coat Type and Grooming: Long, flat to slightly wavy outercoat and short, dense undercoat. Moderate maintenance; the soft fur needs but a weekly brushing. Moderate shedding.
Life Span: 14 to 16 years.

Health Concerns: Cataracts, corneal dystrophy, ear infections, eyelid distichiasis, hip dysplasia, patellar luxation, retinal dysplasia.
Exercise: High; his athleticism and energy demand regular and consistent exercise.
Housing: Best in rural or suburbs with plenty of room to run and hunt.
Sociability: Excellent family dog. Loves to play with children. Gets along well with people. Compatible with other pets.
Trainability: High; easy to train and eager to learn.
Activities: Spaniel hunt tests, spaniel field trials, tracking, agility.

5 Facts

Versatile
Moderate grooming
Excellent family dog
Needs lots of exercise
Easy to train

BRIARD

Origin: France, 1300s; probably the most ancient of the French sheepdogs.

Original Purpose: Shepherding.

Personality: Happy, dominant, devoted, self-assured, lively, strong-willed.

Breed Traits: Makes a superb watchdog and guard dog. If you are looking for pet (not a guard or herding dog), you must find a breeder who breeds for pet temperament. These powerful dogs can easily take over the house if permitted; not for beginners.

Physical Attributes: 22 to 27 in (56 to 68.5 cm); 75 to 100 lb (34 to 45.5 kg). Has double dewclaws on the hind leg. Any solid color except white; mostly commonly black, tawny, fawn, or gray.

Coat Type and Grooming: Long (up to a foot [30.5 cm] long in show dogs, commonly 4 to 6 in [10 to 15 cm] long in pets), slightly wavy, very dry, double; undercoat fine and tight; traditionally likened to a "goat's coat." Very high maintenance, requires lots of brushing; coat continues to grow throughout the life of the dog; some trimming needed. Professional grooming is very desirable. Moderate shedding.

Life Span: 12 to 14 years.

Health Concerns: Hip dysplasia, eye problems (congenital night blindness, cataracts), bloat, von Willebrand's, hypothyroidism.

Exercise: Moderate to high.

Housing: Not suited for an apartment; needs a great deal of space.

Sociability: Excellent with children if socialized early; may attempt to herd them. Very suspicious of strangers. Suspicious of other pets; aggressive with other dogs.

Trainability: High, but they need early socialization.

Activities: Search and rescue, police work, herding, agility, herding trials, Schutzhund.

5 Facts

Good watchdog
Not for novice owners
High-maintenance coat
Suspicious of other pets
Highly trainable

BRITTANY

Origin: Brittany, France, mid-1800s.

Original Purpose: Hunting upland game birds.

Personality: Brave, happy, stubborn, alert, energetic, independent.

Breed Traits: Fast, compact, lots of stamina. Some individuals are timid. Requires close human companionship. Not very reliable off leash.

Physical Attributes: 17 to 20 in (43 to 51 cm); 30 to 40 lb (13.5 to 18 kg). Colors are white and orange, liver and white; roan patterns and with some ticking permitted. Color should be deep and clear.

Coat Type and Grooming: Dense, medium-short, lightly feathered and silky; may be flat or wavy; weather resistant. Moderate care; requires brushing twice a week. Professional grooming is optional; some trimming required. Moderate shedding.

Life Span: 11 to 13 years.

Health Concerns: Hip dysplasia, glaucoma, seizures, VSD.

Exercise: Very high; without exercise several times a day, they can become destructive.

Housing: Not well suited to apartment life; needs a large yard at the very least. This dog does much better in the country than in the city.

Sociability: Tends to bond to one person. Good with children, very playful, needs gentle treatment. Usually extremely friendly to strangers but sometimes suspicious. Generally very good with other pets, although some males dislike other males.

Trainability: High; this dog is easily bored and likes a challenge.

Activities: Field trial, hunting (birds), hunting tests, obedience, agility.

5 Facts

Needs companionship
Moderate grooming
Not for apartments
Bonds with one person
High exercise

BRUSSELS GRIFFON

Origin: Belgium, 1800s. Possible ancestors include Affenpinschers, Pugs, and unknown collaborators.

Original Purpose: Vermin exterminators.

Personality: Cheeky, self-confident, bold, sensitive, lively.

Breed Traits: Active. Due to shortened muzzle, some snore or wheeze.

Physical Attributes: 7 to 8 in (18 to 20 cm); 8 to 11 lb (3.5 to 5 kg). Colors are red, beige, black, black-and-tan.

Coat Type and Grooming: Two coat types: rough (Griffon Bruxellois) and smooth (Petit Brabaçon). Both require minimal care. (Brush once a week.) Rough-coated coats should be hard and wiry and require combing several times a week and stripping a couple of times a year. Professional grooming is recommended for the rough coat; stripping for show dogs, clipping for pets. Low to moderate shedding.

Life Span: 12 to 15 years.

Health Concerns: Patellar luxation, PRA.

Exercise: Fairly low but loves to play.

Housing: Ideal for apartment life.

Sociability: A one-person dog. Not very good with young children but good with older kids. Good with other pets.

Trainability: Average to high; good problem solvers; many, however, are hard to housetrain.

Activities: Obedience.

5 Facts

Cheeky
Ideal for apartments
Bonds with one person
Low shedding
Loves to play

BULLDOG

Origin: England, 1200s.

Original Purpose: Bull- and bear-baiting (a cruel practice that was outlawed in England in 1835); fighting. The whole idea behind the pushed-in muzzle was that the dog could grab the opponent and still breathe, a clever anatomical trick for an absurd purpose.

Personality: Jovial, obstinate, friendly, obstinate, amiable, obstinate, stable, obstinate, lovable, obstinate. (See any patterns?)

Breed Traits: Can be given to sulking. Makes a good watchdog but is not usually protective. An example of a breed that used to be ferocious but whose character has been modified by careful breeding. Does not do well in heat or cold; needs air conditioning or a cooler climate. Drools and snores.

Physical Attributes: 10 to 15 in (25.5 to 38 cm); 40 to 55 lb (18 to 25 kg), with females smaller than males. Colors are brindle, solid white, fawn, red, fallow, or any of these on a white background.

Coat Type and Grooming: Short. Very low maintenance; once-a-week brushing, but the facial wrinkles require regular cleaning to prevent dermatitis. Heavy shedding.

Life Span: 8 to 10 years.

Health Concerns: Eyelid abnormalities (entropion, distichiasis), orthopedic problems (hip dysplasia, OCD), deafness, heart disease (pulmonic stenosis, VSD), obesity, skin problems (allergies), respiratory difficulties, especially in the heat.

Exercise: Very low; can get along with little exercise.

Housing: Can adapt to almost any environment, as long as there are no huge stairs to climb.

Sociability: Wonderful with children. Usually quite tolerant of strangers. Extremely slow to become aroused but could be dangerous if he does. Can be aggressive to other dogs but usually ignores them; usually fine with other pets.

Trainability: Low; early socialization important.

Activities: Companion.

5 Facts

Good with children
Bad for extreme temperatures
Low exercise requirements
Low-maintenance coat
Snores

BULLMASTIFF

Origin: England, 1800s. It is said that the Bullmastiff is about 60-percent Mastiff and 40-percent Bulldog.

Original Purpose: Guard dog to keep away poachers (was known as the "gamekeeper's night dog"); dog of war.

Personality: Independent, fearless, dependable, levelheaded, protective, reserved.

Breed Traits: Large, powerful, sturdy. Enjoys a lot of interaction with family, but not usually playful. Generally considered low-energy, especially indoors. Has very low heat tolerance. Tends to chew as a puppy. Does best with a strong, experienced owner.

Physical Attributes: 24 to 27 in (61 to 68.5 cm); 100 to 135 lb (45.5 to 61 kg). Colors are red, fawn, brindle; muzzle is black.

Coat Type and Grooming: Short. Minimal care; no trimming. Light seasonal shedding.

Life Span: 10 years.

Health Concerns: Orthopedic problems (hip dysplasia, OCD), obesity.

Exercise: Moderate.

Housing: Adaptable to any living situation.

Sociability: Very loving with his family. Usually excellent with children but not playful. Needs proper socialization so that he will not become overprotective of "his" children. Suspicious of strangers. Mostly good with other pets, especially when well-socialized, but can be aggressive with same-sex dogs or with small dogs; does not approve of strange dogs.

Trainability: Low; needs early obedience training. This dog is difficult to train, and some try to dominate the family children.

Activities: Agility, obedience, police and military work.

5 Facts

Protective
Low energy
Minimal grooming
Loving with family
Difficult to train

BULL TERRIER

Origin: England, 1800s. May have Dalmatian and Bulldog in background.

Original Purpose: Dog fighting; bull-baiting.

Personality: Sweet, obstinate, charming, playful, loyal, even-tempered.

Breed Traits: Strong, muscular, solid, symmetrical. Highly territorial; makes a good watchdog. Enjoys being center of interest within the family.

Physical Attributes: 20 to 22 in (51 to 56 cm); 35 to 60 lb (16 to 27 kg). Egg-shaped head and very small eyes. The first Bull Terriers were colored, then all-white ones gained popularity, until that was practically the only color seen. In the 1920s, it was recognized that the white was associated with a gene for deafness, so color (white with red or brindle) has been gradually reintroduced. Today, white and colored Bull Terriers are shown separately, although they are one breed.

Coat Type and Grooming: Smooth. Minimal care; once-a-week brushing with a natural bristle brush or hound mitt. Light shedding.

Life Span: 11 to 14 years.

Health Concerns: Patellar luxation, allergic dermatitis, deafness in white varieties, kidney problems.

Exercise: Moderate to high; needs long walks and exercise; will become destructive if given insufficient exercise.

Housing: Can adapt to almost any living situation with adequate exercise.

Sociability: Good with children, especially if socialized early. May be aloof with strangers. Good with other pets, although often aggressive; usually needs to be raised with other dogs and socialized early.

Trainability: Low. Needs firm training; tends to be disobedient—this dog is nicknamed the "gladiator of the terriers."

Activities: Flyball, agility.

5 Facts

Good watchdog
Minimal grooming
Adaptable
Good with children
Difficult to train

CAIRN TERRIER

Origin: Scottish Highlands and islands, Middle Ages. Related to the West Highland White Terrier, and the two breeds were freely crossed until 1916. In fact, early Cairns, West Highland White Terriers, and Scottish Terriers often came from the same litter and were separated only by color.

Original Purpose: Hunting foxes, rats, otters, and badgers.

Personality: Plucky, courageous, spirited, cheerful, independent, inquisitive.

Breed Traits: Agile, strong, tireless. Superior watchdog, although his bark is bigger than his bite. Can be restless in the house, but given enough room, will self-exercise. Diggers and barkers. Some try to dominate their owners.

Physical Attributes: 9 to 12 in (23 to 30.5 cm); 13 to 15 lb (6 to 7 kg). Colors are cream, wheaten, red, gray, nearly black or brindle; ears, muzzle, and tail usually dark.

Coat Type and Grooming: Harsh, shaggy weatherproof outercoat; undercoat soft and dense. Moderate to high maintenance; once- or twice-weekly grooming with a steel comb. Eyes need special care. Professional grooming is recommended; dead hair should be stripped a couple times a year, even for pets. Slight seasonal shedding.

Life Span: 14 to 15 years.

Health Concerns: Portal systemic shunt (liver problem), blood disorders (von Willebrand's, globoid cell leukodystrophy), CMO, eye problems (PRA, ocular melanosis), allergies.

Exercise: Moderate but needs regular outdoor exercise.

Housing: Adaptable to almost any living situation. Does well in an urban environment if properly exercised.

Sociability: Enjoys the company of human beings but is not much of a snuggler. Not always reliable with toddlers but likes to play with older kids; tends to be bossy with kids. Gets along with other dogs if socialized early but not fond of sharing his household with other pets.

Trainability: Low to moderate; responsive to his owner and a good problem solver.

Activities: Earthdog trials.

5 Facts

Plucky
Good watchdog
Professional grooming
Adaptable
May bark

CANAAN DOG

Origin: Israel.

Original Purpose: Herding and guard dog, sentry.

Personality: Protective, alert, inquisitive, devoted, independent.

Breed Traits: Does not suffer separation anxiety and can be left alone for longer periods than many other dogs. A good watchdog and protection dog. Acute sense of smell and hearing. They are barkers.

Physical Attributes: 20 to 24 in (51 to 61 cm); 35 to 55 lb (16 to 25 kg). Colors are black-and-white; brown-and-white; or solid black, liver, sand, or brown.

Coat Type and Grooming: Medium short, harsh; weather-resistant outercoat, soft undercoat. Moderate care; weekly grooming required. Moderate shedding year round; heavier in spring and fall.

Life Span: 12 to 14 years.

Health Concerns: Because nature has been its breeder for so many years, there are very few health problems associated with this breed.

Exercise: Moderate.

Housing: Adaptable to any living situation.

Sociability: Good with children he is raised with; not fond of strange children. Reserved and cautious with strangers. Good with family animals but dislikes strange cats and dogs; many are same-sex aggressive.

Trainability: High. This dog is a fast learner and is easy to housetrain.

Activities: Tracking, military service, agility, herding trials.

5 Facts

Good watchdog
Very few health problems
Reserved with strangers
Independent
Barky

CANE CORSO

Origin: Italy, antiquity.

Original Purpose: Guard dog.

Personality: Intelligent, even-tempered, loyal, protective, confident, aloof.

Breed Traits: High guarding instincts. Generally quiet around the home if given enough exercise. Not for beginners.

Physical Attributes: 23 to 27.5 in (58.5 to 70 cm); 84 to 110 lb (38 to 50 kg). Colors are black, gray, fawn, red.

Coat Type and Grooming: Short, stiff, shiny, dense outercoat and light undercoat. Low maintenance. Light shedding.

Life Span: 9 to 12 years.

Health Concerns: Allergies, bloat, ectropion, elbow dysplasia, entropion, epilepsy, heart murmur, hip dysplasia.

Exercise: High; needs plenty of exercise.

Housing: Best in rural or suburban, but apartment life is possible with enough exercise.

Sociability: Devoted to his family. Great with children. Suspicious of strangers. Can be territorial and dominant toward other dogs.

Trainability: High. Although highly trainable, they do best with owners experienced in handling protection breeds. They need early and continuing socialization.

Activities: Weight pulling, tracking, agility.

5 Facts

High guarding instinct
Not for beginners
Needs plenty of exercise
Low-maintenance coat
Devoted to family

CARDIGAN WELSH CORGI

Origin: Wales.

Original Purpose: Cattle dog.

Personality: Devoted, stable, alert; more introverted, less playful, and more serious than the Pembroke Welsh Corgi.

Breed Traits: Active, powerful, hardy. Good watchdog. Enjoys family activities. May bark.

Physical Attributes: 10 to 12 in (25.5 to 30.5 cm); 26 to 39 lb (12 to 17.5 kg). Colors are red, sable, brindle, blue merle, black, and tricolored; anything except all white. Usually white around the neck, chest, legs, stomach, and tail tip.

Coat Type and Grooming: Double coat, dense, medium length; outercoat harsh, undercoat soft and thick. Average maintenance; a thorough brushing twice a week is necessary. Moderate to heavy shedding; sheds all year but mostly in fall and spring.

Life Span: 10 to 12 years.

Health Concerns: Orthopedic problems (hip dysplasia, disk problems), blindness.

Exercise: High.

Housing: Can live in urban areas if given frequent exercise.

Sociability: Very devoted to children; can be protective of "his" kids. Reserved with strangers. Not always good with other pets.

Trainability: High.

Activities: Therapy dog, cattle drover, herding, agility.

5 Facts

Adaptable
Very devoted to children
Reserved with strangers
Average maintenance
May bark

CAVALIER KING CHARLES SPANIEL

Origin: England, 1600.

Original Purpose: Flushing small birds.

Personality: Companionable, trusting, friendly, gay, sweet, gentle.

Breed Traits: Elegant. Needs a lot of attention and kisses from his family. Not a good watchdog. Excellent for first-time owner.

Physical Attributes: 12 to 13 in (30.5 to 33 cm); 12 to 18 lb (5.5 to 8 kg). Colors are ruby or mahogany (solid red); Blenheim (red and white); black-and-tan; tricolor.

Coat Type and Grooming: Long, silky, straight or slight wave. Fairly high maintenance; needs regular grooming. Average shedding.

Life Span: 10 to 14 years.

Health Concerns: Heart problems (mitral valve insufficiency), patellar luxation, cataracts.

Exercise: Moderate to high.

Housing: Adaptable to any living situation.

Sociability: Very good with people, including children and older folks. Delighted to meet any strangers. Usually okay with other dogs; very nice with cats.

Trainability: Average.

Activities: Canine freestyle, flyball, tracking. (At the last tracking event I attended, a Cavalier King Charles Spaniel took top honors.)

5 Facts

Needs lots of attention
Regular grooming
Excellent for first-time owner
Adaptable
Good with people

CESKY TERRIER

Origin: Czech Republic, 20th century.

Original Purpose: Vermin hunter.

Personality: Happy, sporty, calm, playful, protective, feisty.

Breed Traits: Good watchdog. High energy. Less aggressive and edgy than many other terriers. Has a deep, loud bark. Digs.

Physical Attributes: 10 to 13 in (25.5 to 33 cm); 13 to 22 lb (6 to 10 kg). Colors are any shade of gray, black, white, brown; may have yellow markings.

Coat Type and Grooming: Long, fine but firm, slightly wavy with silky gloss. High; although his coat is softer than the typical terrier, it still needs plenty of care. He is trimmed, not stripped like other terriers. He needs brushing at least twice a week and trimming every 3 to 5 months.

Life Span: 12 to 15 years.

Health Concerns: Scottie cramp.

Exercise: Moderate to high. This breed needs plenty of exercise that should include interactive play with his owner.

Housing: Adaptable to any living situation. Does well in apartments if given enough outdoor exercise.

Sociability: Loves his family, including children, but does have some typical terrier feistiness. May be reserved toward strangers.

Trainability: Average to high. May be more responsive than some other terriers but does have a stubborn streak and may try to take over the house without strong leadership from his owner. Sensitive and needs positive-based training methods.

Activities: Agility, earthdog, tracking, jogging partner.

5 Facts
Strong minded
Professional grooming
Bonds to one person
Adaptable
Good with children

CHESAPEAKE BAY RETRIEVER

Origin: United States, 1800s. Ancestors may have included Newfoundlands and Labrador Retrievers.
Original Purpose: Hunting and retrieving game (ducks), especially in rough conditions.
Personality: Hardworking, strong-willed, loyal, inquisitive, courageous, protective.
Breed Traits: Hardy, burly, strong, rugged. Excellent watchdog; can be protective and territorial. Calm in the house if properly exercised. Very talkative. Loves water; can handle icy water with ease. Excellent family dogs, although require a strong owner as they can be dominant.
Physical Attributes: 21 to 26 in (53.5 to 66 cm); 55 to 80 lb (25 to 36.5 kg). Colors are brown shades, including a light shade delightfully called "deadgrass." Other shades include red, brown, yellow, tan, and "sedge." He comes in chocolate too, which is considerably more appetizing. White markings are permitted on the chest, belly, toes, or back of feet. The coat tends to fade a bit in the summer. Eyes are amber-colored.
Coat Type and Grooming: Double, water-resistant coat is thick, wavy, and short (not longer than 1 in [2.5 cm]), loaded with natural oils; undercoat is dense and woolly. Moderate maintenance; brushing twice a week. Frequent bathing is unnecessary, as it may strip the coat of its oils. No trimming required. Average shedding.
Life Span: 10 to 13 years.
Health Concerns: Hip and elbow dysplasia, bloat, eye problems (PRA, cataracts), eczema.
Exercise: High; this tireless dog needs a great deal of outside exercise, preferably in water.
Housing: Not suitable for urban life; needs a lot of room to run; preferably near a body of water.
Sociability: Very protective of family. Good with gentle kids. Reserved toward strangers. Will usually accept other dogs, although tries to dominate them; may be aggressive on occasion.
Trainability: Average. Early socialization and regular obedience training is needed to stay in charge of this dominant dog; they can be stubborn. Many do not do well with crate training.
Activities: Field trials, waterfowl retrieving, obedience.

5 Facts
Very "talkative"
Protective of family
Loves water
Needs lots of exercise
Can be stubborn

CHIHUAHUA

Origin: Probably Central Mexico in the 1500s, although some experts think it may have been Malta in the Mediterranean; others suggest China. Ancestry may include the long-coated Techichi, an ancient Toltec breed, and a hairless breed from Asia. Rediscovered in the state of Chihuahua, Mexico, in the 1850s.

Original Purpose: Companion.

Personality: Alert, curious, loyal, mischievous, temperamental, spirited.

Breed Traits: Graceful, agile. Enjoys and requires a lot of attention. Cannot tolerate cold. Barky. Great mousers. Great pets for elderly people.

Physical Attributes: 6 to 10 in (15 to 25.5 cm); 2 to 6 lb (1 to 2.5 kg). Generally considered to be the world's smallest dog. Any color or markings permitted.

Coat Type and Grooming: Chihuahuas come in Smooth and the less common Longhaired varieties. Grooming for the Smooth is minimal; the Longhaired requires brushing a couple of times a week. Light but constant shedding for the Smooth; Longhaired variety sheds seasonally.

Life Span: 16 to 18 years

Health Concerns: Heart disease (pulmonic stenosis, mitral valve insufficiency), cancer, dental problems (gingivitis), orthopedic problems (patellar luxation, fractures), cruciate ligament ruptures, hydrocephalus, enteritis, Cushing's disease, dermatitis. Many have an incomplete closure in the skull; this spot is vulnerable to trauma.

Exercise: Low to moderate.

Housing: Ideal for urban areas or apartment life.

Sociability: Tends to bond to one person. Not suited for homes with kids under the age of 12; good with gentle older children. Many are shy with or dislike strangers. Will get along with other Chihuahuas but not good with other breeds; good with cats and other household pets.

Trainability: Variable—medium to high; needs extensive early socialization. Despite their small size, Chihuahuas can become dominant or nippy if not properly trained.

Activities: Obedience.

5 Facts

**Bonds to one person
Requires lots of attention
Ideal for apartment living
Low exercise needs
Barky**

CHINESE CRESTED

Origin: China, 1200s.

Original Purpose: Ratter; companion.

Personality: Playful, happy, devoted, gay, cheerful.

Breed Traits: Active. Does not do well left alone for long periods. Can be territorial. No cold tolerance. Hairless needs to be protected from the sun. Clean with no doggy odor.

Physical Attributes: 9 to 13 in (23 to 33 cm); 11 to 13 lb (5 to 6 kg).

Color: Any color or combination of colors.

Coat Type and Grooming: Two types: Hairless (no coat at all) and Powderpuff, which is described in the standard as "double soft and silky" with "long, thin guard hairs over the short silky undercoat." Average to high maintenance. The Powderpuff needs regular brushing. Although you would think the Hairless are easy to groom, they are subject to pimples, acne, and even pustules. If they are outside in the summer, they need sunscreen. Professional grooming is not needed except for show dogs. Minimal shedding.

Life Span: 13 to 15 years.

Health Concerns: Legg-Perthes, skin allergies and infections.

Exercise: Low to moderate.

Housing: Ideal for urban areas or apartment life.

Sociability: Both varieties are good with children, although some say the Hairless is somewhat better than the Powderpuff. Excellent with other pets.

Trainability: Average to high; requires gentle handling.

Activities: Obedience.

5 Facts

Needs company
No doggy odor
Ideal for apartment life
Good with children
Minimal shedding

CHINESE SHAR-PEI

Origin: China (Han Dynasty), 1200s.

Original Purpose: Hunting wild boar; dog fighting; herder; protector of livestock and homes.

Personality: Independent, calm, self-assured, alert, regal, friendly.

Breed Traits: Loving to his family but reserved with strangers. Sensitive to heat.

Physical Attributes: 18 to 20 in (45.5 to 51 cm); 45 to 60 lb (20.5 to 27 kg); very wrinkled skin. The tongue is blue-black (like Chow Chows). The original Chinese description of the Shar-pei included a head like a "melon-shaped pear," ears like clamshells, a nose like a butterfly, a back like a shrimp, and a neck like a water buffalo. Solid colors include black, cream, fawn, or red.

Coat Type and Grooming: Short and harsh. The word "shar-pei" means "sandy coat," referring to its texture. Low maintenance; once-a-week brushing. Special care needed for folds of the skin. Needs frequent ironing. (Just kidding!) Moderate shedding.

Life Span: 9 to 12 years.

Health Concerns: Skin allergies, orthopedic problems (OCD, elbow dysplasia), eye problems (entropion).

Exercise: Moderate.

Housing: Can adapt to any living situation.

Sociability: If not socialized, not good with children. Reserved toward strangers. Not good with other dogs but usually gets along fine with other pets.

Trainability: Low to average; this independent breed needs patient training.

Activities: Companion, obedience.

5 Facts

Loving to family
Reserved toward strangers
Adaptable
Special care for skin folds
Independent

CHOW CHOW

Origin: Mongolia, maybe 4,000 years ago; later introduced into China.

Original Purpose: Fighting; guarding; cart-pulling; food.

Personality: Self-contained, independent, dignified, strong-minded, stubborn, loyal, aloof.

Breed Traits: Some individuals are aggressive, and most are highly territorial. Very fine guard dogs; very powerful. Can be dangerous, because they are famously "hard to read" and unpredictable in actions. Not playful. They can handle cold but have no tolerance for heat. Only for experienced dog owners who are well equipped to handle such a dog.

Physical Attributes: 17 to 22 in (43 to 56 cm); 45 to 85 lb (20.5 to 38.5). Black/purple tongues and straight hind legs (for a dog). The deep-set eyes give him limited vision, and the dog should be approached within those limitations. Colors are solid red, black, cream, blue, fawn, and cinnamon.

The baby coat will change at about three months to the color and texture of the adult dog.

Coat Type and Grooming: Two types—rough and smooth; both have thick, plush double coats, with a soft woolly undercoat. High maintenance; brushing four times a week. Professional grooming is optional. Profuse shedding twice a year.

Life Span: 9 to 12 years.

Health Concerns: Hip and elbow dysplasia, eye problems (entropion, glaucoma, cataracts), OCD, color dilution alopecia, eczema.

Exercise: Low to moderate.

Housing: Can adapt to any living situation.

Sociability: Generally picks one person in the family to bond to and may not always be friendly to others. Not good with children outside those in his own family, to whom he is usually devoted. Dislikes or ignores strangers. (Has excellent memory for those he dislikes; for example, one Chow I know disliked any person in a UPS uniform.) Most do not get along with dogs of their own sex and dislike cats.

Trainability: Low to moderate; will challenge his owner for dominance; needs firm early obedience training and thorough socialization; however, extremely easy to housetrain. Needs an experienced trainer.

Activities: Guarding, companion.

5 Facts

Highly territorial
For experienced owners
High-maintenance coat
Dislikes strangers
Adaptable

CLUMBER SPANIEL

Origin: England, 1700s.

Original Purpose: Bird flushing and retrieving.

Personality: Easygoing, friendly, calm, gentle, laid-back, dependable.

Breed Traits: Aristocratic. Somewhat slow. Moderate energy level. Very low watchdog or protection ability or interest. Acute sense of smell, probably the best of all sporting dogs. Some may snore or drool.

Physical Attributes: 17 to 20 in (43 to 51 cm); 50 to 80 lb (22.5 to 36.5 kg). Colors are mostly white with orange or lemon markings.

Coat Type and Grooming: Soft, wavy, silky. High maintenance, needs daily thorough brushing. Professional grooming is desirable; needs trimming about twice a month. Average shedding.

Life Span: 10 to 12 years.

Health Concerns: Autoimmune hemolytic anemia, cataracts, entropion, hip dysplasia.

Exercise: Moderate; not much for vigorous exercise. Enjoys retrieving from water.

Housing: Enjoys being outside so much that he is not suitable for urban life.

Sociability: Very well adapted to family life but may select one person for special attention. Excellent with children and strangers; never aggressive. Friendly with other pets.

Trainability: High.

Activities: Therapy dog, bird flushing, tracking, hunting.

5 Facts

Enjoys being outside
Moderate energy level
Professional grooming
Excellent with children
Dependable

COCKER SPANIEL

Origin: United States, 1800s, although earliest ancestors hail from Spain. The breed came to the US from England between 1870 and 1880; the main split between this breed and the English Cocker took place around 1920.

Original Purpose: Hunting woodcocks and quail; flushing game.

Personality: Curious, upbeat, merry, affectionate, loyal, trustworthy.

Breed Traits: A few individuals can be protective. Some can be very unpredictable and snappish or shy, but that is not the normal temperament for this breed. Quiet in the house. Some are barkers.

Physical Attributes: 14 to 15 in (35.5 to 38 cm); 21 to 30 lb (9.5 to 13.5 kg). The Cocker is the smallest of all the spaniels. Colors are jet black (includes black-and-tan), buff, chocolate, cream, red, parti-color, tricolor.

Coat Type and Grooming: Silky outercoat, enough undercoat for protection. Very high maintenance; two or three times weekly brushing, even for household pets; grooming for show dogs is immense. Professional grooming is necessary every few weeks; dogs who go untrimmed develop unmanageable coats. Regular bathing needed; eyes, ears, and feet need particular attention. Average shedder.

Life Span: 10 to 15 years or more.

Health Concerns: Umbilical hernia, cancer, orthopedic problems (hip dysplasia, patellar luxation), obesity, sebaceous gland tumors, allergies, ear problems, eye problems (cataracts, PRA, distichiasis, glaucoma), autoimmune diseases, heart problems (pulmonary stenosis, mitral valve insufficiency, cardiomyopathy).

Exercise: Moderate to very high; needs regular walks.

Housing: Can adapt to any living situation.

Sociability: Many choose one person for special attention. Still, excellent with all kinds of people, including children (so long as he was bred by a responsible breeder and properly socialized). Friendly to strangers. Usually good with other pets.

Trainability: High; many enjoy learning tricks.

Activities: Retrieving, agility, obedience, flyball.

5 Facts

Affectionate
High-maintenance coat
Adaptable
Excellent with people
Highly trainable

COLLIE

Origin: Scotland (Lowlands), 1800s. The word "Collie" may descend from "Collies" or Scottish Highlands. Others suggest it comes from Colley, a variety of sheep that the dog herded. It has been suggested that Borzoi and Deerhounds may be in the background.

Original Purpose: Sheepherding.

Personality: Patient, sensitive, friendly, independent, gentle, gay.

Breed Traits: Active and lithe. They make good watchdogs. Some (especially the smooth coat) can be quite protective, others not at all. Some are barkers. Some individuals are shy, high-strung, or stubborn. The rough Collie is not well suited to extreme heat but can handle bitter weather with ease.

Physical Attributes: 22 to 26 in (56 to 66 cm); 45 to 75 lb (20.5 to 34 kg). Colors are sable and white, tricolor, blue merle, predominantly white.

Coat Type and Grooming: Two types: rough and smooth. Smooth has a short, dense, straight, flat coat; rough has an abundant, long, straight, harsh outercoat; both have a dense undercoat. The smooth is moderate maintenance. The rough is high maintenance; brushing an hour a week; needs frequent bathing. Professional grooming is desirable for the rough Collie; not necessary for the smooth. Sheds a lot (in clumps) twice a year.

Life Span: 8 to 12 years.

Health Concerns: Bloat, skin problems, cancer (osteosarcoma), PDA, eye problems (Collie eye anomaly, PRA), Collie nose, food allergies, deafness (merle color). This breed is also very sensitive to many kinds of heartworm medication and worm pills in general.

Exercise: High; enjoys regular organized activities.

Housing: Not usually suited for apartment life; however, they have been known to adapt as long as they get plenty of exercise and attention.

Sociability: Excellent with children, especially if raised with them; may try to herd them, though. Quite friendly to strangers. Get along well with other pets.

Trainability: High, although they have an independent streak. They are sensitive, so gentle methods are necessary. Make excellent obedience prospects.

Activities: Herding, obedience, agility.

5 Facts

Active
Not for apartments
High-maintenance coat
Excellent with children
Sensitive

CURLY-COATED RETRIEVER

Origin: England, 1700s. There is obviously Poodle, probably water spaniel, and maybe some St. John's Newfoundland in the background of this breed.

Original Purpose: Hunting both quail and duck.

Personality: Versatile, lively, calm, sensitive, faithful, adaptable.

Breed Traits: Strong, active, sharp. Great watchdogs. Need a lot of attention. Calm and quiet indoors if properly exercised. Considered the most graceful of the retrievers. Can handle any kind of weather. Enjoys swimming. Slow to mature, acting like puppies until three or four years of age.

Physical Attributes: 22 to 27 in (56 to 68.5 cm); 50 to 85 lb (22.5 to 38.5 kg). Colors are solid black or liver.

Coat Type and Grooming: Dense, waterproof, tight, crisp, Poodle-like curls. Low maintenance; this dog is easy to groom despite the curls. They should be combed twice a week rather than brushed so that the curls stay intact. Some trimming is required. Unlike the Poodle, whose coat continues to grow, the Curly's coat is naturally quite short. If shampooed, extra rinsing is essential. One way to get a perfect coat is to take the dog swimming and let the coat dry naturally. Heavy shedding occurs once a year, then not at all.

Life Span: 9 to 13 years.

Health Concerns: Hip and elbow dysplasia, PRA, entropion, bloat, heart murmurs, epilepsy, fleabite dermatitis. The gene pool for this breed is small, so it is essential to go to a good breeder for a puppy to ensure good health.

Exercise: High; needs vigorous daily outdoor exercise, preferably in the water, or he will become destructive.

Housing: Not suitable for urban areas or apartment life.

Sociability: Excellent; bonds to whole family, including kids, if socialized to them early. Generally friendly to strangers. Excellent with other pets.

Trainability: High; this breed is easily bored and does best at high-level work. They can be stubborn and respond best to positive reinforcement.

Activities: Hunting (retrieves) over land and water, service dog, search and rescue, agility, obedience, flyball.

5 Facts

Versatile
Needs attention
Vigorous exercise required
Not for apartment life
Bonds to family

DACHSHUND

Origin: Germany, 1500s.

Original Purpose: Badger hunting.

Personality: Affectionate, bold, lively, alert, confident, determined.

Breed Traits: The Longhaired variety is calmest, the Smooth the liveliest, and the Wirehaired more affectionate and clownish. Many are highly energetic dogs, both in and out of the house. Depend on them to give the alert at the approach of strangers—you can't sneak up on this dog. Most are territorial. Can be barkers and diggers. The Smooth has little tolerance for cold.

Physical Attributes: The smallest of the hounds, he comes in two sizes (standard and miniature). The miniatures are less than 11 lb (5 kg); standards between 16 and 32 lb (7.5 and 14.5 kg). (Dogs in between are known as "tweenies.") There is no height standard for this breed. Known for their long backs, giving them a "hot-dog-like" appearance. Comes in a rainbow of colors: red, black-and-tan, cream, black, sable, chocolate, dapple, double dapple, piebald, and wild boar.

Coat Type and Grooming: Three types: Smooth, Longhaired, and Wirehaired. Minimal grooming for the Smooth; the Longhaired needs to be brushed daily; the Wirehaired should be stripped a couple of times a year. The ears need special attention. Has no doggy odor, but Longhairs benefit from frequent bathing. Professional grooming is not necessary for the Smooth but is preferable for the Longhaired and Wirehaired; only the Wirehaired is trimmed. Seasonal shedding.

Life Span: 15 to 16 years; miniatures live longer—15 to 19 years.

Health Concerns: Orthopedic problems (intervertebral disk disease, patellar luxation, elbow dysplasia), epilepsy, cancer, diabetes, color dilution alopecia, PRA, dermatitis, gastritis, enteritis, von Willebrand's, deafness (in dappled coats).

Exercise: Variable—moderate to high.

Housing: Can adapt well to apartments, especially if few stairs are involved.

Sociability: A very loyal family dog, affectionate without slavishness. Devoted to children in his own family but may not be crazy about other kids. Reserved toward strangers until introduced. Usually all right with other dogs; not good with rodents and other small pets.

Trainability: Average; the Longhaired variety is more obedient than the other types. This breed needs consistent training and confident owners.

Activities: Earthdog trials (the Dachshund is the only hound that is allowed to compete in AKC Terrier go-to-ground events), field trials, tracking, obedience.

5 Facts

Loyal
Good for apartment life
Reserved toward strangers
Needs consistent training
May bark

DALMATIAN

Origin: Whether the breed really comes from Dalmatia or not is debatable, even if you know where Dalmatia is. (It's in what used to be Yugoslavia.)

Original Purpose: Almost everything—hunting dog, vermin exterminator, carriage dog, fire engine dog, guard dog, draft dog, shepherd dog, war dog, and, of course, circus dog.

Personality: Lively, eager, loyal, outgoing, versatile.

Breed Traits: Excellent watchdog. Athletic, extremely active, tireless.

Physical Attributes: 19 to 24 in (48 to 61 cm); 45 to 60 lb (20 to 27 kg). Color is a white base coat, spotted, with round, well-defined black or liver spots (other colors not permitted) distributed evenly over his body. Spots can range from dime-size to half-dollar size. Patches (as opposed to spots) are not permitted, although the spots may overlap. Dalmatian puppies are born pure white and get their spots in two or three weeks.

Coat Type and Grooming: Short, sleek. Low maintenance; brushing three times a week. High shedding, every day year round.

Life Span: 12 to 14 years.

Health Concerns: Epilepsy, hip dysplasia, inhalant and food allergies, bladder stones (urolithiasis), and most common, deafness and partial deafness. One-third of all Dalmatians are deaf; these dogs should not be placed in homes with children.

Exercise: Extremely high; makes a good jogging partner. If not given sufficient exercise, they become restless, destructive, and neurotic.

Housing: Not suitable for urban areas or apartment life.

Sociability: Very loving to his family but not suited to families with young children unless carefully socialized. Okay with introduced strangers but is protective if he senses danger to his owner. May be aggressive to strange dogs but all right with family pets; traditionally likes horses.

Trainability: Average to high; this excitable breed needs firm but kind training.

Activities: Guarding, jogging companion.

5 Facts

Good watchdog
Tireless
Sheds all year
Good jogging partner
Not for apartments

DANDIE DINMONT TERRIER

Origin: The border region between England and Scotland.

Original Purpose: Hunter of mice, foxes, otters, and even badgers.

Personality: Strong-minded, tenacious, "rough-and-tumble," independent, affectionate, persistent.

Breed Traits: Likes to dig. An escape artist.

Physical Attributes: 8 to 11 in (20 to 28 cm); 18 to 21 lb (8 to 9.5 kg). The hind legs are longer than the front legs. Colors are mustard (all shades of reddish brown), pepper (all shades of blue/gray). Puppies tend to be darker than adults.

Coat Type and Grooming: Rough coat with a silky topknot. High maintenance; brush three times a week with a pin brush. Does best with professional care and periodic stripping or plucking, especially for the show dog. Light shedding.

Life Span: 13 to 15 years.

Health Concerns: Intervertebral disk disease, elbow problems.

Exercise: Moderate to high.

Housing: Can adapt to any living situation.

Sociability: Bonds to one person. Fairly good with children, especially if socialized early. Some are shy or unfriendly with strangers. Aggressive with other pets.

Trainability: Average; may try to dominate owner.

Activities: Earthdog trials, obedience.

5 Facts
Strong-minded
Professional grooming
Bonds to one person
Fairly good with children
Adaptable

DOBERMAN PINSCHER

Origin: Germany, 1890s. Original breeder was Louis Dobermann, a tax collector who needed a guard dog while he collected taxes.

Original Purpose: Guard dog; protection dog.

Personality: Alert, energetic, capable, sensitive, biddable, confident, territorial.

Breed Traits: Graceful, muscular, energetic, agile, strong. An excellent watchdog and guard dog. Some individuals may try to dominate family members, so experienced owners are best.

Physical Attributes: 24 to 28 in (61 to 71 cm); 60 to 80 lb (27 to 36.5 kg). Colors are black, red, fawn (Isabella), or blue with tan or rust markings; small white patch on chest permitted. White Dobermans are disqualified from the show ring.

Coat Type and Grooming: Smooth, short, glossy, hard coat. Minimal care. Minimal to moderate shedding seasonally.

Life Span: 10 to 12 years.

Health Concerns: Orthopedic problems (hip dysplasia, OCD, Wobblers), heart disease (cardiomyopathy, arrhythmia), bloat, color dilution alopecia, von Willebrand's, eye problems, skin disorders (acral lick dermatitis), osteosarcoma.

Exercise: Moderate to high; needs a good amount of exercise, although less than you might think for his size. If not given sufficient exercise, this dog can become neurotic, hyperactive, and destructive.

Housing: Adaptable to urban areas if exercised sufficiently.

Sociability: Often a one-person dog. Usually good with children if raised with them but should be supervised; may become overprotective of the family kids. Reserved and quite suspicious of strangers. Not good with dogs he not know; may try to dominate them. Protective of family pets, so long as he is the "boss."

Trainability: High. Most are highly trainable, but all need firm handling and very careful training. Some individuals make superior obedience prospects.

Activities: Tracking, police dog, obedience.

5 Facts

Guard dog
Needs experienced owner
Minimal grooming
Bonds to one person
Agile

DOGUE DE BORDEAUX

Origin: France, Middle Ages.

Original Purpose: Dog of war; fighting dog.

Personality: Vigilant, courageous, affectionate, balanced, formidable, loyal, playful, even-tempered, self-assured.

Breed Traits: Territorial nature makes them excellent patrol dogs. They drool and slobber. Not for novice owners.

Physical Attributes: 22.5 to 27 in (57 to 68.5 cm); at least 110 lb (50 kg) for males, and at least 99 lb (45 kg) for females. Colors are all shades of fawn.

Coat Type and Grooming: Fine, short, soft. Minimal care except for the wrinkles, which need to be kept clean. Moderate shedding.

Life Span: 8 to 12 years.

Health Concerns: Bloat, elbow and hip dysplasia, heart problems, hypothyroidism, panosteitis, skin problems.

Exercise: Moderate.

Housing: Due to his size, this breed does best in the suburbs or country.

Sociability: Devoted to and protective of his family. If properly socialized can be well-behaved with children, but his large size means he's better with older children. Suspicious of strangers. Aggressive toward other dogs.

Trainability: Moderate; he needs firm training from someone he can respect and must be socialized from an early age; can be stubborn.

Activities: Carting, obedience, weight-pulling, tracking, search and rescue work.

5 Facts

Territorial
Not for novice owners
Minimal coat care
Not for apartments
Devoted to family

ENGLISH COCKER SPANIEL

Origin: England, 1800s. Ancestors may have come from Spain (hence "spaniel").

Original Purpose: Flushing woodcock.

Personality: Obedient, exuberant, cheerful, joyful, gentle, loving.

Breed Traits: Elegant. Bigger and more houndlike than the American Cocker Spaniel. Makes a good watchdog. Needs plenty of human companionship and doesn't do well if left alone for long periods. Very family oriented and enjoy traveling.

Physical Attributes: 15 to 17 in (38 to 43 cm); 25 to 35 lb (11.5 to 16 kg). Colors are solid black, red (gold), liver, black-and-tan, buff, liver-and-tan; any of the foregoing on a white background, either parti-colored, ticked, or roan.

Coat Type and Grooming: Silky, flat, or wavy. High maintenance, though he has less coat than the American Cocker Spaniel. Unless carefully groomed, this dog looks messy. Ears and feet need special care. Professional grooming is recommended; some trimming required. Moderate shedding year round.

Life Span: 12 to 15 years.

Health Concerns: Eye problems (PRA, cataracts, glaucoma, distichiasis), hip dysplasia, ear problems, cardiomyopathy, obesity, deafness (parti-colors). Some solid colors have a history of rage syndrome.

Exercise: High; they need a lot of exercise, much more than the American Cocker. They calm down as they mature.

Housing: Can adapt to any living situation.

Sociability: Excellent, very good with children and new people alike if properly bred and healthy. Gets along with most other pets, as long as they are introduced properly.

Trainability: High.

Activities: Hunting, obedience, tracking, agility.

5 Facts

Family oriented
High exercise requirements
Needs companionship
Professional grooming
Adaptable

ENGLISH FOXHOUND

Origin: Great Britain, 1600s.

Original Purpose: To hunt foxes over varied terrain.

Personality: Amiable, friendly, calm, stubborn, lively.

Breed Traits: Extremely strong, symmetrical, and solid. Very active, but his stable character prevents hyperactivity. Although he is a very fine watchdog, he is not protective.

Physical Attributes: 23 to 27 in (58.5 to 68.5 cm); 60 to 90 lb (27 to 41 kg). Any hound color, usually black, tan, and white (tricolor) or tan-and-white (bicolor).

Coat Type and Grooming: Short, glossy, dense. Low maintenance. Minimal to moderate shedding.

Life Span: 10 to 13 years.

Health Concerns: Some epilepsy, hip dysplasia, pancreatitis, kidney and heart disease; however, one of the very healthiest breeds.

Exercise: High.

Housing: Not suitable for urban areas or apartment life; needs a very large fenced area in which to run.

Sociability: Gets along well with everyone, although a bit reserved with strangers. Tolerant of children. Gets along with other pets supremely well; a true pack animal and is happiest with other dogs.

Trainability: Low unless it's for foxhunting. Training should start early.

Activities: Hunting.

5 Facts

Active
High exercise requirements
Low-maintenance coat
Not for apartments
Friendly

ENGLISH SETTER

Origin: England, 1300s; fully developed in England and Wales in the 1800s. Ancestors may have included the Spanish Pointer.

Original Purpose: Hunting pheasant, grouse, and partridge.

Personality: Quiet, gentle, friendly, patient, well-mannered, mild.

Breed Traits: Active, aristocratic, graceful, rugged. Prefers to be with people; should not be left alone. This is a slow-maturing breed.

Physical Attributes: 24 to 27 in (61 to 68.5 cm); 50 to 70 lb (22.5 to 31.5 kg); the smallest of the setters and comparatively slight in build to others. English Setters come in two basic types: Lavarack (show style) and Llewellin (field model). Show dogs are larger and have a more luxuriant coat. Colors are tricolor, orange, blue, lemon, or silver belton (white with flecks or shading of the stated color). Patches of color are acceptable on field dogs but are discouraged on show dogs.

Coat Type and Grooming: Long, silky. High maintenance; coat requires daily brushing. Professional grooming is recommended; trimming required. Moderate shedding.

Life Span: 10 to 14 years.

Health Concerns: Deafness, hip and elbow dysplasia, some cancers, allergies, hypothyroidism.

Exercise: High; requires a lot of outdoor activity every day.

Housing: Suited only to country living.

Sociability: Likes everyone, including strangers. Very sociable and gentle with children. Very playful and friendly with other dogs.

Trainability: Average.

Activities: Hunting, therapy dog, field trials.

5 Facts

Slow maturing
Needs outdoor activity
High-maintenence coat
Very sociable
Not for apartments

ENGLISH SPRINGER SPANIEL

Origin: England, 1800s.

Original Purpose: Springing birds, which is how he got his name.

Personality: Energetic, friendly, merry, vivacious, loyal, eager to please.

Breed Traits: Fast. Hunts farther and faster than other spaniels. Needs a great deal of attention. Field-bred dogs are more energetic than show types. Some individuals can be shy or aggressive. Can handle cold and wet with no difficulty.

Physical Attributes: 19 to 20 in (48.5 to 51 cm); 45 to 55 lb (20.5 to 25 kg). Show-stock Springers are heavier, stockier, with more dramatic coats than field dogs. (Today, very few Springers work in both field and show events.) Colors are black or liver with white; either the white or the color can predominate; some have ticking.

Coat Type and Grooming: Smooth, silky, wavy, weather-resistant, long. High maintenance, especially in dogs from show lines. Needs regular brushing once a week because the coat picks up everything. The pendulous ears need special care. Professional grooming is recommended. Average seasonal shedding.

Life Span: 10 to 14 years.

Health Concerns: Obesity, gastritis, ear infections, orthopedic problems (hip dysplasia, OCD), eye problems (PRA, eyelid abnormalities), hemophilia, heart problems (PDA, VSD, cardiomyopathy), anemia.

Exercise: High; a tireless dog.

Housing: Adaptable to apartment life if special care is given to their very considerable exercise needs, but best suited to the country.

Sociability: Excellent with the whole family and always happy to meet new friends. Some lines are not good with children. May on occasion be aggressive to other dogs, although usually well-behaved with other pets.

Trainability: Very high; learns quickly; does well with professional training.

Activities: Flushing upland game birds, field trials, hunting tests, obedience, agility, tracking, flyball, therapy dog.

5 Facts

Energetic
High-maintenance coat
High exercise requirements
Friendly
Learns quickly

ENGLISH TOY SPANIEL

Origin: England, 1600s.

Original Purpose: Lapdogs; flushing small birds.

Personality: Sweet, haughty, gentle, stubborn, quiet, affectionate.

Breed Traits: Rather inactive inside and outside of the home. Because of short muzzle, are not well suited to heat. Some snore.

Physical Attributes: 10 to 11 in (25.5 to 28 cm); 8 to 14 lb (3.5 to 6.5 kg). Colors are red or burgundy (ruby), black-and-tan (King Charles), red-and-white (Blenheim), tricolor (Prince Charles).

Coat Type and Grooming: Long, soft, silky, flowing. Average to high maintenance; requires grooming two or three times a week. Professional grooming is optional; feet and whiskers need trimming. Light to moderate shedding.

Life Span: 10 to 13 years.

Health Concerns: Patellar luxation, juvenile cataracts, hernia, PDA, sensitivity to anesthesia. Heart murmurs, which can escalate into a serious difficulty, are a special problem for this breed. Because the gene pool is very small, the propensity for this problem is hard to eliminate.

Exercise: Low.

Housing: Ideal for urban areas or apartment life.

Sociability: Devoted to his family and reserved with strangers. May not be good with very young children, fine with older ones. Excellent with other pets.

Trainability: Average.

Activities: Companion, obedience.

5 Facts

Devoted to family
Not suited to hot weather
Ideal for apartments
Regular grooming
Low energy

ENTLEBUCHER MOUNTAIN DOG

Origin: The valley of Entlebuch, Switzerland.

Original Purpose: Driving cattle to market.

Personality: Courageous, alert, cheerful, independent, self-confident, loyal.

Breed Traits: Protective but not aggressive. Tuned in to family and needs to be with them in order to be happy.

Physical Attributes: 16.5 to 19.5 in (42 to 50 cm); 55 to 65 lb (25 to 29.5 kg). Color is tricolor (black, white, and tan or black, white, and yellow).

Coat Type and Grooming: Double coat with short, close-fitting, harsh, shiny outercoat and dense undercoat. Low maintenance; needs little more than occasional brushing. Moderate shedding.

Life Span: 10 to 12 years.

Health Concerns: Hip dysplasia, PRA.

Exercise: Moderate. He thrives in the great outdoors and enjoys exercising while doing a job, such as cart-pulling.

Housing: Adaptable, as long as he's given enough time outdoors.

Sociability: Great family dog. Gets along well with children and other pets.

Trainability: High. He is a quick learner and eager to please.

Activities: Cart-pulling, herding.

5 Facts

**Cheerful
Devoted to family
Moderate exercise
Adaptable
Highly trainable**

FIELD SPANIEL

Origin: England, 1800s. A close relative of the Cocker Spaniel and Springer Spaniel.

Original Purpose: Bird flushing and retrieving.

Personality: Diligent, friendly, even-tempered, willing, eager, noble.

Breed Traits: Hardy, agile. Needs a lot of attention from his family. Can be very active in the house. Has a keen nose. Escape artist. Will announce visitors.

Physical Attributes: 17 to 18 in (43 to 45.5 cm); 35 to 48 lb (16 to 22 kg). Liver is the most common color, but can also be black, roan, golden liver, mahogany red.

Coat Type and Grooming: Medium-long, slightly wavy, glossy; feathering on chest, body, and legs. Moderate to high maintenance; brushing twice a week. Frequent bathing is beneficial; ears must be carefully attended. Professional grooming is optional; some trimming on head, ears, throat, and feet. Moderate shedding.

Life Span: 11 to 14 years.

Health Concerns: Orthopedic problems (hip dysplasia), eye problems (PRA, cataracts, entropion, ectropion), thyroid disease, SAS.

Exercise: Moderate to high; needs regular exercise, preferably where he is able to run.

Housing: Not suitable for apartment life; needs room to run.

Sociability: Excellent with nearly everyone, including children. A few may be reserved with strangers. Gets along extremely well with other dogs and other pets if socialized with them.

Trainability: High; these are highly intelligent dogs and good problem solvers.

Activities: Bird flushing, spaniel field trials.

5 Facts

Active
Regular grooming
Not for apartments
Very sociable
Highly trainable

FINNISH LAPPHUND

Origin: Finland.

Original Purpose: Herding reindeer.

Personality: Versatile, eager to please, courageous, faithful, affectionate, amenable.

Breed Traits: All-weather dog. Alert; he will bark but is a bit less noisy than many other spitz-type dogs.

Physical Attributes: 16 to 20.5 in (40.5 to 52 cm); 33 to 53 lb (15 to 24 kg). Colors are black, blonde, brown, golden, sable tan, white, all with black, cream, gold, tan, gray, white, white-and-tan markings.

Coat Type and Grooming: Double coat with profuse, long, straight, coarse outercoat and soft, dense undercoat. Weatherproof. Average maintenance; needs regular brushing to keep the undercoat free of mats and dead hair. Annual shedding.

Life Span: 12 to 16 years.

Health Concerns: Cataracts, PRA.

Exercise: Average. He is keen to stay busy and part of any family activities.

Housing: Adaptable to any living situation; loves the outdoors and needs to get outside daily.

Sociability: Family-oriented dog who loves children. Friendly to strangers. Gets along very well with other dogs.

Trainability: High. He is very tuned in to his owner and picks up easily what is expected of him.

Activities: Herding, agility, tracking, obedience.

5 Facts

Versatile
All-weather dog
Moderate exercise
Family-oriented
Highly trainable

FINNISH SPITZ

Origin: Finland.

Original Purpose: Hunting waterfowl, small mammals, elk/moose, grouse.

Personality: Cooperative, friendly, obedient, independent, active, lively.

Breed Traits: Very little doggy odor. Easily startled; known for his acute hearing. This is a very vocal, active dog.

Physical Attributes: 15 to 20 in (38 to 51 cm); 29 to 36 lb (13 to 16.5 kg). Elegant and foxlike. Colors are orange, pale honey, golden red, or red. Puppies are born with a black overlay that disappears at about eight weeks of age.

Coat Type and Grooming: Stand-off stiff coat. Low maintenance; brushing once or twice a week. Moderate shedding.

Life Span: 12 to 15 years.

Health Concerns: No major concerns; this is a very healthy breed.

Exercise: Moderate.

Housing: Not suited for urban areas or apartment life.

Sociability: Devoted to their families. Playful with children. May be shy around strangers and other pets.

Trainability: Average.

Activities: Hunting.

5 Facts

Little doggy odor
Few health concerns
Not for apartment life
Devoted to family
Very vocal

FLAT-COATED RETRIEVER

Origin: England, 1800s.
Original Purpose: Retriever.
Personality: Cheerful, good-natured, intuitive, steady, sweet, loving, sociable, adaptable.
Breed Traits: Active. Quiet indoors if given enough exercise; if not, you have a very unhappy retriever. Needs human companionship. Among the most affectionate of all dogs. Some individuals are a bit territorial. These dogs are slow to mature.
Physical Attributes: 22 to 24 in (56 to 61 cm); 55 to 76 lb (25 to 34.5 kg). Graceful. Color is black, although some individuals are liver.
Coat Type and Grooming: Dense, glossy, and flat; feathering at the legs. Low to moderate maintenance; brushing twice a week. Some trimming required. Average seasonal shedding.
Life Span: 9 to 13 years.

Health Concerns: Cancer; a widespread problem among Flatties—about 65 percent of all Flat-Coated Retrievers die of cancer. Other concerns include hip dysplasia, patellar luxation, bloat, eye problems (cataracts, PRA).
Exercise: High; this breed needs a great deal of exercise, preferably near water.
Housing: Not suited for an urban environment.
Sociability: Very good with people. Especially good with kids; however, may be too rambunctious for children under four. Loves everyone, including strangers. Gets along with all other animals.
Trainability: High. Very trainable but sensitive; early training important.
Activities: Hunting (both land and water retrieval), search and rescue, avalanche dog, service dog, obedience, agility, flyball.

5 Facts

Cheerful
Moderate grooming
High exercise requirements
Highly sociable
Sensitive

FRENCH BULLDOG

Origin: France, 1800s.
Original Purpose: Companion.
Personality: Well-behaved, mild-mannered, playful, amiable, affectionate, cheerful.
Breed Traits: Very good watchdog. Due to short muzzle, does not handle hot weather well. Some wheeze and snore.
Physical Attributes: 11 to 13 in (28 to 33 cm); under 28 lb (12.5 kg). Sturdy. Most famous for his "bat" ears and perfectly flat skull. Colors are fawn, brindle, white, brindle-and-white.
Coat Type and Grooming: Short. Minimal care required; no trimming. Slight shedding.
Life Span: 9 to 11 years.
Health Concerns: Back problems, respiratory problems.

Exercise: Low to moderate.
Housing: Can adapt to any living situation.
Sociability: Often a one-person dog. Not always good with children. Does not care for strangers. Can get along well with other pets.
Trainability: Average.
Activities: Companion, obedience.

5 Facts

Amiable
Bonds to one person
Minimal grooming
Adaptable
May snore

GERMAN PINSCHER

Origin: Germany, 1700s.

Original Purpose: Vermin control, home protection.

Personality: Intense, alert, independent thinker, deliberate, intelligent, assertive, fearless.

Breed Traits: Makes a good guard dog, warning people away with a loud bark, but is generally not barky otherwise.

Physical Attributes: 17 to 20 in (43 to 51 cm); 31 to 44 lb (14 to 20 kg). Colors are all solid colors from fawn to stag red in various shades, black and blue with reddish-tan markings.

Coat Type and Grooming: Short, dense, smooth, shiny, close lying. Minimal care required. Average shedding.

Life Span: 12 to 14 years.

Health Concerns: Cataracts, hip dysplasia, von Willebrand's.

Exercise: High. He needs a job to provide him with the physical and mental stimulation to keep him satisfied.

Housing: Can adapt to most living situations if sufficiently exercised.

Sociability: Protective of family. Usually good with older children but needs socialization and supervision. Naturally wary and guarded with strangers. Not reliable with smaller pets.

Trainability: Highly trainable; needs a firm and fair trainer to handle him.

Activities: Agility, tracking, obedience, rally.

5 Facts

Assertive
Needs a job to do
Minimal grooming
Protective of family
Adaptable

GERMAN SHEPHERD DOG

Origin: Germany, 1800s.

Original Purpose: Military and guard dog; sheepherding; farm work.

Personality: Self-confident, loyal, versatile, hardy, intent, responsive, protective.

Breed Traits: Graceful, strong, agile, active. Highly territorial; very protective of their families; good watchdog and guard dog. Some poorly bred individuals may be shy or inappropriately aggressive. Best with experienced owners, because they may challenge their owners for leadership.

Physical Attributes: 22 to 26 in (56 to 66 cm); 70 to 95 lb (31.5 to 43 kg), with males usually larger than females. Excessive size is not desirable in this breed. Chiseled head, bushy tail. Colors are black-and-tan, gray sable, red sable, black, black-and-red, black-and-cream, black-and-silver, solid black.

Coat Type and Grooming: Double coat, medium length; outercoat dense, undercoat downy. Coats can go from short to long, but long coats are a fault in the show ring. Moderate to high maintenance; needs brushing two or three times a week. Professional grooming is optional. Heavy constant shedding.

Life Span: 10 to 12 years.

Health Concerns: Orthopedic problems (hip and elbow dysplasia, panosteitis, hypertrophic osteodystrophy, OCD), eye problems (cataracts, Collie eye anomaly), heart problems (SAS, PDA, cardiomyopathy), enteritis, ear infections, skin problems (nodular dermatofibrosis, food allergies, acral lick dermatitis), gastritis, epilepsy, cancer (osteosarcoma), von Willebrand's, exocrine pancreatic insufficiency, arthritis.

Exercise: High; needs lots of exercise and a lot of room. If he doesn't get enough exercise, he can become neurotic and even aggressive.

Housing: Not suited for apartment life, unless he receives an enormous amount of exercise.

Sociability: Very good with children he knows. Wary of strangers. Usually good with other pets once he accepts them as part of the family.

Trainability: High, but needs early training and socialization. It is extremely important to get a puppy of the right temperament from a reputable breeder.

Activities: Obedience, guide dog for the blind, herding, Schutzhund, agility, drug detection, therapy dog, search and rescue, police work.

5 Facts

Versatile
Best with experienced owner
Protective
Needs lots of exercise
Highly trainable

GERMAN SHORTHAIRED POINTER

Origin: Germany, 1600s. Possible Spanish Pointer and Bloodhound in the background.

Original Purpose: Hunting fowl.

Personality: Gentle, friendly, even-tempered, adaptable, proud, excitable.

Breed Traits: Hardy, versatile, powerful, active, with lots of endurance. Needs lot of attention from his owner. Excellent watchdog. Will bark if ignored. Enjoys the water.

Physical Attributes: 21 to 25 in (53.5 to 63.5 cm); 46 to 70 lb (21 to 31.5 kg). Colors range from solid liver to any combination of liver and white, including ticked, spotted, roan.

Coat Type and Grooming: Short, sleek, water-repellent outercoat; thick, short undercoat. Very low maintenance; twice a week quick brushing; no trimming; ears need special attention. Moderate shedding.

Life Span: 13 to 16 years.

Health Concerns: Lymphedema, hip and elbow dysplasia, localized eczema around paws, juvenile cataracts, epilepsy, hypothyroidism.

Exercise: High; if not exercised enough, can be extremely destructive in the house.

Housing: Not suitable for urban areas or apartment life; needs a lot of room.

Sociability: Very loving, although this breed needs to be supervised with smaller kids. Most like strangers, although a few may be somewhat suspicious. Very good with other dogs; some individuals may chase cats.

Trainability: Very high.

Activities: Hunting, field trials, tracking, obedience.

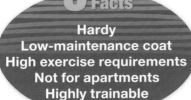

5 Facts

Hardy
Low-maintenance coat
High exercise requirements
Not for apartments
Highly trainable

GERMAN WIREHAIRED POINTER

Origin: Germany, 1800s.

Original Purpose: Versatile gundog.

Personality: Loyal, stubborn, friendly, goofy, energetic, aloof.

Breed Traits: Rugged, energetic, sturdy. Seems to have a sense of humor. Can be hard to handle in the house, especially if not properly exercised. Will warn of approaching strangers; barks in general. Can be protective. Can handle cold and wet weather with no trouble.

Physical Attributes: 21 to 26 in (53.5 to 66 cm); 55 to 75 lb (25 to 34 kg). Slightly larger on the average than the German Shorthaired Pointer. Colors are solid liver, liver-and-white.

Coat Type and Grooming: Short, wiry. Moderate maintenance; brushing twice a week. For best look, should be hand-stripped occasionally. Professional grooming is optional; some trimming is helpful. Moderate shedding.

Life Span: 11 to 14 years.

Health Concerns: Hip and elbow dysplasia.

Exercise: Very high.

Housing: Not suitable for urban areas or apartment life.

Sociability: Bonds to one person. Not always good with kids, unless socialized early. Aloof with strangers. May try to dominate other dogs.

Trainability: High, but it takes some patience. Can be dominant if not properly trained.

Activities: Hunting, retrieving, field trials.

5 Facts

Rugged
High exercise requirements
Moderate grooming
Bonds to one person
May bark

GIANT SCHNAUZER

Origin: Germany, Middle Ages.

Original Purpose: Driving cattle; carting; guarding; police work.

Personality: Confident, loyal, playful, exuberant, reliable, spirited.

Breed Traits: Territorial. Makes a good watchdog and is very protective of his family. Not overtly affectionate. When left alone too long, may become destructive. Not recommended for first-time owners.

Physical Attributes: 23 to 27 in (58.5 to 68.5 cm); 65 to 95 lb (29.5 to 43 kg). Colors are black or salt and pepper.

Coat Type and Grooming: Outercoat hard and wiry; undercoat soft. High maintenance; trimming around eyes and ears. Whiskers should be cleaned after meals. Professional grooming is recommended; coat needs to be stripped twice a year. Low to moderate shedding.

Life Span: 11 to 12 years.

Health Concerns: Hip dysplasia, OCD, PRA.

Exercise: Moderate to high.

Housing: Not suitable for urban areas or apartment life; this big dog needs a lot of room.

Sociability: Lives to be near people and is usually very good with them. Tends to bond with one person. Tolerant and protective of family kids but may be too rough for small children; may also try to "herd" kids. Can be reserved and suspicious of strangers, including strange children. May be all right with other pets if socialized early but will attempt to dominate.

Trainability: High; all Giant Schnauzers should be taken to puppy kindergarten and later to obedience classes. These dogs require firm handling and an experienced owner.

Activities: Police work, search and rescue, tracking, obedience, bomb squad, therapy dog, canine assistant, Schutzhund.

5 Facts

Protective
Not for novice owners
Professional grooming
Bonds to one person
Needs room

GLEN OF IMAAL TERRIER

Origin: Ireland, 1700s.

Original Purpose: Hunting badger, foxes, and rats; "turn-spit" dogs.

Personality: Spirited, brave, stubborn, rambunctious, stoic, hardy, independent, playful.

Breed Traits: Like to dig. Rarely bark without a reason.

Physical Attributes: 12.5 to 14 in (31.5 to 35.5 cm); males approx. 35 lb (16 kg), females slightly less. Colors are wheaten, blue, brindle.

Coat Type and Grooming: Medium-length, harsh outercoat and soft undercoat. Fairly high maintenance; does best with stripping or professional clipping; some trimming required. Light shedding.

Life Span: 12 to 14 years.

Health Concerns: Skin allergies.

Exercise: Low to moderate.

Housing: Can adapt to most living arrangements.

Sociability: Devoted to his family. Gentle with children of all ages. Gets along with most other pets but can't be trusted around small animals like guinea pigs, ferrets, and hamsters.

Trainability: Low to moderate. Intelligent but has a stubborn streak in the face of training.

Activities: Earthdog, agility, rally.

5 Facts

Spirited
Professional grooming
Adaptable
Devoted to family
Stubborn

GOLDEN RETRIEVER

Origin: England/Scotland, 1800s. The modern breed was developed by an English nobleman with the interesting name of Lord Tweedmouth. (His estate was on the Tweed River near Inverness, Scotland.) Ancestors include setters, water spaniels, and the Curly-Coated Retriever.

Original Purpose: Gundog, hunting and retrieving shot waterfowl.

Personality: Eager to please, trustworthy, outgoing, versatile, self-confident, friendly, calm, kindly.

Breed Traits: Solid, strong, rugged, active. Requires human attention. Not protective but may bark to welcome strangers. Can handle extremes of heat and cold better than many other breeds but does best in a colder climate. Enjoys swimming. Quite reliable off leash, because he is very responsive to his owner. Superb first dog.

Physical Attributes: 21 to 25 in (53.5 to 63.5 cm); 55 to 75 lb (25 to 34 kg). Working lines somewhat smaller than show lines. Colors are golden or "lion" color, all shades from pale to reddish. Originally, darker, redder shades were favored, but nowadays, lighter, more "golden" shades are more common.

Coat Type and Grooming: Either flat or wavy, moderately long; undercoat dense and water-repellent. Fairly high maintenance; two or three times a week brushing. Some trimming. Moderate shedding.

Life Span: 10 to 14 years.

Health Concerns: Bloat, orthopedic problems (hip dysplasia, OCD), epilepsy, eye problems (distichiasis, PRA, cataracts), von Willebrand's, enteritis, cancer, heart problems (cardiomyopathy, SAS) skin problems (hot spots, dermatitis, inhalant and food allergies), ear infections, diabetes, obesity.

Exercise: Moderate to high. Needs moderate outdoor exercise but perhaps not as much as some of the other retrievers; however, if he doesn't get a sufficient amount, can have behavior problems.

Housing: Not a good apartment dog; needs room to run.

Sociability: Very affectionate to the entire family. Excellent with children; however, may be too rambunctious for very small kids. Likes strangers, so don't expect the well-bred Golden to guard your property. Very friendly with other pets.

Trainability: Extremely high; very easy to train. Goldens hang around and wait to be told to do something.

Activities: Guide dog, search and rescue, hunting, therapy dog, flyball, obedience, agility.

5 Facts

Friendly
Excellent for novices
High-maintenance coat
Devoted to family
Highly trainable

GORDON SETTER

Origin: Scotland, 1600s. Daniel Webster imported the first one to the United States.

Original Purpose: Field dog.

Personality: Good-humored, conscientious, capable, lively, devoted to family, faithful.

Breed Traits: Immense endurance; simply tireless. Slower and heavier but more powerful than other setters. Excellent watchdog; more protective of family than other setters. Generally quiet and pleasant in the house. Reliability off leash is low.

Physical Attributes: 23 to 27 in (58.5 to 68.5 cm); 55 to 80 lb (25 to 36.5 kg); dramatic long wavy coat. The Gordon is a slow-maturing breed that goes thorough a gangling adolescence; however, the results are worth the wait. Colors are black with tan, chestnut, or gold markings.

Coat Type and Grooming: Wavy, long, silky. High maintenance; daily grooming is necessary to prevent mats. Professional grooming is recommended; trimming required. Low to moderate seasonal shedding.

Life Span: 10 to 12 years.

Health Concerns: Hip dysplasia, bloat, PRA.

Exercise: High. Needs a lot of strenuous hard exercise every day. Most become calmer as they mature, although mine is five years old, gets unlimited amounts of exercise every day, and is still a handful.

Housing: Not suitable for urban areas or apartment life.

Sociability: A very good dog with children. Some are suspicious of strangers. Amiable for the most part with other pets but wants to be boss; some are aggressive to other dogs.

Trainability: Average. The Gordon is a "soft" dog who responds to gentle but firm handling.

Activities: Hunting upland game birds, field trials, therapy dog, agility, obedience.

5 Facts

Good watchdog
Needs strenuous exercise
High-maintenance coat
Not for apartments
Good with children

GREAT DANE

Origin: Germany, Middle Ages. Despite his name, the Great Dane has nothing to do with Denmark; he is a refined version of a Mastiff.

Original Purpose: Dog of war; boarhound; guarding; drafting.

Personality: Regal, stable, good-natured, affectionate, friendly, dignified.

Breed Traits: Strong, powerful, and elegant. Calm in the house with moderate daily outdoor exercise. Makes a fine watchdog. Some are dominant and will not back down if threatened. Does not fare well in extremely cold weather. Best with an experienced owner; otherwise can become dominant and try to challenge the owner.

Physical Attributes: At least 28 in (71 cm) for females and at least 30 in (76 cm) for males; 100 to 180 lb (45.5 to 81.5 kg). Colors are fawn (tan) with a black mask, brindle, black, blue, harlequin (white with black patches).

Coat Type and Grooming: Short, thick, smooth, glossy. Minimal care; twice-a-week brushing. Moderate to high shedding, but there's a lot of dog.

Life Span: 8 to 10 years.

Health Concerns: Bloat, allergies, orthopedic problems (hip dysplasia, OCD, hypertrophic osteodystrophy, Wobblers), color dilution alopecia, heart disease (cardiomyopathy, SAS, arrhythmia), thyroid problems (hyperthyroidism), cancer (osteosarcoma), entropion, deafness (in white and harlequin), acral lick dermatitis.

Exercise: Moderate to high; lower as the dog matures.

Housing: Adaptable to any living situation if given sufficient exercise. Generally does better in the suburbs than in the city.

Sociability: Bonds to the entire family. Very good with children, although his great size merits supervision; best if raised with them. Very friendly with other pets; may be somewhat suspicious of other dogs.

Trainability: High; because of his great size, this dog should be given obedience training early.

Activities: Therapy dog, obedience.

5 Facts
Calm in house
Best with experienced owner
Minimal grooming
Bonds to entire family
Adaptable

GREATER SWISS MOUNTAIN DOG

Origin: Switzerland, antiquity.

Original Purpose: Guarding, drafting, herding, cattle driving.

Personality: Sensitive, dominant, gentle, calm, attentive, patient, affectionate.

Breed Traits: Sturdy, powerful. Can be territorial. A superior watchdog.

Physical Attributes: 24 to 29 in (61 to 73.5 cm); 90 to 130 lb (41 to 59 kg). The ground color is jet black; markings are rich rust and white.

Coat Type and Grooming: Dense outercoat and thick undercoat. Minimal care required; weekly brushing. Low seasonal shedding.

Life Span: 8 to 10 years.

Health Concerns: Hip, elbow, or shoulder dysplasia.

Exercise: Moderate to high.

Housing: Not well suited to urban life, although his exercise needs are fairly moderate. The country is the best home; he enjoys being outdoors.

Sociability: Very gentle with children but may be too large for toddlers. Wary of strangers until introduced, then friendly. Very good with other pets.

Trainability: Average to high.

Activities: Weight-pulling, carting, herding.

5 Facts

Good watchdog
Not for apartments
Minimal grooming
Gentle with children
Affectionate

GREAT PYRENEES

Origin: Pyrenees Mountains between Spain and France. Fossil remains estimated to date as far back as 1800 BCE, and some estimates place the breed's origins back 11,000 years.

Original Purpose: Guarding sheep from wolves and bears; later guard dogs for people.

Personality: Independent, sedate, affectionate, confident, serene, patient.

Breed Traits: Imposing, elegant. One of the strongest of all dogs. Territorial; protective; a superior watchdog. Has great endurance and loves the cold but cannot handle heat. An escape artist; should be kept within a secure area. This breed drools. Experienced owner recommended.

Physical Attributes: 26 to 32 in (66 to 81 cm); 99 to 132 lb (45 to 60 kg). Double dewclaws on the hind legs. Color is white or white with markings of gray, badger, reddish brown, or tan. These markings may appear on the ears, head, tail, and a few body spots.

Coat Type and Grooming: Outercoat long, thick, and coarse; undercoat downy. High maintenance; daily grooming and occasional trimming required. Professional grooming is desirable. Profuse shedding twice a year.

Life Span: 10 to 12 years.

Health Concerns: Hip (although less common than in other large breeds) and elbow dysplasia, deafness, patellar luxation, Factor XI deficiency (a bleeding disorder), bloat, bone cancer, sensitivity to anesthesia.

Exercise: Moderate. Needs regular walks, but moderate exercise will suit him fine.

Housing: Not suitable for urban areas or apartment life; needs a lot of space and a fenced yard.

Sociability: Adapts well to family life; may become a one-person or one-family dog. Gentle, tolerant, and protective of the family children. Wary of strangers; can be aggressive. Often antagonistic to dogs of their own sex; may protect other pets in "their" family.

Trainability: Low; needs strong motivational training and an experienced owner. Some individuals attempt to dominate members of the family.

Activities: Rescue dog, avalanche dog, drafting, carting, backpacking, guard dog.

5 Facts

Territorial
Needs experienced owner
Protective of children
Cannot handle heat
Daily grooming

GREYHOUND

Origin: Middle East; ancestors are supposedly seen on Egyptian tomb paintings dating to 2900 BCE, and the Greyhound is the only breed of dog specifically mentioned in the Bible.

Original Purpose: Coursing hares and rabbits; racing.

Personality: Independent, even-tempered, sensitive, lovable, strong-willed, gentle.

Breed Traits: The fastest of all dogs, can run up to 40 miles an hour (63 kph). Very quiet and well-behaved in the house. Older dogs are quite sedate. Must be kept on a leash or inside a safe fenced area. Little tolerance for cold.

Physical Attributes: 23 to 30 in (58.5 to 76 cm); 60 to 80 lb (27 to 36.5 kg). Most common colors are black, brindle, and fawn, but any color accepted, including red, white, and blue.

Coat Type and Grooming: Thick, short, and smooth. Minimal care required; weekly brushing. Light to moderate shedding.

Life Span: 9 to 14 years.

Health Concerns: Bloat, brittle bones, PRA, hypothyroidism, deafness, allergic dermatitis, may be sensitive to anesthesia and certain flea treatments.

Exercise: Moderate to high; these dogs need large fenced-in exercise areas.

Housing: Adaptable to any living situation with sufficient exercise.

Sociability: Good, although some are not suited to small children; usually, however, they are very gentle and biddable. Typically good with strangers, although some may be shy. Good, even submissive, with other dogs. May be all right with smaller pets and cats if raised with them, but need to be watched. They have a natural instinct to chase small animals.

Trainability: Low; easily distracted; early socialization required to prevent shyness.

Activities: Racing, lure-coursing.

5 Facts

Quiet
Minimal grooming
Adaptable
Gentle with children
No cold tolerance

HARRIER

Origin: Great Britain; probably derived from the English Foxhound. The first pack was established by Sir Elias de Midhope in 1260; descendants of the pack existed for 500 years.

Original Purpose: Hunting rabbits and hares.

Personality: Amiable, mild, easygoing, alert, active.

Breed Traits: Makes a fine watchdog but is not a protection dog. Very active; may be hyperactive in the house without sufficient exercise. More playful than his larger cousin the Foxhound, but less so than the smaller Beagle. Has a superlative sense of smell.

Physical Attributes: 19 to 21 in (48.5 to 53.5 cm); 45 to 60 lb (20.5 to 27 kg). Any hound color, usually black, tan, and white.

Coat Type and Grooming: Short. Minimal care required. Light to moderate shedding.

Life Span: 10 to 12 years.

Health Concerns: Hip dysplasia (about 16 percent in this breed), elbow dysplasia, PRA, anal fissures.

Exercise: High; needs room to exercise in a large, high fenced area.

Housing: Not suitable for urban areas or apartment life.

Sociability: Excellent with children. Reserved with strangers. Excellent with other pets.

Trainability: Average.

Activities: Hunting.

5 Facts

Active
Needs room to exercise
Minimal grooming
Good with children
Amiable

HAVANESE

Origin: Cuba; closely related to the Maltese and Bichon Frise.

Original Purpose: Lapdog, companion.

Personality: Affectionate, playful, clownish, merry, willing to please.

Breed Traits: Sturdy, agile, and vocal. Will give a welcoming bark to strangers. Craves attention. Has a lot of energy. Can handle both heat and cold. Makes a good pet for the first-time dog owner.

Physical Attributes: 8 to 11 in (20 to 28 cm); 7 to 14 lb (3 to 6.5 kg). All colors and combinations of colors, including champagne and chocolate (which I think is a great combination under any circumstances).

Coat Type and Grooming: Double wavy, undulating, or curly. Fairly high maintenance; needs to be groomed two to four times a week. Professional grooming is optional. Practically non-shedding, but the long hair can tangle and mat all too easily.

Life Span: 12 to 15 years.

Health Concerns: PRA, juvenile cataracts, patellar luxation.

Exercise: Moderate. Energetic but does not need a great deal of room in order to be properly exercised.

Housing: Can adapt to any living situation.

Sociability: Loves everyone, including strangers and young children. Good with other pets.

Trainability: High; this breed will perform on command.

Activities: Obedience, agility.

5 Facts

Needs company
Non-shedding
Ideal for apartment life
Highly sociable
Willing to please

IBIZAN HOUND

Origin: Ibiza (Balearic Islands in the Mediterranean) or Egypt; probably developed from the Pharaoh Hound.

Original Purpose: Chase prey.

Personality: Energetic, gentle, loving, curious, restless, adaptable.

Breed Traits: Graceful, tireless, strong, fast. Some individuals are shy, especially around loud noises. Not a protection dog, although he appears daunting. An amazing jumper; needs a safe, fenced area. Has an acute sense of smell and hearing. Naturally clean. Not suited to cold weather.

Physical Attributes: 23 to 27 in (58.5 to 68.5 cm); 45 to 50 lb (20.5 to 22.5 kg). Colors are red or white, chestnut, tawny, solid or in combination. One tawny-red shade is called "lion."

Coat Type and Grooming: Two types: one smooth and short, and one longer and more wiry (seen mostly in Spain). Low maintenance; both types just need occasional brushing. Minimal shedding.

Life Span: 12 to 14 years.

Health Concerns: Axonal dystrophy, cardiopathy, deafness, seizures, sensitive to anesthesia.

Exercise: Moderate to high.

Housing: Adaptable if given sufficient exercise. Because the Ibizan is such a good jumper, fences need to be very high.

Sociability: Gets along with the whole family. Very good with children. Very good with other pets; unlike many sighthounds, gets along with small animals and cats.

Trainability: Average; however, this breed requires very careful and thorough socialization.

Activities: Therapy dog, lure-coursing, search and rescue, tracking, agility.

5 Facts

Adaptable
Graceful
Minimal grooming
Naturally clean
Needs secure yard

ICELANDIC SHEEPDOG

Origin: Iceland, 10th century.

Original Purpose: Herding livestock.

Personality: Playful, inquisitive, courageous, alert, active, gentle.

Breed Traits: He can be barky, and barks while he herds.

Physical Attributes: 16 to 18 in (40.5 to 45.5 cm); 20 to 30 lb (9 to 13.5 kg). Colors are tan shades, chocolate brown, gray, black, all with white markings.

Coat Type and Grooming: Two varieties: shorthaired (medium-length, weatherproof outercoat and thick, soft undercoat) and longer-haired (longer-length, weatherproof outercoat and thick, soft undercoat). High maintenance; both types need frequent brushing and combing. Seasonal heavy shedding.

Life Span: 11 to 14 years.

Health Concerns: Cataracts.

Exercise: High. Requires vigorous exercise to keep him physically and mentally fit. If he's not being used as a working dog, his daily routine should include long walks and lots of play.

Housing: Does best in a home with lots of outdoor space.

Sociability: An enthusiastic and friendly dog who gets along well with everyone and adores children. Gets along well with other pets.

Trainability: High. He is an eager learner and enthusiastic participant in training.

Activities: Agility, flyball, obedience, herding.

5 Facts

Playful
High-maintenance coat
Needs vigorous exercise
Adores children
May bark

IRISH RED AND WHITE SETTER

Origin: Ireland, 1700s.

Original Purpose: Locating and retrieving birds.

Personality: Friendly, energetic, lively, boisterous, mischievous.

Breed Traits: Wonderful companion for an active family.

Physical Attributes: 24 to 26 in (61 to 66 cm); 50 to 75 lb (22.5 to 34 kg). Color is white with solid red patches.

Coat Type and Grooming: Long, straight, flat, silky, fine, with feathering. High maintenance; regular brushing—especially the feathering on his tail, legs, and underside. Moderate shedding.

Life Span: 12 to 14 years.

Health Concerns: Bloat, canine leukocyte adhesion deficiency (CLAD), posterior polar cataract (PPC), von Willebrand's.

Exercise: High. He needs to be able to extend himself in wide-open spaces.

Housing: Best in the country with lots of places to exercise.

Sociability: Friendly to all. Enjoys children but may be too energetic for very small children. Gets along with other pets.

Trainability: Average. His exuberance can make it difficult for him to focus on his training. Patient repetition is the way to get results.

Activities: Hunting, field trials, therapy dog.

5 Facts

Good for active family
High exercise requirements
Needs outdoor space
High-maintenance coat
Friendly

IRISH SETTER

Origin: Ireland, 1700s.
Original Purpose: Locating and retrieving birds.
Personality: Tireless, sweet, energetic, playful, gay, happy.
Breed Traits: Very fast, graceful, aristocratic. Highly energetic. Acute sense of smell. Not protective but will bark to welcome guests. Needs a lot of attention. Has a wonderful zest for life. Slow to mature and is quite long-lived. A well-bred Irish, given sufficient exercise, is a wonderful pet and a perfect show dog.
Physical Attributes: 24 to 27 in (61 to 68.5 cm); 55 to 70 lb (25 to 31.5 kg). Colors are deep red or chestnut to mahogany, although many of the first Irish setters were white and red. By the 1870s, however, the dogs became solid red, although a very tiny patch of white is allowed on the chest.

Coat Type and Grooming: Silky, long, feathery, wavy, with heavy feathering on the legs, tail, and ears. High maintenance; brushing three times a week. Coat tends to tangle, especially behind the ears. Professional grooming is recommended; some trimming required. Moderate shedding.
Life Span: 12 to 14 years.
Health Concerns: Eye problems (PRA, entropion, cataracts), bloat, osteosarcoma, epilepsy, skin problems (allergies, acral lick dermatitis), hypothyroidism, orthopedic problems (hip dysplasia, hypertrophic osteodystrophy), ear infections.
Exercise: High; a place to run freely is absolutely essential.
Housing: Cannot live happily in an apartment and really does best in the country.
Sociability: Excellent but rambunctious with people. My Irish was terribly fond of babies, but many are too joyfully wild for very small children. Excellent with other pets; my Irish Setter would chase unknown cats but was fond of her own.
Trainability: Average. Slow to train but remembers lessons well. Extremely sensitive and responds only to positive reinforcement; needs very soft handling.
Activities: Hunting (not common nowadays, but some breeders are working to return the breed to its original use), therapy dog, field trials, obedience.

5 Facts

Energetic
Needs attention
High-maintenance coat
Not for apartment life
Highly sociable

IRISH TERRIER

Origin: Southern Ireland, 1700s; one of the oldest terrier breeds.

Original Purpose: Hunting foxes and otters.

Personality: Bold, fearless, intuitive, playful, loyal, adaptable.

Breed Traits: Graceful. Loves to play. An excellent watchdog. Will protect his family. Quiet in the house. Can be an escape artist. Can handle any climate. They require a strong owner; terriers in general can be tough to own, but once you train one, they are excellent pets.

Physical Attributes: 18 to 19 in (45.5 to 48.5 cm); 25 to 27 lb (11.5 to 12 kg). Colors are red and wheaten solid colors.

Coat Type and Grooming: Harsh, wiry, weather-resistant. Fairly high maintenance. Professional grooming is recommended; hand-stripping for show dogs, clipping for pets. Light shedding, if groomed correctly.

Life Span: 13 to 16 years.

Health Concerns: Bladder or kidney stones.

Exercise: High; daily exercise needed.

Housing: Adaptable to any living situation; does well in the city.

Sociability: Very good with kids. Reserved with strangers. Will probably be aggressive or dominate strange dogs; may tolerate family pets if socialized early.

Trainability: High but may try to dominate his owner.

Activities: Vermin elimination, terrier trials.

5 Facts

Protective
Professional grooming
High exercise requirements
Adaptable
Quiet in house

IRISH WATER SPANIEL

Origin: Ireland, 1800s. Some say the breed is 6,000 years old; obviously some Poodle blood (or at least curls) in the background.

Original Purpose: Water retriever.

Personality: Playful, courageous, willing, sense of humor, gentle, loyal.

Breed Traits: A very good watchdog. Active but heat intolerant. Has lots of endurance. Needs to be around water to be happy and has many retriever qualities. Some individuals drool. Known as "The Clown of Spaniels."

Physical Attributes: 21 to 24 in (53.5 to 61 cm); 55 to 65 lb (25 to 29.5 kg). The tallest of the spaniels and is often confused with a Poodle, although the Irish Water Spaniel has a rat tail. Color is liver.

Coat Type and Grooming: Tight curls. Moderate to high maintenance; oily coat can give off a characteristic smell. Professional grooming is recommended; trimming required. Negligible shedding.

Life Span: 10 to 12 years.

Health Concerns: Hip dysplasia, von Willebrand's, autoimmune diseases.

Exercise: High, especially as a puppy. Likes to swim and happiest around water.

Housing: Not suited to urban areas or apartment life.

Sociability: Fair with children. Initially rather standoffish to and suspicious of strangers, but gradually becomes friendly. Very good with other pets; a few unaltered males dislike other males.

Trainability: Highly trainable but requires early socialization.

Activities: Hunting, obedience, field trials, tracking, agility, service dog.

5 Facts

Active
Oily coat
High exercise requirements
Not for apartment life
Loves water

IRISH WOLFHOUND

Origin: Ireland, antiquity.

Original Purpose: Hunting boar, Irish elk, and wolves. (Was apparently so good at this that wolves are extinct in Ireland.)

Personality: Adaptable, fearless, peaceful, willing to please, calm, gentle.

Breed Traits: A low-energy dog. Quiet in the house. Known as the "gentle giant." Has very little tolerance for heat. Best with an experienced owner

Physical Attributes: At least 30 in (13.5 cm) for females and at least 32 in (81 cm) for males; 105 to 120 lb (47.5 to 54.5 kg). One of the tallest of all dogs. Any color, but gray, brindle, red, black, white, and fawn are most common.

Coat Type and Grooming: Rough, hard, and wiry; short to medium. Moderate maintenance. Professional grooming necessary for a show dog, who needs to be stripped occasionally; not necessary for a pet. Some trimming advised. Light shedding if coat is correctly maintained.

Life Span: 6 to 8 years.

Health Concerns: Bloat, von Willebrand's, OCD, heart problems (arrhythmia, cardiomyopathy).

Exercise: Moderate; needs daily exercise.

Housing: Not suited to small apartments but can be happy in an urban area with a lot of exercise.

Sociability: Tends to be a one-person dog. Very calm, reliable, and sociable with children but not playful, at least as an adult; puppies can overwhelm a child with good-natured exuberance. Very good with other pets; benefits from the company of other dogs.

Trainability: High, especially for a sighthound.

Activities: Lure-coursing.

5 Facts

Adaptable
Low energy
Bonds with one person
Moderate grooming
Gentle giant

ITALIAN GREYHOUND

Origin: Italy, Greece, or Turkey, antiquity; Romans bred them for pets.

Original Purpose: Companion.

Personality: Gentle, devoted, calm, sensitive, alert, vivacious.

Breed Traits: Elegant, quick-footed. Likes to be the center of attention. Thrives on human companionship; however, he does not need constant attention. Sedate in the house, especially as he matures. Should not be allowed to play roughly, as he could be injured. Tends to jump on people. Has no doggy odor. No cold tolerance. Slow to mature.

Physical Attributes: 13 to 16 in (33 to 40.5 cm), 7 to 13 lb (3 to 6 kg). So delicately built that he is considered a toy dog. Colors are usually black, fawn, red, cream blue, with or without broken white. Any color but brindle or black-and-tan allowed.

Coat Type and Grooming: Short, soft, and glossy. Minimal grooming; once a week. Very minimal shedding.

Life Span: 13 to 16 years.

Health Concerns: Periodontal problems, PRA, fractures, color dilution alopecia, patellar luxation, sensitivity to anesthesia and barbiturates.

Exercise: Moderate to high; enjoys running.

Housing: Suitable for any type of living environment.

Sociability: Good with older, gentle children; too fragile for toddlers. Reserved with strangers. Good with larger dogs; likes familiar pets, including cats. May chase very small pets or quarrel with dogs his own size.

Trainability: Average; some are hard to housetrain.

Activities: Agility.

5 Facts

Elegant
Good for apartment life
Reserved with strangers
Minimal grooming
Sedate in house

JAPANESE CHIN

Origin: China (despite its name), antiquity.
Original Purpose: Companion. (Early types were supposedly sometimes kept in hanging birdcages.)
Personality: Playful, devoted, sensitive, alert, cheerful.
Breed Traits: Enjoys human company. Does not tolerate heat or cold. Some can climb. Some snore. A naturally clean dog.
Physical Attributes: 8 to 11 in (20 to 28 cm); 4 to 7 lb (2 to 3 kg). Colors are black-and-white, red-and-white, or tricolor.
Coat Type and Grooming: Long, profuse, and silky. Moderate grooming; two or three times a week. Professional grooming is optional. Moderate shedding; heavy seasonally.

Life Span: 12 to 14 years.
Health Concerns: Respiratory problems, patellar luxation, mitral valve insufficiency, sensitive to anesthesia.
Exercise: Low.
Housing: Ideal for urban areas and apartment life.
Sociability: Tends to bond to one person. Very good with gentle, well-behaved children. A few are reserved around strangers; others enjoy meeting new friends. Very good with other pets.
Trainability: Variable, often very high. Has been known to make up his own tricks.
Activities: Therapy dog.

5 Facts

Needs company
Moderate grooming
Ideal for apartment life
Bonds with one person
Playful

KEESHOND

Origin: Holland, 1700s.

Original Purpose: Barge guard; watchdog; rat-killer.

Personality: Confident, bold, happy, adaptable, stubborn, friendly.

Breed Traits: One of the most delightful of the spitz-type dogs. Handles cold and damp well, but not good in the heat. Good swimmer. Can be barky. Best with experienced owners.

Physical Attributes: 17 to 18 in (43 to 45.5 cm); 38 to 40 lb (17 to 18 kg). Solidly built. The tail is carried over the back, and a double curl is preferred. They are also known for their Keeshond smile, a real grin. Color is gray with black-tipped overcoat, the undercoat colored pale gray or cream. The dark puppy coat gradually lightens as they mature.

Coat Type and Grooming: Double undercoat and lion-like mane. High maintenance; vigorous grooming three or four times a week. Professional grooming is recommended. Heavy shedding; the undercoat "blows" in big clumps twice a year.

Life Span: 12 to 14 years.

Health Concerns: Hip dysplasia, heart problems (VSD), von Willebrand's, epilepsy.

Exercise: Moderate.

Housing: Adaptable to any living situation.

Sociability: Quite good with both adults and children. Usually good with other pets but aggressive on occasion.

Trainability: Average; needs an experienced trainer. Some have housetraining problems.

Activities: Agility, obedience, tracking.

5 Facts

Confident
Professional grooming
Needs experienced trainer
Adaptable
May bark

KERRY BLUE TERRIER

Origin: Ireland (County Kerry, of course), 1700s. Its ancestry is a mystery. There are tales of Russian shipwrecks and more plausible stories of breeding from Soft Coated Wheatens and Irish Terriers.

Original Purpose: Ratting; hunting.

Personality: Hardworking, fun-loving, adaptable, game, intense, fearless.

Breed Traits: Elegant, powerful. Superior watchdog. Territorial. Best with an experienced owner.

Physical Attributes: 17 to 19 in (43 to 48.5 cm); 33 to 39 lb (15 to 17.5 kg). Color is any shade of blue-gray, including light silver and dark slate. Puppies are born almost black but must show a color change by 18 months of age.

Coat Type and Grooming: Silkier coat than most terriers; can mat overnight. High maintenance; combing two or three times a week. Professional grooming is recommended; monthly shaping and scissoring. Low shedding.

Life Span: 13 to 16 years.

Health Concerns: Cataracts, bleeding disorders, progressive neuronal abiotrophy, sebaceous cysts, hip dysplasia.

Exercise: Fairly high but does not need large amounts of open space.

Housing: Adaptable to any living situation.

Sociability: Attaches himself to the whole family. Very good with well-behaved children, if socialized. Not friendly to strangers but very amiable once he gets used to them. Bad with other dogs and not good with other pets, including birds, unless socialized very early.

Trainability: Average; needs a great deal of early, firm socialization. They are easily housetrained and good problem solvers; however, they may try to dominate their owner.

Activities: Police dog, ratting, obedience.

5 Facts

Professional grooming
Best with experienced owner
Bonds to whole family
Good watchdog
Adaptable

KOMONDOR

Origin: Hungary, antiquity.

Original Purpose: Flock guarding.

Personality: Serious, independent, aloof, stubborn, bold, wary.

Breed Traits: Powerful. Excellent watchdog. Strong protective instincts. Loves the outdoors but does not tolerate heat. An experienced and strong owner is required; this independent dog can be dangerous if not handled properly.

Physical Attributes: 21 to 31 in (53.5 to 78.5 cm); 79 to 130 lb (36 to 59 kg). Males are considerably larger than females. Color is white.

Coat Type and Grooming: Corded, long. High maintenance. The coat tends to get dirty very easily, and it takes about two hours to wash; furthermore, it takes about a full day to dry. Professional grooming is necessary for the show dog; pets are easiest clipped. Practically non-shedding, but coat tends to knot.

Life Span: 12 years.

Health Concerns: Hip dysplasia, bloat.

Exercise: Moderate to high; needs intense exercise for a fairly long period.

Housing: Adaptable to urban areas or apartment life with effort.

Sociability: Not good with children; although he may get along well with his own family, he may be too protective. Reserved with strangers. Aggressive toward strange dogs; amenable with his "own" pets and will guard them.

Trainability: High; however, this dog may challenge his owner for dominance. Needs a very experienced owner and extensive early socialization.

Activities: Sheep guarding, agility.

5 Facts

Protective
Needs experienced owner
Loves outdoors
High-maintenance coat
Powerful

KUVASZ

Origin: Hungary, by way of Tibet.

Original Purpose: Sheepherder and protector of flocks.

Personality: Gentle, loyal, brave, wary, spirited.

Breed Traits: Strong, sturdy. Likes cold weather. Looks soft but is a very tough customer. Not especially demonstrative. Very protective; highly territorial; high watchdog and guarding ability. Can be restless in the house. Escape artist. Frequently tries to dominate, so must have an experienced owner.

Physical Attributes: 26 to 30 in (66 to 76 cm); 84 to 130 lb (38 to 59 kg). Color is white with no markings.

Coat Type and Grooming: Thick, medium length, wavy. Moderate grooming; no trimming. Heavy shedding.

Life Span: 10 years.

Health Concerns: Hip and elbow dysplasia, OCD, von Willebrand's.

Exercise: Moderate. Needs a lot of space to exercise.

Housing: Not well suited for urban areas or apartment life.

Sociability: A one-family dog. Very protective of family children but not trustworthy around strange kids. Suspicious of strangers. Fine, even protective, with family dogs; can be aggressive toward other pets.

Trainability: Low; requires strong training. Since the ancestors of this breed were sheep guarders and were bred to bond to sheep, not people, this dog must be very well socialized early.

Activities: Livestock guarding.

5 Facts

High guarding instinct
Not for novice owners
Moderate grooming
Likes cold weather
One-family dog

LABRADOR RETRIEVER

Origin: Newfoundland, Canada, 1800s. Others say the breed actually originated in Greenland. All Labradors can be traced back to a certain Tramp, owned by Lord Malmsbury, who supposedly arrived in a ship carrying salted codfish.

Original Purpose: Water retriever.

Personality: Loyal, outgoing, playful, confident, hardworking, easygoing.

Breed Traits: Active, strong. Fine sense of smell. Can be a good watchdog, notifying the family of strangers. Some can be barkers and diggers. Most become obese easily. Very reliable off leash. Makes an ideal family dog and is generally calm in the house. A good dog for first-time dog owners;

Physical Attributes: 21 to 24 in (53.5 to 61 cm); 55 to 75 lb (25 to 34 kg). His tail is said to resemble that of an otter. Colors are black, yellow, chocolate. The yellow can range from pale cream to a reddish hue.

Coat Type and Grooming: Short, straight dense outercoat; soft water-repellant undercoat. Moderate maintenance. No trimming. Weekly brushing. Moderate to heavy shedding.

Life Span: 11 to 13 years.

Health Concerns: Orthopedic problems (hip and elbow dysplasia, cruciate ligament injuries, arthritis, OCD), ear infections, gastritis/enteritis, obesity, cardiomyopathy, bloat, eye problems (cataracts, retinal dysplasia, PRA), skin problems (inhalant and food allergies, acral lick dermatitis), cancer (osteosarcoma).

Exercise: High, especially when young. If exercise needs are not met, can become destructive, chewing anything in their path.

Chocolate Labradors have a reputation of being more active than yellow or black.

Housing: Not suited for apartment life. Happiest in homes where he has access to swimming.

Sociability: Very friendly to children, but young Labs may be too exuberant for toddlers. This is a great family dog who loves the rough-and-tumble games of children. One of the best "people" dogs; loves everyone. Also good with other pets.

Trainability: Exceptionally high; these dogs are eager to please. Early training is important.

Activities: Guide dog, hunting and retrieving, obedience, flyball, sniffer dog, therapy dog, search and rescue.

5 Facts

Ideal family dog
High exercise requirements
Moderate grooming
Exceptionally trainable
Highly sociable

LAKELAND TERRIER

Origin: Lake District of England, 1700s.
Original Purpose: Killing vermin.
Personality: Frisky, spunky, clever, playful, curious, self-confident.
Breed Traits: Energetic, agile. Quiet for a terrier. Likes to be the center of attention. Superb watchdog but too small to be really protective.
Physical Attributes: 13 to 14 in (33 to 35.5 cm); 16 to 20 lb (7.5 to 9 kg). Colors are blue, red, black, wheaten, or liver; may have a saddle of black, blue, liver, or grizzle.
Coat Type and Grooming: Short, wiry. Moderate to high maintenance required; brushing three times a week. Professional grooming is necessary; pets need to be clipped and show dogs stripped regularly. Light shedding.

Life Span: 12 to 13 years.
Health Concerns: Legg-Perthes, cataracts.
Exercise: Moderate to high.
Housing: Adaptable to any living situation.
Sociability: Bonds to one person. Enjoys playing with children; may be too active for toddlers. Reserved with strangers. Not always good with other pets but better than many other terriers.
Trainability: Low; can be stubborn.
Activities: Earthdog trials, varmint eradication.

5 Facts
Frisky
Professional grooming
Bonds to one person
Quiet for a terrier
Adaptable

LEONBERGER

Origin: Germany, 1800s.

Original Purpose: Companion.

Personality: Affectionate, intelligent, noble, even-tempered, patient, loving, loyal.

Breed Traits: Requires lots of interaction with his owner.

Physical Attributes: 25.5 to 31.5 in (65 to 80 cm); 80 to 150 lb (36.5 to 68 kg). Colors are lion yellow, golden to red-brown, sand, and all combinations in between.

Coat Type and Grooming: Long, medium-soft to coarse, close-fitting, water-resistant outercoat and thick, soft undercoat; feathering; mane. High maintenance required; brushing required several times a week or the long hair tangles. Profuse seasonal shedding.

Life Span: 8 to 10 years.

Health Concerns: Addison's disease, bloat, ectropion, entropion, hip dysplasia, OCD, osteosarcoma, panosteitis.

Exercise: High; he needs to be kept busy.

Housing: Best in rural or suburban areas where he can get enough room to exercise.

Sociability: Family-oriented and especially loves children. Can do well with other dogs and animals as long as he's properly socialized.

Trainability: Average. Sensitive and need positive-based training; they also need lots of socialization from puppyhood.

Activities: Agility, carting, water work, therapy dog.

5 Facts

Affectionate
Requires a lot of interaction
Family-oriented
High-maintenance coat
Sensitive

LHASA APSO

Origin: Tibet, antiquity.

Original Purpose: Indoor watchdog; companion.

Personality: Creative, playful, bold, loyal, companionable, independent.

Breed Traits: Needs plenty of attention but less than other small breeds. Small as he is, he is not in the Toy Group and does not have a "toy" personality. Protective of his family, sometimes too much so. Acute hearing. Can handle cold weather. Good as a family dog or companion for one person.

Physical Attributes: 10 to 11 in (25.5 to 28 cm); 14 to 16 lb (6.5 to 7.5 kg). Any color: golden, dark grizzle, black, parti-color, sandy, honey, white, brown are all acceptable.

Coat Type and Grooming: Long (floor length), hard, straight, heavy. Very high maintenance required; brushing every other day; lots of shampooing to bring out the shine. The hair over the eyes was protective against Tibetan winds but serves little purpose now. The coat is parted in the middle. Pet owners often have their dogs clipped and tie the hair back. Light shedding.

Life Span: 12 to 15 years.

Health Concerns: Allergies.

Exercise: Low to moderate.

Housing: Adaptable to any living situation; can be noisy.

Sociability: All right with older children if they are well behaved; some are snappish with toddlers. Reserved or very wary with strangers. Not always good with other dogs; good with other pets.

Trainability: Low; responds to positive reinforcement; needs a lot of repetition.

Activities: Companion, obedience.

5 Facts

Protective
High-maintenance coat
Low exercise requirements
Reserved with strangers
Adaptable

LÖWCHEN

Origin: France, Germany, 1500s.

Original Purpose: Companion.

Personality: Willing to please, devoted, alert, affectionate, fun-loving, spunky.

Breed Traits: Needs a lot of human company and attention. Some are barkers and diggers.

Physical Attributes: 12 to 14 in (30.5 to 35.5 cm) (shorter in Europe); 8 to 18 lb (3.5 to 8 kg) (lower range in Europe). Any color or combination.

Coat Type and Grooming: Long, silky, soft. Fairly high maintenance. Professional grooming is necessary; groomed in a traditional lion clip for shows, but pet owners usually leave the dog in a puppy clip. Light to moderate shedding.

Life Span: 13 to 15 years.

Health Concerns: Patellar luxation, eye problems (PRA and cataracts).

Exercise: Low.

Housing: Adaptable to any living situation.

Sociability: Very good with children and strangers. Compatible with other pets.

Trainability: Average to high.

Activities: Obedience, therapy dog.

5 Facts

Needs attention
Professional grooming
Ideal for apartment life
Good with children
Willing to please

MALTESE

Origin: Malta or possibly Melita (Sicily), antiquity. One of the oldest breeds. (Yes, there are Egyptian tomb paintings of Maltese, or something vaguely like them.) The Maltese arrived in Britain with the Romans. It is odd to think of Roman legions carrying fluffy little Maltese around with them, but there you are.

Original Purpose: Lapdog.

Personality: Fearless, lively, sweet-natured, loyal, sparkly.

Breed Traits: Likes to be pampered. Cannot handle severe weather. Will alert to the presence of strangers. Some are barkers.

Physical Attributes: 5 to 10 in (12.5 to 25.5 cm); 3 to 7 lb (1.5 to 3 kg). Color is white.

Coat Type and Grooming: Long, silky, single; even a hint of a double coat would ruin the outline for a show dog. Very high maintenance; brushing every day. Maintenance for a show coat even more, including "wrapping" the hair in cloth to keep it from matting. Professional grooming recommended. Minimal shedding.

Life Span: 12 to 15 years.

Health Concerns: Heart problems (PDA, mitral valve insufficiency), patellar luxation.

Exercise: Low; gets along with little exercise.

Housing: Adaptable to any living situation.

Sociability: Attached to whole family. Fine with older kids and strangers, although some individuals are reserved; most Maltese should not be placed in home with toddlers. Some are not good with other animals.

Trainability: Average to high; may be hard to housetrain.

Activities: Therapy dog, agility, obedience, tracking.

5 Facts
Needs companionship
High-maintenance coat
Attached to family
Low exercise
Adaptable

MANCHESTER TERRIER

Origin: England, 1500s.
Original Purpose: Ratting; coursing rabbits.
Personality: Independent, companionable.
Breed Traits: Sleek, quick. Good watchdog. Some individuals may be shy. Usually quiet, although some poorly breed individuals can be non-stop barkers. Cannot handle cold.
Physical Attributes: 16 in (40.5 cm); 12 to 22 lb (5.5 to 10 kg). Color is black with mahogany or tan points.
Coat Type and Grooming: Short, smooth, glossy. Low maintenance; this breed is so clean it has been called "catlike." Low to average seasonal shedding.
Life Span: 15 to 17 years; some have been known to live more than 20 years.
Health Concerns: Legg-Perthes, PRA, von Willebrand's.

Exercise: Moderate.
Housing: Suited for apartment life and urban areas.
Sociability: Bonds to whole family. Good with gentle children; may be overprotective; some can be snappish. Can be shy or reserved with strangers. Good with other dogs, especially other Manchester Terriers; most chase cats and smaller pets.
Trainability: Average to high; responds better than many terriers.
Activities: Earthdog trials, obedience, agility.

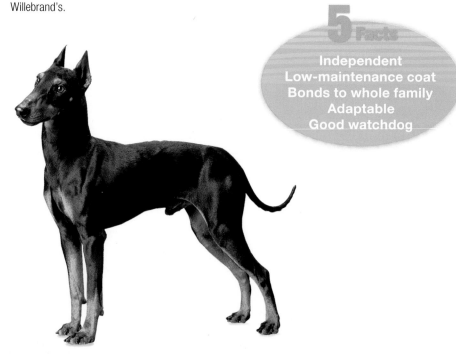

5 Facts

Independent
Low-maintenance coat
Bonds to whole family
Adaptable
Good watchdog

MASTIFF

Origin: England, antiquity. Ancestors came from Asia, and there exists the typical Egyptian tomb painting of a breed resembling a Mastiff.

Original Purpose: Guard dog; fighting dog; dog of war.

Personality: Affectionate, even-tempered, faithful, mellow, good-natured, steady.

Breed Traits: Quiet in the house. Very low energy level. Makes a reliable watchdog. Some lines can be protective or aggressive, but even Mastiffs who are not protective ward off miscreants by sheer size. Not demonstrative. Dislikes the heat.

Physical Attributes: At least 30 in (76 cm); 120 to 225 lb (54.5 to 102 kg); show Mastiffs are often a good deal bigger than the pet variety. Colors are fawn, apricot, silver fawn, or brindle; muzzle, mask, and ears must be very dark.

Coat Type and Grooming: Short, close-lying. Minimal grooming required, although there is a lot of dog here. No trimming; eyes need special care. Moderate shedding; tends to be constant rather than seasonal.

Life Span: 5 to 10 years.

Health Concerns: Obesity, bloat, hip dysplasia, OCD, von Willebrand's.

Exercise: Moderate; needs frequent moderate walks and a lot of room.

Housing: Adaptable to most living situations if given enough room to move around.

Sociability: Enjoys being around people; bonds to the entire family. Usually very good with children but not playful; however, some lines not good with kids. Usually very tolerant of other dogs.

Trainability: Average.

Activities: Therapy dog, weight-pulling.

5 Facts

Reliable watchdog
Bonds to whole family
Quiet in house
Easy coat care
Adaptable

MINIATURE BULL TERRIER

Origin: England, 1800s.
Original Function: Ratting; dog fighting.
Personality: Comical, playful, friendly.
Breed Traits: Good watchdog. Extremely playful. Similar to the Bull Terrier.
Physical Attributes: 11 to 14 in (28 to 35.5 cm); 25 to 40 lb (11.5 to 18 kg). Colors are solid white and colored (any color).
Coat Type and Grooming: Short, flat, harsh. Minimal care required; should be brushed once a week. No trimming. Moderate shedding.
Life Span: 12 to 14 years.

Health Concerns: Eye problems (glaucoma, lens luxation), allergies, mood swings, obsessive-compulsive disorders, epilepsy, deafness in whites, patellar luxation, heart problems.
Exercise: Low to moderate.
Housing: Ideal for urban areas and apartment life.
Sociability: Tends to bond to one person. Good with kids if well socialized. Usually accepting of less dominant dogs; not good with cats or small pets.
Trainability: Average.
Activities: Earthdog trials, obedience.

5 Facts

Very playful
Minimal grooming
Bonds to one person
Adaptable
Good watchdog

MINIATURE PINSCHER

Origin: Germany, 1600s. Contrary to what some may think, the Miniature Pinscher is not a toy Doberman. Both the Miniature Pinscher and the Doberman come from older stock, but the "Min Pin" is not a descendant; nor is the Miniature Pinscher related to the Manchester Terrier, although there is a physical resemblance between the two.

Original Purpose: Hunting small vermin.

Personality: Self-possessed, stubborn, curious, spunky, lively, alert.

Breed Traits: Small and quick. Despite his diminutive size, definitely not a lapdog. A good watchdog. Has little tolerance for cold. A barker, climber, and escape artist.

Physical Attributes: 11 to 12 in (28 to 30.5 cm); 8 to 10 lb (3.5 to 4.5 kg). Colors are clear or solid red, stag, red, black-and-tan (or rust), black-and-rust, or chocolate-and-rust.

Coat Type and Grooming: Hard, smooth, short. Minimal grooming required. Light shedding.

Life Span: 12 to 15 years.

Health Concerns: PRA, mitral valve insufficiency, orthopedic problems (fractures, patellar luxation, Legg-Perthes).

Exercise: Very high.

Housing: Adaptable to any living situation; perfect for apartment dwellers.

Sociability: Tends to bond to one person. Good with gentle older children but probably too small for rough toddlers. Reserved with strangers. May be all right with other dogs and cats if socialized carefully; will chase smaller animals.

Trainability: Low to average; this is a tough, self-possessed dog who needs firm handling.

Activities: Agility.

5 Facts

Good watchdog
Minimal grooming
Ideal for apartment life
Bonds with one person
Barky

MINIATURE SCHNAUZER

Origin: Southern Germany, 1800s. The Miniature Schnauzer is not only "bred down" from the Standard size but also has some Affenpinscher or possibly Miniature Pinscher in him.

Original Purpose: Ratting; watchdog.

Personality: Friendly, sweet, fearless, devoted, strong-willed, tenacious.

Breed Traits: Energetic, sturdy. Some are high-strung. Not as dominant as bigger Schnauzers. Some are barkers.

Physical Attributes: 12 to 14 in (30.5 to 35.5 cm); 15 to 20 lb (7 to 9 kg). Colors are pepper and salt, black-and-silver, or solid black.

Coat Type and Grooming: Harsh, wiry. High maintenance; needs brushing three times a week. Professional grooming is recommended. Slight shedding.

Life Span: 12 to 15 years.

Health Concerns: Eye problems (juvenile cataracts, PRA, rheumy eyes), pancreatitis, pulmonary stenosis, arrhythmia, von Willebrand's, skin problems (allergies), diabetes.

Exercise: Moderate to high; needs regular exercise; well-mannered in the house.

Housing: Adaptable to any living situation; however, some are too vocal for neighbors.

Sociability: Bonds to the whole family. Very good with people, less dominant than the bigger Schnauzers. Likes children but better with older kids; best when socialized early. Good with other dogs; okay with cats; not good with small pets.

Trainability: Very high; some may attempt to challenge their owners for dominance.

Activities: Earthdog trials, obedience.

5 Facts

Energetic
Professional grooming
Bonds to whole family
Adaptable
May bark

NEAPOLITAN MASTIFF

Origin: Italy, antiquity.

Original Purpose: Dog of war; fighting dog.

Personality: Protective, calm, sensitive, independent, loyal, steady, wary.

Breed Traits: Relatively inactive indoors. Doesn't bark much. Drools and snores. Can't tolerate hot weather. Needs an experienced owner who understands protection breeds.

Physical Attributes: 23.5 to 31 in (59.5 to 78.5 cm); 110 to 154 lb (50 to 70 kg). Colors are gray, lead, black, brown, fawn, deep fawn.

Coat Type and Grooming: Short, hard, stiff, glossy, dense. Minimal coat care; however, the generous folds around his face, neck, and ears all require regular attention to keep them clean and dry. Average shedding.

Life Span: Up to 10 years.

Health Concerns: Bloat, cherry eye, hip dysplasia, hypothyroidism, panosteitis.

Exercise: Low to moderate; need a long daily walk.

Housing: Not a good apartment dog; does better in suburban home or country.

Sociability: Although protective of and loyal to their family, they are not recommended for families with young children. Suspicious of strangers. Aggressive with other dogs, especially of the same sex.

Trainability: Average; needs an experienced trainer; needs extensive socialization.

Activities: Weight-pulling, police work.

5 Facts

Protective
Not for beginners
Low-maintenance coat
Not for apartments
Drools

NEWFOUNDLAND

Origin: Canada, 1700s. Probably derived ultimately from the Molossian Mastiffs, although a few historians give credit to the Algonquin Indians.

Original Purpose: Water dog (helped fishermen), draft dog, towing lines and nets. Today, they save people from drowning.

Personality: Benevolent, calm, adaptable, sweet, easygoing, docile.

Breed Traits: Not protective, but size is daunting. Loves the water; to be happy, these dogs need frequent access to a lake or river. Cannot tolerate heat and need to be kept cool. Very heavy droolers. Have a deep, loud bark.

Physical Attributes: 26 to 32 in (66 to 81 cm); 100 to 150 lb (45.5 to 68 kg). Colors are solid black, brown, bronze-and-blue, or gray, with small white markings permissible. One variety, the Landseer, is black-and-white.

Coat Type and Grooming: Profuse, dense, flat, waterproof, slightly oily; medium long. Fairly high maintenance; twice-a-week thorough combing desirable; no trimming. Professional grooming is optional. Heavy shedding, seasonally.

Life Span: 10 to 12 years.

Health Concerns: Orthopedic problems (hip and elbow dysplasia, OCD), heart problems (SAS, cardiomyopathy, VSD) heatstroke, seizures, allergies, hypothyroidism.

Exercise: Moderate. They are lazy by nature and must be encouraged to exercise; otherwise, they will become obese.

Housing: Best in suburban or rural areas. They need a lot of room and enjoy swimming.

Sociability: Bonds to the whole family. Should be placed in a family with kids, often preferring their company to that of adults; however, because of their great size, must be supervised. Excellent with other pets, often protecting them.

Trainability: High; of all the giant breeds, the Newfoundland makes the best obedience prospect; a fast learner.

Activities: Water search and rescue, drafting, obedience.

5 Facts

Easygoing
Cannot tolerate heat
Needs plenty of room
High-maintenance coat
Highly trainable

NORFOLK TERRIER

Origin: England, 1800s.

Original Purpose: Ratting; farm dog.

Personality: Lively, feisty, spunky, amiable, alert, game, outgoing.

Breed Traits: Energetic. Very playful. Excellent watchdog but not protective. Requires attention. Not reliable off leash. A digger and barker.

Physical Attributes: 11 to 12 in (28 to 30.5 cm); 8 to 10 lb (3.5 to 4.5 kg). Colors are various shades of red, wheaten, black-and-tan, or grizzle.

Coat Type and Grooming: Short and wiry. High maintenance; requires a comb-out every week and stripping of dead hair a few times a year. Professional grooming is very desirable, especially for a show coat. Moderate shedding.

Life Span: 12 to 15 years.

Health Problems: Allergic dermatitis, collapsing trachea, mitral valve insufficiency.

Exercise: Moderate.

Housing: Well suited to apartment life and urban areas.

Sociability: Bonds to whole family. Good with children if socialized early; not good with toddlers. Good with other pets.

Trainability: Low.

Activities: Earthdog trials, agility.

5 Facts

Spunky
Professional grooming
Bonds to whole family
Adaptable
May bark

NORWEGIAN BUHUND

Origin: Norway, Middle Ages.
Original Purpose: Herder; guardian.
Personality: Adaptable, intelligent, self-confident, lively, affectionate.
Breed Traits: Keen watchdog; vigilant but not excessively noisy. Weather-resistant coat enables him to enjoy himself in almost any conditions.
Physical Attributes: 16 to 18.5 in (40.5 to 47 cm); 26 to 40 lb (12 to 18 kg). Colors are wheaten, black.
Coat Type and Grooming: Hard, thick, smooth-lying outercoat and soft, dense undercoat. Moderate maintenance; regular brushing and combing required. Seasonally heavy shedder.
Life Span: 13 to 15 years.
Health Concerns: Hip dysplasia.
Exercise: High.

Housing: Does best in rural or suburban areas.
Sociability: Gets along well with children. Doesn't mind other dogs or pets.
Trainability: Average to high. He has an independent streak, but his strong desire to please makes him receptive and responsive to requests.
Activities: Obedience, agility, service dog.

5 Facts

Keen watchdog
Moderate grooming
Not for apartments
Independent
All-weather dog

NORWEGIAN ELKHOUND

Origin: Norway, originally bred by the Vikings.

Original Purpose: Elk and moose hunting; also bear and rabbit.

Personality: Independent, strong-willed, bold, loyal, energetic, friendly.

Breed Traits: Strong, solid, compact, nimble. Good eyesight. A spitz-type dog. Makes a fine watchdog and can be protective if he feels his owner is being threatened. They can be barkers, but the bark is said to have a bell-like quality. Can handle extreme cold but very little heat. Definitely does best with a strong owner.

Physical Attributes: 19 to 20 in (48.5 to 51 cm); 40 to 55 lb (18 to 25 kg). Color is gray tipped with black.

Coat Type and Grooming: Straight, thick, coarse, abundant, long, weather resistant. Moderate maintenance. Professional grooming is optional. Heavy shedding.

Life Span: 10 to 12 years.

Health Concerns: Hip dysplasia, eye problems (PRA, glaucoma).

Exercise: High; needs daily exercise.

Housing: Adaptable to any living situation.

Sociability: Tends to bond with one person. He is very friendly, if rambunctious with kids, which is an unusual trait in a hound. Friendly with strangers. Not good with other pets; especially bad with cats.

Trainability: Average; difficult to train for obedience and is a natural puller; however, very quick to learn what he wants to know.

Activities: Hunting, tracking.

5 Facts

Independent
Can handle cold weather
Needs plenty of exercise
Bonds with one person
May bark

NORWEGIAN LUNDEHUND

Origin: Norway

Original Purpose: Puffin hunting

Personality: Tenacious, courageous, single-minded, lively, charming, playful, stubborn, devoted, cheerful, inquisitive.

Breed Traits: Excellent climbing ability and tracking instincts. Sure-footed. Cannot be trusted off lead. Loves to dig. Barky. Not for novice owners.

Physical Attributes: 12 to 15 in (30.5 to 38 cm); 13 to 15.5 lb (6 to 7 kg). Colors are fallow to reddish brown to tan with white markings, white with red or dark markings. This breed has some of the most unusual physiology in the dog world—at least six toes on each foot, many of which are triple jointed; the front legs can turn at 90-degree angles to the side; the head can be bent back to the point where it nearly touches his back; and he can close his ears to protect the ear canal from moisture and debris.

Coat Type and Grooming: Double coat with harsh, dense outercoat and soft, dense undercoat. Average maintenance; regular brushing required. Heavy shedder.

Life Span: About 12 years.

Health Concerns: Lundehund syndrome.

Exercise: High. These are active, busy dogs who need to be stimulated mentally and physically.

Housing: Best in a home where he has safe outdoor space to play in and explore.

Sociability: Fine with children they are raised with, but may not tolerate rough treatment from young children. Wary of strangers. Gets along well with other dogs. Their strong prey drive means they are not compatible with small animals.

Trainability: Low. Although they are intelligent, Lundehunds don't have an inborn willingness to please. Training them must be done in a positive manner with lots of patience. May be difficult to housetrain. Extensive socialization is necessary.

Activities: Hiking, tracking, agility.

5 Facts

Tenacious
Needs outdoor space
Experienced owner
High energy
Barky

NORWICH TERRIER

Origin: England, 1800s.
Original Purpose: Ratting.
Personality: Protective, loyal, pert, game, gay, alert.
Breed Traits: Quick. A good watchdog. Some may be barkers. Does not do well in heat.
Physical Attributes: 10 in (25.5 cm); 10 to 13 lb (4.5 to 6 kg). Colors are shades of red, wheaten, black-and-tan, and grizzle.
Coat Type and Grooming: Short, wiry coat. High maintenance; requires combing two or three times a week and stripping a few times a year for show dogs. Professional grooming is very desirable. Light shedding.
Life Span: 12 to 15 years.

Health Concerns: Allergic dermatitis, patellar luxation, mitral valve insufficiency.
Exercise: Moderate to high; needs frequent walks or a run every day.
Housing: Adaptable to any living situation.
Sociability: Bonds to the whole family. Good with children if exposed early. Good with other dogs; some chase smaller pets, but most are fine with cats.
Trainability: Low.
Activities: Earthdog trials, agility.

5 Facts

Pert
Professional grooming
Bonds to whole family
Adaptable
May bark

NOVA SCOTIA DUCK TOLLING RETRIEVER

Origin: Canada, 1800s.

Original Purpose: Hunting and retrieving ducks; decoy dog.

Personality: Intelligent, alert, outgoing, affectionate, devoted, playful.

Breed Traits: Happiest when working. Can adapt to all kinds of weather and environments.

Physical Attributes: 17 to 21 in (43 to 53.5 cm); 37 to 51 lb (17 to 23 kg). Smallest of the retrievers. Colors are various shades of red, orange; may have white markings.

Coat Type and Grooming: Water-repellent, medium-length outercoat and soft, dense undercoat; whiskers; feathering. Moderate maintenance; must be brushed regularly. Moderate shedding.

Life Span: 13 to 16 years.

Health Concerns: Addison's disease, autoimmune thyroiditis, Collie eye anomaly, PRA.

Exercise: High; an athletic and energetic dog who can animatedly retrieve in and out of the water for hours at a time.

Housing: Best in situations with a lot of room and outdoor space, but he is adaptable and can live in an apartment if properly exercised.

Sociability: Devoted to family members and patient with children. Good with other pets.

Trainability: High; a responsive and eager learner.

Activities: Field trials, obedience, agility, hunting.

5 Facts
Happiest when working
Adaptable
High exercise requirements
Devoted to family
Playful

OLD ENGLISH SHEEPDOG

Origin: England, the West Country; ancestors may include the Bearded Collie. Despite the name, the breed is not very old.

Original Purpose: Sheep and cattle drover.

Personality: Bold, adaptable, lovable, affectionate, friendly, home-loving.

Breed Traits: Well-mannered at home. Some individuals may be timid or aggressive. Can handle hot weather better than you might think. This is a fairly slow-maturing breed.

Physical Attributes: 22 in (56 cm) or more; 75 to 90 lb (34 to 41 kg). Bear-like motion. Colors are any shade of gray, grizzle, or blue, often with white markings.

Coat Type and Grooming: Long, shaggy, harsh-textured, profuse. High maintenance; requires combing every other day to prevent mats. House pets are frequently clipped down to a short coat, but show dogs must be shown in a full coat. Professional grooming is recommended; some trimming. Heavy shedding.

Life Span: 10 to 12 years.

Health Concerns: Hip dysplasia, cataracts, deafness, cardiomyopathy.

Exercise: Moderate to high. These dogs need lots of outdoor exercise, at least twice a day.

Housing: Not suited for apartment life; they need plenty of room.

Sociability: Bonds to whole family. Good with children. Highly sociable with everyone, including strangers. Compatible with other pets.

Trainability: Average to high; this breed benefits from early obedience training.

Activities: Herding, obedience, therapy dog.

5 Facts

Well-mannered
Not for apartments
Professional grooming
Good with children
Affectionate

OTTERHOUND

Origin: England, antiquity; may have some large terriers in his ancestry. May be related to the French Wendy Hound.

Original Purpose: Otter hunting, which was outlawed in Britain in 1978.

Personality: Affectionate, persistent, laid-back, cheerful, sociable, devoted.

Breed Traits: Big-boned, strong. Will alert owners to newcomers. Some are territorial and have guarding ability. Persistent hunter, good nose. Good swimmer with webbed feet. This is a slow-maturing breed.

Physical Attributes: 23 to 27 in (58.5 to 68.5 cm); 65 to 115 lb (29.5 to 52 kg). All colors acceptable; black-and-tan, grizzle, red, liver-and-tan, tricolor, wheaten are common.

Coat Type and Grooming: Rough, long, crisp, shaggy outercoat; woolly water-resistant undercoat. High maintenance. Professional grooming is desirable. Moderate to heavy seasonal shedding.

Life Span: 12 to 14 years.

Health Concerns: Orthopedic disorders (hip dysplasia, OCD), bloat, seizures.

Exercise: Moderate to high, especially when young.

Housing: Not well suited to urban areas or apartment life.

Sociability: Excellent with people, including children and strangers. Good with other dogs; sometimes object to unfamiliar cats.

Trainability: Average; needs firm training.

Activities: Tracking, water search and rescue.

5 Facts

Good swimmer
Professional grooming
Needs plenty of exercise
Highly sociable
Affectionate

PAPILLON

Origin: Central Europe, some say France or Spain, 1500s. The breed is related to toy spaniels. Some claim a Roman statue depicts one.

Original Purpose: Companion; lapdog.

Personality: Devoted, gentle, a "royal" attitude, happy, perky, lively.

Breed Traits: Lithe, elegant. They desire constant companionship; demand attention and cuddling. Some individuals are timid—look for a dog who does not exhibit this trait. Intolerant of cold.

Physical Attributes: 8 to 11 in (20 to 28 cm); 9 to 10 lb (4 to 4.5 kg). Known for "butterfly" ears, although some kinds have drop or "phalene" ears. ("Phalene" means "moth" in French.) Color is predominantly white with patches of any other color; a white blaze is preferred.

Coat Type and Grooming: Long and silky, no undercoat. Low maintenance; once or twice a week. Minimal shedding.

Life Span: 12 to 15 years or more.

Health Concerns: Patellar luxation, eye problems, fractures.

Exercise: Low to moderate; however, requires more than many toy breeds.

Housing: Adaptable to any living situation; enjoys both city and country.

Sociability: Likes everyone, including strangers. Good with children, but because they are so small, they are not suited for families with toddlers. Good with other pets.

Trainability: Extraordinarily high; one of the best of the toy breeds. A good obedience prospect. Some are hard to housetrain.

Activities: Obedience, agility, tracking.

5 Facts

Needs company
Low-maintenance coat
Ideal for apartment life
Sociable
Highly trainable

PARSON RUSSELL TERRIER

Origin: England, late 1800s. Same basic stock as the Fox Terrier.

Original Purpose: Bred to follow red foxes, both over- and underground.

Personality: Cheeky, outgoing, playful, independent, spunky, bold.

Breed Traits: Demand a lot of attention from their owners. Excellent watchdogs. Some individuals are shy. Not reliable off leash. Most dig and bark. Need an owner experienced with both terrier and hunting dogs.

Physical Attributes: 10 to 15 in (25.5 to 38 cm); 10 to 16 lb (4.5 to 7.5 kg). All colors permitted; most are white with black, tan, or brown markings.

Coat Type and Grooming: Two types: smooth and broken. Minimal grooming for the smooth, more for the broken coat. Professional grooming not necessary for smooth; optional for broken.

Life Span: 14 to 15 years.

Health Concerns: This is a very healthy breed and has no unusual health problems.

Exercise: Very high. Will get fat if not given sufficient exercise, and they need a tremendous amount of it. They will hunt, play, chase, and run around all day long.

Housing: Not suitable for apartments.

Sociability: Likes to play with kids but is not especially tolerant and will not stand teasing; if irritated, they will nip. Reserved with strangers. May show same-sex aggression; prefers other Parson Russells. Not good with cats or small animals.

Trainability: Average; can learn quickly but tends to be independent-minded.

Activities: Hunting, earthdog trials, agility.

5 Facts

Spunky
High exercise requirements
Moderate grooming
Demands attention
Most are barky

PEKINGESE

Origin: China, antiquity.

Original Purpose: Companion; sacred dog; lapdog.

Personality: Courageous, determined, stubborn, loyal, companionable, aloof.

Breed Traits: A good watchdog. Needs a lot of attention from his family, but not particularly playful. This heavy-coated, compact breed cannot handle heat. Due to shortened muzzle, may snore (mine did).

Physical Attributes: 6 to 9 in (15 to 23 cm); 8 to 13 lb (3.5 to 6 kg). All colors and patterns except albino and liver.

Coat Type and Grooming: Long, profuse, thick. High maintenance; a lot of brushing at least once a week to prevent matting. Face and eyes need special attention. Professional grooming is desirable. Light shedding.

Life Span: 13 to 15 years.

Health Concerns: Umbilical hernia, eye problems (corneal ulcer, distichiasis, entropion, "dry eye"), breathing problems, stenotic nares (pinched nostrils), cysts, phobias, elongated soft palate, patellar luxation, skin allergies, congestive heart failure, arthritis, seizures, ear infections.

Exercise: Low.

Housing: Adaptable to any living situation; perfect for apartment life.

Sociability: Tends to bond to one person. Not good with children. Aloof with strangers. Can be jealous of other pets.

Trainability: Low; some may be hard to housetrain.

Activities: Therapy dog, agility.

5 Facts

Needs company
Ideal for apartment life
Bonds with one person
Professional grooming
Cannot handle heat

PEMBROKE WELSH CORGI

Origin: Pembrokeshire, Wales.

Original Purpose: Cattle herder; cattle drover.

Personality: Alert, lively, devoted, bold, workmanlike, intuitive.

Breed Traits: Excellent watchdog. Good family dog. Can be barky.

Physical Attributes: 10 to 12 in (25.5 to 30.5 cm); 17 to 30 lb (7.5 to 13.5 kg). Color is usually red but can also be fawn, sable, black-and-tan, sometimes with white markings.

Coat Type and Grooming: Outercoat is short to medium, rather coarse and water-resistant; undercoat is thick and dense. Moderate maintenance. Professional grooming is optional. Moderate shedding.

Life Span: 12 to 14 years.

Health Concerns: Degenerative myelopathy, hot spots, eye problems (cataracts, glaucoma, PRA), PDA, epilepsy, intervertebral disk disease, von Willebrand's.

Exercise: Moderate to high; needs daily vigorous exercise; many will self-exercise.

Housing: Adaptable to any living situation.

Sociability: Bonds to whole family. Very playful with older children, probably less apt to "nip" than the Cardigan, who has kept more of his cattle-herding proclivities. Usually accepting of strangers. Usually all right with other pets, although some may fight with same-sex dogs.

Trainability: High; early socialization needed.

Activities: Obedience, agility, herding.

5 Facts

Excellent watchdog
Good family dog
Adaptable
Moderate grooming
May bark

PETIT BASSET GRIFFON VENDÉEN

Origin: Vendée France, 1700s.

Original Purpose: Small game hunter.

Personality: Affectionate, merry, inquisitive, happy, determined, busy.

Breed Traits: Loudly vocal. Sturdy. Requires a lot of attention.

Physical Attributes: 12 to 15 in (30.5 to 38 cm); 25 to 45 lb (11.5 to 20.5 kg). Color is white with markings of lemon, orange, black, grizzle, or tricolor.

Coat Type and Grooming: Hard, rough, wiry outercoat; short, dense undercoat. Moderate maintenance. While the breed standard charmingly requests that the PBGV be "casual" and have a "rough, unrefined outline," owners should not interpret that request as "scruffy." These dogs require weekly grooming and a little trimming for show dogs. Professional grooming is optional. Minimal shedding.

Life Span: 10 to 14 years.

Health Concerns: Orthopedic problems (hip dysplasia, patellar luxation), eye problems (PRA, lens luxation), aseptic meningitis, heart murmurs.

Exercise: High; needs a good deal of exercise in a fenced area.

Housing: Does best in the country.

Sociability: Bonds to the whole family. Very good with children, although perhaps too exuberant for very young kids. Friendly to strangers but might bark at a newcomer. Good, but sometimes pushy, with other pets.

Trainability: Average; some say that males are more trainable than females.

Activities: Hunting, tracking, agility.

5 Facts

Affectionate
Moderate grooming
Bonds to whole family
High exercise
Vocal

PHARAOH HOUND

Origin: Malta, antiquity; they have come from Egypt as the name indicates; one of the oldest breeds.

Original Purpose: Rabbit hunting.

Personality: Alert, eager to please, friendly, playful, affectionate.

Breed Traits: Sturdy, graceful, elegant. Lots of stamina. Quiet in the house. Not a protective dog but a very good watchdog. Cannot handle cold weather (35°F [2°C] or lower) for more than 20 or 30 minutes; ears and feet are especially prone to frostbite. Must be kept on a leash outside a fenced area. These dogs are escape artists of the highest order; they can unlock gates. Known to blush when agitated or happy. Clean breed with no doggy odor.

Physical Attributes: 21 to 26 in (53.5 to 66 cm); 40 to 60 lb (18 to 27 kg). Colors are tan, rich tan, or chestnut, with some white markings allowed; white tail tip preferred.

Coat Type and Grooming: Short, smooth, glossy. Minimal care required; brush once a week with a hound mitt. Minimal shedding.

Life Span: 11 to 15 years.

Health Concerns: Optic nerve hypoplasia.

Exercise: Moderate to high; needs large exercise yard and lots of playtime (30 minutes four times a day).

Housing: Does best in the country.

Sociability: Bonds to whole family. Very good with people. Enjoys active playing with children. Good with other pets, not quarrelsome.

Trainability: Average to high.

Activities: Lure-coursing, obedience.

5 Facts

**Elegant
Quiet in house
Enjoys children
Not for apartments
Minimal shedding**

PLOTT

Origin: United States, 1700s.

Original Purpose: Cold trailing, baying, and treeing bear and other large game; hunting raccoons.

Personality: Tough, intelligent, curious, tenacious, courageous, playful.

Breed Traits: Has a tendency to drool. Excellent for families who want a hunting dog and a companion.

Physical Attributes: 20 to 27 in (51 to 68.5 cm); 40 to 75 lb (18 to 34 kg). Colors are any shade of brindle, including yellow, buckskin, tan, brown, chocolate, liver, orange, red, light or dark gray, blue or Maltese (slate gray), dilute black, black.

Coat Type and Grooming: Single coat is smooth, fine, glossy. Minimal grooming. Light shedding.

Life Span: 12 to 14 years.

Health Concerns: Bloat.

Exercise: High. He is large and athletic and needs plenty of exercise, without which he will become bored and restless.

Housing: Does best in rural or suburban homes.

Sociability: Gentle and kind with people of all ages. Gets along well with other pets.

Trainability: Average to high. Eager and responsive but can be single-minded about hunting.

Activities: Hunting, coonhound trials.

5 Facts

Tenacious
High exercise requirements
Not for apartments
Excellent hunting dog
Gentle

POINTER

Origin: England, 1600s; ancestors probably include the Foxhound and Greyhound.

Original Purpose: Finding hares for Greyhound to chase.

Personality: Adaptable, obedient, willing to please, independent, gentle, congenial.

Breed Traits: Aristocratic, clean-cut, fluid, built for both speed and endurance; great stamina. Tireless, energetic, very active. Excellent sense of smell. Clean with little odor. Well-behaved in the house if given sufficient exercise, but otherwise can be hyper and destructive. A good watchdog but not a protective breed. The field variety is a "hard" dog and relentless (read "stubborn"); show-line dogs are softer with a more even temper.

Physical Attributes: 23 to 28 in (58.5 to 71 cm); 50 to 90 lb (22.5 to 41 kg). As is usual with pointers and setters, the dogs used for hunting and field trials tend to run smaller than dogs from show lines. Colors are lemon, liver, black, orange, usually with white. They say, "A good Pointer can never be a bad color."

Coat Type and Grooming: Short. Low maintenance; easy to care for; no trimming. Moderate to high shedding.

Life Span: 12 to 15 years.

Health Concerns: Entropion, PRA, cataracts, hip and elbow dysplasia.

Exercise: Immense; this dog is happiest if he can hunt, as he was intended to do. Dogs from show lines are calmer and less energetic than field dogs.

Housing: Needs a good amount of room and is not suited to urban life.

Sociability: Good but rambunctious with people. Tolerant of kids. Gets along very well with other dogs.

Trainability: High; easy to housetrain.

Activities: Hunting dog, obedience, field trials, agility, tracking, service dog.

5 Facts

Tireless
Minimal grooming
High exercise requirements
Congenial
Rambunctious

POLISH LOWLAND SHEEPDOG

Origin: Poland, 1500s. Possibly related to the Bearded Collie and Puli.

Original Purpose: Sheepherder.

Personality: Stable, gentle, friendly, dominant, lively, alert.

Breed Traits: Agile, hardy. Best with experienced owners.

Physical Attributes: 17 to 20 in (43 to 51 cm); 35 to 50 lb (16 to 22.5 kg). Any color acceptable.

Coat Type and Grooming: Long, thick, harsh outercoat; dense, soft undercoat. High maintenance required; the coat needs to be thoroughly brushed every two or three days to prevent matting. Professional grooming is recommended. Low to moderate shedding.

Life Span: 12 to 15 years.

Health Concerns: Hip dysplasia.

Exercise: High; regular exercise is needed.

Housing: Not suitable for urban areas or apartment life.

Sociability: Very playful with children. Reserved with strangers. Gets along well with other pets.

Trainability: High; however, this dog needs very firm handling and an experienced trainer because of his tendency to dominate.

Activities: Agility, obedience, herding.

5 Facts

Hardy
Needs experienced trainer
Professional grooming
Reserved with strangers
Playful with children

POMERANIAN

Origin: Germany (Pomerania is on the shore of the Baltic Sea), 1800s.

Original Purpose: Lapdogs; companions.

Personality: Bouncy, loyal, curious, bold, alert, happy, extroverted.

Breed Traits: Good watchdog. Well-behaved in the house. Can be very vocal. A good breed for the first-time owner.

Physical Attributes: 6 to 7 in (15 to 18 cm); 4 to 6 lb (2 to 2.5 kg); the smallest of the spitz breeds, miniaturized from larger cousins. They have small feet, even for their tiny size. The earliest Pomeranians were all white. Today all colors and patterns are allowed, including chocolate and white.

Coat Type and Grooming: Heavy, dense, harsh, double, abundant. High maintenance required; daily grooming when shedding; twice a week the rest of the year; some trimming. Professional grooming is recommended. Heavy seasonal shedding.

Life Span: 12 to 16 years.

Health Concerns: Patellar luxation, PDA.

Exercise: Low; able to self-exercise.

Housing: Adaptable to any living situation, but the breed can be noisy.

Sociability: Tends to bond to one person. Okay with older well-disciplined children but are not suited for rough play. Reserved and wary of strangers; some individuals may be snappish. Often suspicious of other pets and may be aggressive.

Trainability: Variable—low to high; responds well to consistent training. I have a friend with a pair of Poms that can do anything.

Activities: Agility, flyball, obedience.

5 Facts

Extroverted
Good for novice owners
Adaptable
Bonds with one person
Vocal

POODLE

Origin: Central Europe (maybe Russia) or Germany, 1500s.

Original Purpose: Water retriever; truffle finder.

Personality: Friendly, great sense of fun, proud, loyal, intuitive, sparky.

Breed Traits: Standard Poodles tend to be more docile than smaller varieties. Toy Poodles may be high-strung and barky. They have no doggy odor.

Physical Attributes: Poodles come in three sizes, Standard, Miniature, and Toy, but except for size, the standard for each is exactly the same. Toy Poodles are under 10 in (25.5 cm); 7 to 12 lb (3 to 5.5 kg). Miniatures are 11 to 15 in (28 to 38 cm); 16 lb (7.5 kg). Standards are usually over 21 in (53.5 cm); 45 to 55 lb (20.5 to 25 kg). Any solid color including black, white, silver, blue, apricot, brown.

Coat Type and Grooming: Single, harsh, curly coat. High maintenance; all need daily grooming and regular clipping. Professional grooming is recommended; however, you are not required to have a Continental or English Saddle clip as show dogs do. Ask for a sensible, easy-care trim. Very low shedding.

Life Span: 13 to 15 years—higher for smaller dogs.

Health Concerns: PRA (Miniature and Toy), distichiasis, Legg-Perthes (Miniature and Toy) glaucoma, patellar luxation (Toy and Miniature), cancer, epilepsy (Miniature and Toy), sebaceous adenitis (Standard), sebaceous gland tumors, ear infections, conjunctivitis, enteritis, entropion, color dilution alopeica (Standard), PDA, cardiomyopathy (Standard), mitral valve insufficiency (Toy and Miniature), hip dysplasia (Standard and Miniature), hypothyroidism, allergies.

Exercise: Moderate to high.

Housing: All sizes of Poodles can accommodate themselves to apartment living.

Sociability: Superior family dog but may be reserved around strangers. Smaller Poodles, who may be timid, do better in a calm household. All are excellent with family children, with the Standard being the best; some Toys are too excitable for kids. Variable with other pets; they seem to enjoy the company of other Poodles most.

Trainability: Very high; very responsive; these dogs enjoy obedience work.

Activities: Agility, retrieving, obedience, hunting, therapy dog.

5 Facts

Intuitive
Professional grooming
Adaptable
Highly trainable
May bark

PORTUGUESE WATER DOG

Origin: Algarve, Portugal, Middle Ages. The Goths may have originally brought the breed to Portugal, although others trace the origin of the breed to Russia.

Original Purpose: Retrieving fish for fishermen.

Personality: Bouncy, adaptable, fun-loving, spirited, calm, stubborn.

Breed Traits: Active, strong, compact. Need a lot of attention. Great swimmers; need access to a body of water. Can catch anything in their mouths. Can be protective.

Physical Attributes: 17 to 23 in (43 to 58.5 cm); 35 to 60 lb (16 to 27 kg). Colors are solid black, brown, white, parti-color.

Coat Type and Grooming: Wavy or curly, profuse. Very high maintenance required; brushing three times a week; professional clipping every six to eight weeks. Ears need special attention, particularly after swimming. Professional grooming is recommended. Practically non-shedding.

Life Span: 9 to 15 years.

Health Concerns: Hip dysplasia, PRA, glycogen storage disease.

Exercise: High; this dog is tireless; needs a lot of exercise.

Housing: Not suited to apartment life but can adapt if given an extreme amount of exercise.

Sociability: Tends to bond to one person. Good with children if well socialized but tends to play very hard. May be somewhat reserved with strangers. Good with other pets; some individuals can be jealous.

Trainability: Average to very high; needs consistency.

Activities: Obedience, agility, water sports.

5 Facts

Spirited
Professional grooming
Needs plenty of exercise
Bonds with one person
Great swimmer

PUG

Origin: Uncertain, possibly China; others suggest a Russian origin. The breed may be more than 1,000 years old.

Original Purpose: Lapdog.

Personality: Good-natured, confident, affectionate, stable, lively, willful.

Breed Traits: Needs a lot of attention. Enjoys showing off. Calm in the house. Not good in very hot or cold weather. Snores.

Physical Attributes: 11 to 13 in (28 to 33 cm); 14 to 24 lb (6.5 to 11 kg). Compact; a double twist in the tail is especially prized. Although the skin is loose, there are no wrinkles except on the head. Colors are red, sable, apricot, fawn, silver fawn, black-and-tan, silver; with or without white markings. Back moles on cheeks; black mask.

Coat Type and Grooming: Short, fine, glossy; outercoat is water-resistant; undercoat is dense and velvety soft. Low maintenance; eyes need special care. Moderate shedding.

Life Span: 12 to 15 years.

Health Concerns: Obesity, breathing problems, eye and eyelid abnormalities (prolapse of the eye), dental problems, orthopedic problems (patellar luxation, hip dysplasia), Pug Dog encephalitis, seizures, allergies.

Exercise: Low.

Housing: Adaptable to any living situation; ideal for apartment life.

Sociability: Does equally well as family dog or a sole companion. Good with older children. Aloof with strangers. Good with other pets but doesn't mind being an only dog.

Trainability: Average; obedience training is useful.

Activities: Obedience, therapy dog.

5 Facts

Needs attention
Ideal for apartment life
Low exercise requirements
Easy coat care
Snores

PULI

Origin: Hungary, Middle Ages; ancestors possibly from Central Asia.

Original Purpose: Herding sheep; hunting in marshy areas; later used as a police dog.

Personality: Energetic, lively, devoted, stubborn, affectionate, busy.

Breed Traits: Fast, agile. Good watch and guard dog. Restless in the house if not given sufficient exercise. These dogs are barkers.

Physical Attributes: 15 to 18 in (38 to 45.5 cm); 29 to 33 lb (13 to 15 kg). Colors are rusty black, dull black, black, white, gray, apricot; specks of other colors permitted, but overall impression should be that of a solid color.

Coat Type and Grooming: Long (ground-length), corded, weather-resistant; outercoat wavy or curly, but not silky; undercoat soft, woolly, dense. Very high maintenance required; professional grooming is recommended. Beginning very early, cords must be separated out. Dog may be shown either corded or brushed out. The corded coat requires at least 45 minutes of grooming a week, including care every day. Brushed coats need grooming every other day; no trimming. A damp Puli, especially one with a correctly corded coat, is a smelly Puli. To avoid the smell, the dog must be dried as fast as possible with a dryer. Light shedding.

Life Span: 12 to 16 years.

Health Concerns: Eye problems.

Exercise: Very high.

Housing: Adaptable to any living situation with a great deal exercise; best in the country.

Sociability: Bonds to whole family. Not good with young kids. Aloof and wary with strangers. Likes other Pulik but aggressive to other breeds.

Trainability: Low to average for obedience work, but a clever dog in things that matter to him; easily housetrained.

Activities: Sheep guard dog, herding trials.

5 Facts

Good watchdog
High exercise requirements
Professional grooming
Not for young kids
May bark

PYRENEAN SHEPHERD

Origin: France, antiquity.

Original Purpose: Sheepherding.

Personality: Lively, alert, cheerful, adaptable, fearless, vigilant, devoted, mischievous.

Breed Traits: Alert; makes a good watchdog, barking at any unfamiliar noises.

Physical Attributes: 15 to 19 in (38 to 48 cm); 15 to 32 lb (7 to 14.5 kg). Colors are shades of fawn, gray, black, black with white markings, merles of diverse tones, brindle.

Coat Type and Grooming: Two types: Rough-Faced and Smooth-Faced. The Rough has a long, almost flat or slightly wavy, harsh outercoat and minimal undercoat. The Smooth has a semi-long, fine, soft outercoat, a muzzle covered with short, fine hair, and a modest ruff. Both types are low maintenance; brushing about twice a month to prevent matting. The Rough's coat will naturally cord if not tended to. Light to moderate shedding.

Life Span: 10 to 14 years.

Health Concerns: Epilepsy, hip dysplasia, patellar luxation.

Exercise: High; it's almost impossible to tire him out.

Housing: Can adapt to city living provided he's given enough exercise, but rural or suburban living is preferable.

Sociability: Loyal and devoted to his family, both adults and children. Naturally wary of strangers. Gets along with other pets in the family but is suspicious of strange dogs.

Trainability: High; quick study. Needs plenty of socialization to be comfortable with strange pets, children, and adults.

Activities: Agility, herding, rally, flyball, tracking, obedience.

5 Facts

Alert
High exercise requirements
Minimal grooming
Devoted to family
Quick learner

REDBONE COONHOUND

Origin: United States, 1800s.

Original Purpose: Trailing and treeing game (especially raccoon).

Personality: Good-natured, kindhearted, even-tempered, versatile, intelligent, loyal.

Breed Traits: Fast, agile. Good dog for an active family. Exceptional hunting dog. Some have a tendency to drool.

Physical Attributes: 21 to 27 in (53.5 to 68.5 cm); 45 to 70 lb (20.5 to 31.5 kg). When it comes to color, solid red is preferred.

Coat Type and Grooming: Short, smooth, and coarse. Minimal care, but their ears need to be cleaned regularly. Light shedding.

Life Span: 12 to 14 years.

Health Concerns: Eye problems, hip dysplasia, obesity.

Exercise: Moderate to high; dedicated hunting dog who needs to be in the great outdoors, preferably trailing and tracking game.

Housing: Not suited for apartment life; enjoys the outdoors.

Sociability: Gets along wonderfully with children and other animals.

Trainability: Average. He is open to formal training and wants to please his owner.

Activities: Hunting, coonhound trials.

5 Facts

Versatile
Needs active family
Dedicated hunting dog
Not for apartments
Sociable

RHODESIAN RIDGEBACK

Origin: Southern Africa, 1800s. The original Ridgebacks were owned by Hottentots. Other ancestors include Great Danes, Mastiffs, Greyhounds, Salukis, and Bloodhounds.

Original Purpose: General farm dog; guarding; hunting lion and other game. (Rhodesian Ridgebacks did not kill lions. They merely found out where they were and alerted the hunters.)

Personality: Loyal, proud, dignified, bold, aloof, strong-willed.

Breed Traits: Strong, active, elegant, stylish, powerful. Make good watch and guard dogs. Cannot handle very cold weather. Not recommended for novice owners.

Physical Attributes: 24 to 27 in (61 to 68.5 cm); 70 to 85 lb (31.5 to 38.5 kg). The ridged line of hair along the back is the predominant feature. Colors are light to red wheaten; a small amount of white on the chest or toes is permitted.

Coat Type and Grooming: Short, hard, sleek, dense, with a ridge along the spine. Minimal care; brushing once a week with a curry comb; no trimming. Moderate shedding.

Life Span: 10 to 12 years.

Health Concerns: Hip dysplasia, hypothyroidism, dermoid sinus.

Exercise: High, especially when young; can be destructive if not given enough of it.

Housing: Not suitable for urban areas or apartment life.

Sociability: Tends to bond with one person. Generally fine with older family children; however, this energetic dog may be too rambunctious for toddlers. Very reserved with strangers. Not always good with dogs he does not know well; may try to dominate; not good with small pets like rabbits and cats.

Trainability: Average; can be distracted; positive reinforcement necessary. Some individuals have a tendency to be dominant. This dog needs an experienced owner and early socialization.

Activities: Therapy dog, lure-coursing, obedience, tracking. They also seem to be quite good at herding, although they don't have AKC approval for this activity yet.

5 Facts

Good watchdog
Not for novice owners
High exercise requirements
Minimal grooming
Bold

ROTTWEILER

Origin: Rottweil, Germany, Middle Ages.
Original Purpose: Boar hunting; cart-pulling; cattle driving; guardian; later, police work. (Early drafting dogs were larger than today's version, who are descended from the shepherding type.)
Personality: Bold, calm, headstrong, stern, somewhat aloof, courageous.
Breed Traits: Rugged, strong. Very territorial; may be aggressive. Extremely good watchdog and guard dog, but can be overprotective. Not right for the first-time dog owner; will try to dominate. Everyone in the family should be dog savvy.
Physical Attributes: 22 to 27 in (53.5 to 68.5 cm); 75 to 125 lb (34 to 57 kg). Color is black with rust or mahogany markings.
Coat Type and Grooming: Shiny, thick, medium-short double coat. Minimal grooming required—once a week brushup; no trimming. Average to heavy shedding.
Life Span: 8 to 9 years.

Health Concerns: Orthopedic problems (hip and elbow dysplasia, panosteitis, OCD), eye problems (PRA, entropion), aortic stenosis, seizures, allergies, bone cancer, von Willebrand's.
Exercise: Moderate to high; enjoys outdoor exercise.
Housing: Surprisingly good in apartments or urban areas with adequate exercise.
Sociability: A one-person dog. Not good with young children; tends to dominate them; good with older children if well-socialized. Wary of strangers; may be aggressive. Will try to dominate strange dogs or dogs of the same sex.
Trainability: High; this dog needs early obedience training and strong early socialization.
Activities: Guard dog, herding, weight-pulling, carting, obedience, agility, search and rescue, therapy dog, Schutzhund.

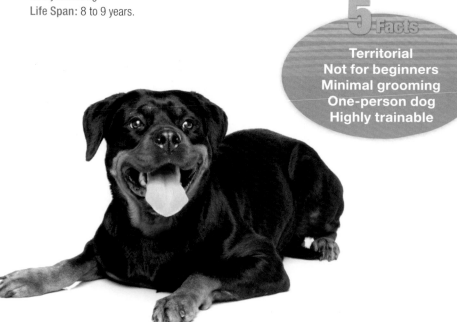

5 Facts

Territorial
Not for beginners
Minimal grooming
One-person dog
Highly trainable

SAINT BERNARD

Origin: Switzerland, Middle Ages; developed further during the 17th century. Originally accompanied Roman armies to the region; ancestors include the Molossian Mastiff.

Original Purpose: Guarding; herding.

Personality: Faithful, quiet, obedient, easygoing, steady, gentle.

Breed Traits: Adapts very well to family life. Little tolerance for heat but can handle very cold weather. Great sense of smell. They drool and snore.

Physical Attributes: 25 to 34 in (63.5 to 86.5 cm); 140 to 190 lb (63.5 to 86 kg). Color is white with varying shades and amounts of orange or red; never solid white or completely without white.

Coat Type and Grooming: Two types, long- and shorthaired. Longhaired variety has a thick, rather wavy coat (and is really medium in length, despite the name). The shorthaired coat is dense and short. Moderate to high maintenance; the longhaired variety needs brushing three times a week. Eyes, face, and ears need special care. Professional grooming is optional. Heavy seasonal shedding.

Life Span: 8 to 10 years.

Health Concerns: Bloat, hip dysplasia, eye problems (distichiasis, entropion, ectropion), OCD, osteosarcoma, cardiomyopathy.

Exercise: Moderate; needs lots of room and regular, although not excessive, exercise.

Housing: Due to his large size and need for regular exercise, this breed does best with a fenced-in yard or room to run.

Sociability: Well-bred Saints are excellent with people and very patient with children, although too big for toddlers. Excellent with other pets, especially if brought up with them.

Trainability: Average; some attempt to dominate their owners.

Activities: Search and rescue work, weight-pulling, agility, obedience, draft dog.

5 Facts

Faithful
Needs room
Moderate grooming
Patient with children
Drools

SALUKI

Origin: Middle East (probably Sumer), antiquity. Named after the Arabian city of Saluk. Migrated to Europe during the Crusades.

Original Purpose: Hunting gazelle and foxes.

Personality: Loyal, responsive, independent, sensitive, companionable, affectionate.

Breed Traits: Graceful, elegant, fast. Generally quiet indoors. Some individuals can be shy. Sensitive to loud noises. Very clean and do not have a doggy smell. Need to be kept on a leash when in an unfenced area, as they can easily leap a 5-foot (1.5-m) fence.

Physical Attributes: 21 to 28 in (53.5 to 71 cm); 35 to 60 lb (16 to 27 kg); naturally thinner than most dogs. Colors are white, cream, fawn, golden red, red grizzle, black-and-tan, grizzle-and-tan.

Coat Type and Grooming: Two coat types: short, and, more commonly, short with long silky feathering. Low maintenance. Light to moderate shedding.

Life Span: 10 to 12 years.

Health Concerns: Phobias, glaucoma, sensitivity to anesthesia (like most sighthounds).

Exercise: Moderate to high; needs outdoor exercise.

Housing: Does best in the country but can adapt to any situation if given sufficient exercise.

Sociability: Usually attaches to one person and remains steadfast. Good with family kids, especially if raised with them; not good with toddlers. Quite reserved with strangers (and almost everybody except the family remains a stranger—even some people in the family stay strangers). Okay with other dogs, not good with small pets, including cats.

Trainability: Average; need gentle handling and early socialization; regular obedience classes are must. They tend to be easily distracted.

Activities: Lure-coursing, obedience, agility.

5 Facts

Graceful
Quiet indoors
Low-maintenance coat
Bonds to one person
Sensitive

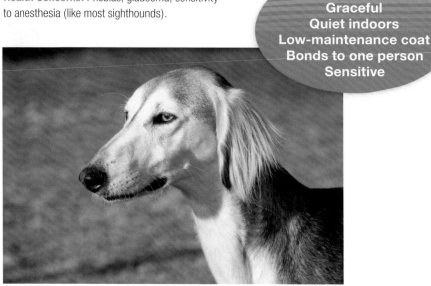

SAMOYED

Origin: Northeast Siberia, antiquity; developed by the nomadic Samoyed people.

Original Purpose: Reindeer herding; pulling sleds; guarding from bears.

Personality: Independent, vivacious, full of fun, dominant, person-oriented, alert.

Breed Traits: Active, sturdy. Human companionship is critical to this breed. An excellent watchdog. Calm in the house. Loves cold weather but has no tolerance for heat. (Some liken them to small polar bears.) Can be vocal and may dig. Will wander off if not kept in a secure fenced area.

Physical Attributes: 18 to 24 in (45.5 to 61 cm); 38 to 70 lb (17 to 31.5 kg). Known for their beautiful Samoyed smile. Colors are pure white, cream white, silver white, white-and-biscuit, or all biscuit. (Originally the dog came in dark colors, but those were gradually weeded out.)

Coat Type and Grooming: Heavy, harsh, bushy, weather-resistant outercoat; undercoat is short, thick, soft. High maintenance required; brushing at least every other day. Professional grooming is recommended. Heavy seasonal shedding.

Life Span: 10 to 12 years.

Health Concerns: Hip dysplasia, eye problems (PRA, glaucoma), hypothyroidism, deafness, pulmonary stenosis, VSD.

Exercise: Moderate to high.

Housing: Adaptable to any living situation with plenty of exercise.

Sociability: Bonds to the entire family. Extremely good with children. Very good with people, including strangers. Good with other pets.

Trainability: Low to average; not a great obedience prospect because of independent nature.

Activities: Herding trials, skijoring, sledding, obedience, therapy dog.

5 Facts

Good watchdog
Needs companionship
High-maintenance coat
Bonds to whole family
Adaptable

SCHIPPERKE

Origin: Belgium, 1600s.

Original Purpose: Hunting; guarding; ratting. The original dogs were larger than today's specimens.

Personality: Confident, independent, fearless, bold, headstrong, quick-thinking, amiable.

Breed Traits: Fast, nimble. A superior watchdog; very acute hearing. Can handle extremes of weather.

Physical Attributes: 10 to 13 in (25.5 to 33 cm); 12 to 18 lb (5.5 to 8 kg). The silhouette is the most pronounced aspect of the breed's appearance. Color is black.

Coat Type and Grooming: Double coat is slightly harsh and forms a mane around the neck. Moderate maintenance; weekly grooming necessary (more when shedding). Professional grooming is optional. Moderate to heavy shedding; gets much worse if grooming is not attended to.

Life Span: 14 to 16 years. Some individuals live until they are 20.

Health Concerns: Eye problems, hypothyroidism.

Exercise: Low to moderate.

Housing: Adaptable to any living situation.

Sociability: Mostly gentle with kids; some can be snappish. Not fond of strangers. Very good with other pets; loves to play with them.

Trainability: High; may have housetraining problems; may guard possessions. Firm training needed.

Activities: Obedience, agility.

5 Facts

Superior watchdog
All-weather dog
Adaptable
Suspicious of strangers
Nimble

SCOTTISH DEERHOUND

Origin: Scotland; may descend from the Greyhound or the Irish Wolfhound.

Original Purpose: Hunting red deer.

Personality: Stable, courageous, companionable, dignified, alert, quiet.

Breed Traits: Strong, graceful. Not a watchdog, but his size is intimidating to people who don't know what they're looking at. Some individuals are timid.

Physical Attributes: At least 27 in (68.5 cm) for the female and 30 in (13.5 cm) for the male (most are 32 in [81 cm]); 75 to 110 lb (34 to 50 kg). Colors are dark blue-gray (preferred), pastel shades of gray, dark gray. Light shades of yellow, brindle, fawn were formerly seen but have now been practically eliminated.

Coat Type and Grooming: Hard, harsh, wiry, ragged, shaggy coat; medium length. Minimal grooming required, although there's lot of dog there; some trimming. Professional grooming is optional. Average shedding.

Life Span: 8 to 10 years.

Health Concerns: Bloat, osteosarcoma, OCD, cardiomyopathy.

Exercise: Needs a good deal of supervised exercise; not a "self-starter." Generally a calm and quiet dog but needs to run.

Housing: Due to their size, they are not well suited to apartment life or urban areas.

Sociability: Excellent with people. Very sociable with older children especially; generally prefer children to everyone else in the family but need proper socialization with toddlers. Friendly with strangers. The one I know best likes to stand up and hug everybody. Okay with family pets if introduced carefully; may chase strange cats.

Trainability: Average.

Activities: Lure-coursing.

5 Facts

Dignified
Minimal grooming
Not for apartments
Very sociable
Calm

SCOTTISH TERRIER

Origin: Scottish Highlands, 1800s; closely related to the Cairn Terrier and West Highland White Terrier.

Original Purpose: Hunting rodents, foxes.

Personality: Alert, inquisitive, fearless, assured, sophisticated, bold.

Breed Traits: Lots of stamina, agile, active. Superior watchdog; territorial. Some members of this breed can be aggressive, an unacceptable trait that good breeders are trying successfully to eliminate. Cannot abide heat. Some individuals are barkers. Needs an experienced owner.

Physical Attributes: 10 in (25.5 cm); 18 to 22 lb (8 to 10 kg). This breed comes in a mix of colors, including wheaten, steel, and brindle, not just the commonly seen black.

Coat Type and Grooming: Harsh, wiry, long, weatherproof. High maintenance required; brushing three times a week. Professional grooming is recommended at least four times a year; clipping for pets and stripping for show dogs. Light shedding.

Life Span: 12 to 15 years.

Health Concerns: Bladder cancer, CMO, von Willebrand's, allergies, hypothyroidism.

Exercise: High; they need a considerable amount.

Housing: Adaptable to any living situation.

Sociability: Bonds strongly to one person. Not good with young children, all right with respectful school-aged kids. Aloof with strangers. Usually all right with dogs of opposite sex if socialized early.

Trainability: Low; needs early obedience training; difficult to train; many will challenge their owners for dominance.

Activities: Earthdog trials.

5 Facts

Good watchdog
Bonds with one person
Needs experienced trainer
Professional grooming
May bark

SEALYHAM TERRIER

Origin: Wales (Sealyham), 1800s.
Original Purpose: Hunting badger, otter, and fox.
Personality: Cheerful, stubborn, stable, alert, fearless, sociable.
Breed Traits: Calmer and more laid-back than many other terriers. Quiet in the house. Good watchdog, but not protective. Not reliable off leash.
Physical Attributes: 10 to 12 in (25.5 to 30.5 cm); 18 to 24 lb (8 to 11 kg). Colors are all white, or with lemon, tan, or badger markings.
Coat Type and Grooming: Wiry, longer than many other terriers. Moderately high maintenance, brushing several times a week. Professional grooming is recommended; clipping for pets, stripping for show. Light shedding.
Life Span: 11 to 14 years.

Health Concerns: Eye problems, allergies, deafness.
Exercise: Moderate.
Housing: Adaptable to urban areas but prefers the country.
Sociability: Bonds to one owner. Not good with young children; good with kind older kids. Somewhat reserved with strangers. Not great with other pets but tolerant if socialized early.
Trainability: Low; works best with food rewards. Some will attempt to dominate their owners; require an experienced hand.
Activities: Earthdog trials.

5 Facts

Good watchdog
Quiet in house
Professional grooming
Bonds to one person
Adaptable

SHETLAND SHEEPDOG

Origin: Shetland Islands, 1800s.

Original Purpose: Sheepherding; chicken guarding.

Personality: Kind, watchful, loyal, obedient, sensitive, affectionate.

Breed Traits: Agile. The lightest of the working breeds. Needs affection. This breed barks a lot.

Physical Attributes: 13 to 16 in (33 to 40.5 cm); 16 to 21 lb (7.5 to 9.5 kg); resembles a rough-coated Collie in miniature. Colors are sable, brown, black, tricolor, or blue merle with white markings.

Coat Type and Grooming: Double coat; outercoat long, straight, bushy; undercoat thick, soft. High maintenance, brushing at least twice a week. He is a very clean dog who tries to look after himself. Professional grooming is recommended. Sheds heavily in the spring and fall.

Life Span: 12 to 15 years.

Health Concerns: Eye problems (PRA, Collie eye anomaly), PDA, thyroid disease, dermatomyositis, deafness, von Willebrand's.

Exercise: Moderate to high.

Housing: Can adapt to urban areas (if the neighbors can handle the barking) as well as the country, but needs long walks and other strenuous exercise.

Sociability: Bonds to whole family. Good with children, if the children are gentle. May be shy or reserved with strangers. Good with other pets.

Trainability: Very high—excellent obedience and agility dogs.

Activities: Obedience, herding, agility, therapy dog.

5 Facts

Adaptable
High-maintenance coat
Highly trainable
Bonds to whole family
Barks

SHIBA INU

Origin: Honshu, Japan, antiquity.

Original Purpose: Hunting and flushing small game.

Personality: Determined, active, courageous, loyal, alert, bold.

Breed Traits: Territorial. Good jumpers. Quiet in the house. Not barkers, but they can make weird noises. Have many catlike qualities. Naturally clean. Escape artists.

Physical Attributes: 14 to 16 in (35.5 to 40.5 cm); 18 to 22 lb (8 to 10 kg). Well-balanced. Any color; the most common colors include red, black, sesame, red sesame, black sesame.

Coat Type and Grooming: Soft double coat. Low maintenance. Moderate shedding.

Life Span: 12 to 15 years.

Health Concerns: Some patellar luxation; usually a healthy breed.

Exercise: High.

Housing: Adaptable to any living situation but are escape artists who need a fenced yard.

Sociability: Aloof. Not good with children. May be aggressive with other dogs, especially those of the same sex; will chase small animals.

Trainability: Moderate to high.

Activities: Hunting, therapy dog.

5 Facts

Territorial
Naturally clean
Adaptable
Escape artist
Quiet in house

SHIH TZU

Origin: Probably Tibet, 600s; later, China, 1800s.
Original Purpose: Pet; sacred dog.
Personality: Outgoing, sweet, independent, spunky, stable, friendly.
Breed Traits: Sturdy. Likes everyone. Enjoys participating in family events and does not care to be left alone all day. Cannot handle hot weather. Quiet in the house. Combines attributes of the Lhasa Apso and Pekingese.
Physical Attributes: Up to 10 in (25.5 cm); 10 to 16 lb (4.5 to 7.5 kg). All colors permitted.
Coat Type and Grooming: Long, dense. High maintenance required; daily brushing to prevent tangles. The hair grows upward on the bridge on the nose, purportedly giving it a chrysanthemum look. Professional grooming is recommended. Light shedding.

Life Span: 11 to 15 years.
Health Concerns: Pinched nostrils, eye problems (distichiasis, conjunctivitis), obesity, allergies and dermatitis, ear infections, cancer, nephritis, congestive heart failure.
Exercise: Low.
Housing: Can adapt well to town or country.
Sociability: Bonds to whole family. Very good with children; in very rare cases may be snappish. Good with other pets.
Trainability: Low; can be obstinate. However, with patience he can be trained. Housetraining may be difficult.
Activities: Companion, therapy dog.

5 Facts

Outgoing
Needs companionship
High-maintenance coat
Bonds to whole family
Adaptable

SIBERIAN HUSKY

Origin: Siberia, antiquity. Developed by the nomadic Chukchi people for a variety of tasks.

Original Purpose: Sled-pulling, reindeer herding.

Personality: Gentle, friendly, fun-loving, loyal, eager, outgoing.

Breed Traits: Fast, agile, hardy, great stamina. Not a guard dog. Suffers separation anxiety if left alone for long periods. Cannot tolerate heat but can handle the worst winters with aplomb, even pleasure. Wonderful howlers. Must be kept on a leash outside a fenced area; he is a roamer, a digger, and an escape artist. Not the best dog for a first-time dog owner.

Physical Attributes: 21 to 23 in (53.5 to 58.5 cm); 35 to 60 lb (16 to 27 kg). The smallest and fastest of the purebred sled dogs. Colors are white, black, sable, red, gray, "wild color." Many have a white mask. Eyes may be blue, brown, or one of each.

Coat Type and Grooming: Medium-length outercoat and soft, dense undercoat. Moderate to high maintenance; needs thorough brushing three times a week. Heavy shedding, especially in the spring and fall.

Life Span: 12 to 14 years.

Health Concerns: Hip dysplasia, eye problems (PRA, cataracts), VSD.

Exercise: Very high; needs a couple hours of vigorous exercise every day. Will become very destructive if not given sufficient exercise.

Housing: Not suitable for apartment life or urban areas.

Sociability: Bonds to whole family. Especially good with children. Likes everyone, including strangers. Great with the family dogs, may not be crazy about strange dogs; not good with small pets or cats.

Trainability: Low; not easy to train to do things outside his original purpose and will complain vociferously if asked.

Activities: Sled racing, backpacking.

5 Facts

Great stamina
Escape artist
Sheds all year
Not for apartments
Sociable

SILKY TERRIER

Origin: Australia, late 1800s; ancestors include Australian and Yorkshire Terriers.

Original Purpose: Vermin (rats and snakes) extermination.

Personality: Outgoing, stubborn, spunky, lively, friendly.

Breed Traits: Can be territorial; a super watchdog. Quite barky. Demands a great deal of attention. Some individuals reserved or shy

Physical Attributes: 9 to 10 in (23 to 25.5 cm); 8 to 11 lb (20 to 28 kg). Color is blue-and-tan.

Coat Type and Grooming: Long, silky. Moderate to high maintenance. Professional grooming is recommended. Light shedding.

Life Span: 11 to 14 years.

Health Concerns: No major concerns. Some individuals have orthopedic problems.

Exercise: Moderately high; needs more exercise than most toy breeds.

Housing: Adaptable to any living situation; perfect for apartment life.

Sociability: Tend to bond to one person. Most do best in a home without small children, although they are fine with older kids; some individuals can be snappish. Can be aggressive to other dogs and small pets.

Trainability: Average; this dog does best with obedience training; can be hard to housetrain.

Activities: Earthdog trials.

5 Facts

Good watchdog
Demands attention
Little shedding
Adaptable
May bark

SKYE TERRIER

Origin: Scotland, 1500s; from the same basic stock as the Scottish Terrier.

Original Purpose: Fox, rodent, badger, and otter hunting.

Personality: Devoted, sensitive, fearless, good-tempered.

Breed Traits: Agile, elegant, dignified, stylish, strong. A good watchdog; too small to be protective.

Physical Attributes: 9 to 12 in (23 to 30.5 cm); 19 to 22 lb (8.5 to 10 kg); long, low, and level. Colors are black, gray, blue, silver, fawn, or cream, preferably with black points. Adult color may not clear until the dog is 18 months old.

Coat Type and Grooming: Long, hard, shiny, straight. High maintenance; frequent (at least three times a week) grooming to prevent mats. Careful cleaning needed around the eyes and mouth. Professional grooming is recommended. Moderate shedding.

Life Span: 10 to 13 years.

Health Concerns: Premature closure of ulna and radius, allergies.

Exercise: Moderate.

Housing: Ideal for apartment life; low-key enough to live happily in the city.

Sociability: A one-person dog. Most are okay with gentle children, but not the best breed to have with toddlers. Wary and cautious with strangers; can be snappish. Not good with household dogs; can be unfriendly to strange dogs. Can learn to tolerate cats, but small animals are in grave danger.

Trainability: Average.

Activities: Earthdog trials, tracking.

5 Facts

Dignified
Professional grooming
Ideal for apartments
One-person dog
Low-key

SMOOTH FOX TERRIER

Origin: England, 1700s.

Original Purpose: Hunting fox and badger; ratting.

Personality: Dynamic, energetic, inquisitive, alert, friendly, gay.

Breed Traits: Active. Territorial; a super watchdog. Barks and digs. Does best with experienced owners.

Physical Attributes: 14 to 17 in (35.5 to 43 cm); 16 to 20 lb (7.5 to 9 kg). Show dogs tend to be smaller than pets. Color is white with tan or black markings; red, brindle, or liver markings not desirable.

Coat Type and Grooming: Short, flat, hard. Low maintenance; brushing once a week. Light seasonal shedding.

Life Span: 12 to 14 years.

Health Concerns: Legg-Perthes, pulmonary stenosis.

Exercise: High but not demanding.

Housing: Adaptable to any living situation.

Sociability: Good with playful older children. Rather reserved with strangers. Not good around livestock. Usually okay around bigger dogs but may try to dominate smaller ones; okay around family cats if exposed early.

Trainability: Average; best with an experienced trainer.

Activities: Earthdog trials, obedience.

5 Facts

Good watchdog
Minimal grooming
Adaptable
Not for novice trainers
May bark

SOFT COATED WHEATEN TERRIER

Origin: Ireland, 1700s
Original Purpose: Vermin extermination, hunting; general farm dog.
Personality: Affectionate, happy, good-natured, spirited, friendly.
Breed Traits: Powerful, athletic. Requires lots of attention. Active in the house. Low heat tolerance. These dogs may dig or jump. Has a tendency to be dominant, and some individuals can be aggressive. They need an owner who can provide discipline. Not for first-time owners.
Physical Attributes: 17 to 19 in (43 to 48.5 cm); 30 to 40 lb (13.5 to 18 kg). Color is wheaten (what a surprise!); ranges from reddish gold to silver. Puppies may be darker (red or brown) and have black tipping. By age two, the correct color should appear.
Coat Type and Grooming: Single coat; soft, abundant, and silky; very unterrier-like; medium long. Very high maintenance required; needs to be combed out every couple of days to prevent matting. The hair grows about an inch (2.5 cm) a month. Professional grooming is optional; they can use a bath and a trim every month. Negligible shedding.

Life Span: 12 to 14 years.
Health Concerns: Kidney problems (protein-losing nephropathy, renal dysplasia), PRA, protein-losing enteropathy.
Exercise: Moderate to high.
Housing: Adaptable to any living situation if given a great deal of exercise.
Sociability: Very sociable family dog. Excellent with older children; can be too rambunctious and dominant for smaller children; needs supervision. Likes strangers. Good with other pets—much better than other terriers; not good with cats.
Trainability: High; quick learner. Best with experienced trainer.
Activities: Obedience, agility, therapy dog, herding.

5 Facts

Athletic
Not for novice owners
High-maintenance coat
Sociable
Adaptable

SPINONE ITALIANO

Origin: Italy, 1200s; perhaps German Pointer in the background.

Original Purpose: Hunting, both in forests and swamps.

Personality: Curious, gentle, courageous, gregarious, playful, willing.

Breed Traits: Vigorous, muscular, athletic. Calm inside; calmer than many other pointing breeds. Preeminent hunting dog. Must be involved in household life.

Physical Attributes: 22 to 26 in (56 to 66 cm); 60 to 85 lb (27 to 38.5 kg). Colors are white, or white with yellow, light brown, liver, or chocolate, or orange patches; black not permitted. There is a preferred shade of brown, called "Capuchin Friar's Frock."

Coat Type and Grooming: Rather short, rough, hard, weatherproof; no undercoat. Moderate to high maintenance; needs brushing thoroughly once a week. Mouth area needs special care. Professional grooming is optional.

Life Span: 12 to 13 years.

Health Concerns: Cerebellar ataxia, hip dysplasia.

Exercise: High.

Housing: Best on a farm but can get by with regular exercise elsewhere.

Sociability: Good with people. May be too large for small children. Good with both cats and dogs but may try to retrieve them.

Trainability: High.

Activities: Hunting, obedience, agility, flyball, tracking.

5 Facts

Calm indoors
High exercise requirements
Sociable
Athletic
Highly trainable

STAFFORDSHIRE BULL TERRIER

Origin: England, 1800s.

Original Purpose: Bull-baiting; bear-baiting; dog fighting; ratting.

Personality: Stubborn, fun-loving, affectionate, companionable, fearless, loyal.

Breed Traits: An excellent watchdog. Needs an experienced owner.

Physical Attributes: 14 to 18 in (35.5 to 45.5 cm); 30 to 40 lb (13.5 to 18 kg). Strong jaws. Colors are red, fawn, black, or blue, either solid or with white. Any shade of brindle or brindle and white.

Coat Type and Grooming: Smooth and shiny. Minimal care; brushing with a curry comb. Light to moderate shedding.

Life Span: 12 to 14 years.

Health Concerns: Cataracts. (Note: This breed's famously high pain threshold may prevent him from showing symptoms from disease or trauma.)

Exercise: Moderate to high.

Housing: Adaptable to any living situation.

Sociability: Good with people, usually including children, although can be very rambunctious. If angrily aroused, can be aggressive, so needs to be carefully supervised. Likes strangers but tends to bond with one person. Dislikes other dogs, although can sometimes adjust to other dogs in the household; should be supervised. Most are bad with cats.

Trainability: Average; needs firm obedience training and very careful early socializing, especially if he is to be around other animals.

Activities: Obedience.

5 Facts

Good watchdog
Needs experienced owner
Minimal grooming
Rambunctious
Adaptable

STANDARD SCHNAUZER

Origin: Germany, Middle Ages. The Standard Schnauzer is the one from which the Miniature and Giant Schnauzers were developed.

Original Purpose: Ratter.

Personality: Alert, clever, reliable, devoted, adaptable, fearless.

Breed Traits: Territorial; makes an excellent watchdog or protection dog. Does not have the typical doggy odor.

Physical Attributes: 17 to 19 in (43 to 48.5 cm); 45 lb (20.5 kg). This is the middle-sized Schnauzer. Colors are pepper and salt, black.

Coat Type and Grooming: Hard, wiry outercoat and soft, dense undercoat. Fairly high maintenance; show dogs require hand-stripping by a professional. Light to moderate shedding.

Life Span: 12 to 14 years.

Health Concerns: Pulmonary stenosis.

Exercise: High; needs a good bit of daily exercise.

Housing: Does best in a house with a yard for exercise but can adapt to apartment living.

Sociability: Tends to bond with one person. Reliable and tolerant with children. Does not like strangers. Not good with other pets, unless socialized early; will try to dominate strange dogs; very aggressive with small animals. (In Germany, they hold ratting trials to see which Schnauzer can kill the most rats in the least amount of time.)

Trainability: High; quick learner but may try to dominate owner. Needs thorough socialization.

Activities: Agility, obedience, tracking, bomb squad, service dog.

5 Facts

Protective
High-maintenance coat
Bonds with one person
Quick learner
No doggy odor

SUSSEX SPANIEL

Origin: Sussex, England, 1800s; ancestor of the Field Spaniel.

Original Purpose: Hunting in heavy coverts.

Personality: Dignified, kindly, serious, conscientious, cheerful, gentle, tractable.

Breed Traits: Slow-moving, methodical hunter. Less energetic and playful than most other spaniels. Calm in the house. These dogs drool and slobber.

Physical Attributes: 13 to 16 in (33 to 40.5 cm); 35 to 45 lb (16 to 20.5 kg). Color is golden liver.

Coat Type and Grooming: Medium long, wavy. Fairly high maintenance; regular brushing and some trimming required. Professional grooming is optional. Moderate shedding.

Life Span: 11 to 14 years.

Health Concerns: Bloat, autoimmune diseases, hypothyroidism, heart problems.

Exercise: Moderate.

Housing: Adaptable to any living situation.

Sociability: Excellent with both children and strangers; may be protective of family children. Gets along well with other pets.

Trainability: Low to average; although he learns quickly, he has a tendency to assert himself.

Activities: Hunting, tracking.

5 Facts

Calm in house
High-maintenance coat
Adaptable
Good with children
Drools

SWEDISH VALLHUND

Origin: Sweden, may have been developed by Vikings.

Original Purpose: Cattle droving; watchdog; ratter.

Personality: Clever, plucky, even-tempered, watchful, energetic, fearless, alert, affectionate, intelligent.

Breed Traits: An excellent watchdog. He does not hesitate to vocalize his pure happiness in being alive.

Physical Attributes: 11.5 to 14 in (29 to 35.5 cm); 20 to 35 lb (9 to 16 kg). Colors are steel gray, grayish brown, grayish yellow, reddish yellow, reddish brown.

Coat Type and Grooming: Medium-length, harsh, water-repellent outercoat and woolly, dense undercoat. Low maintenance, except during periods of seasonal shedding.

Life Span: 13 to 15 years.

Health Concerns: Cryptorchidism, hip dysplasia, patellar luxation, renal dysplasia.

Exercise: Moderate. A brisk walk at least once a day will help keep him physically and mentally fit.

Housing: Can adapt to any living situation.

Sociability: Calm and affectionate with family. Excellent with children. May be dominant with other dogs; strong prey drive with small animals.

Trainability: High. Extremely responsive, bright, and devotedly takes to training readily.

Activities: Agility, obedience, therapy, flyball.

5 Facts

Clever
Good watchdog
Low-maintenance coat
Excellent with children
May bark

TIBETAN MASTIFF

Origin: Tibet (China), antiquity.

Original Purpose: Flock guard; guard dog.

Personality: Devoted, protective, independent-minded, self-reliant, strong-willed, reserved.

Breed Traits: Very protective of family and territory. Active outdoors but typically settles down inside. Cannot be trusted off leash. Not for first-time owners.

Physical Attributes: 26 in (66 cm) minimum for males, 24 in (61 cm) minimum for females; 75 to 160 lb (34 to 72.5 kg) or more. Colors are rich black with or without tan markings, blue with or without tan markings, shades of gold, brown.

Coat Type and Grooming: Long, straight, thick, coarse outercoat and heavy, soft undercoat (winter) or sparse undercoat (warmer months). High maintenance; needs regular brushing and combing, and during shedding season, may need to be gone over every day. Seasonal shedding.

Life Span: 13 to 16 years.

Health Concerns: Hip dysplasia, skin problems, thyroid problems.

Exercise: Moderate.

Housing: Not suited for apartment living.

Sociability: Not suited for families with an active social life. While affectionate with the children in his family, can be overprotective of them. Naturally aloof with strangers and may not let strange people (including children) enter the house. May not tolerate other dogs, especially of the same sex.

Trainability: Low. Not for novice trainers; an independent thinker and a large dog, he needs someone with experience managing a guard dog. Socializing him is an absolute necessity so that his protective instincts do not get out of control.

Activities: Protection work.

5 Facts
Protective
Not for novice owners
High-maintenance coat
Independent thinker
Moderate exercise

TIBETAN SPANIEL

Origin: Tibet, antiquity.

Original Purpose: Watchdog, companion.

Personality: Loving (but not cuddly), gay, independent, outgoing, enthusiastic, assertive, somewhat catlike in temperament.

Breed Traits: Active, alert. Quiet indoors. Likes to be center of attention. Playful. A good watchdog. Some may be nervous. Naturally clean.

Physical Attributes: 10 in (25.5 cm); 9 to 15 lb (4 to 7 kg). All colors and combinations permitted, but golden red is the most common.

Coat Type and Grooming: Double silky coat, moderate length; neck has a mane of longer hair. Moderate maintenance; brush once a week.

Moderate shedding most of the year; heavier seasonal shedding.

Life Span: 12 to 15 years.

Health Concerns: PRA, patellar luxation.

Exercise: Low.

Housing: Adaptable to any living situation; perfect for apartment life.

Sociability: Tends to bond to one person. Good with children. Reserved with strangers. Good with other pets.

Trainability: Average.

Activities: Agility, obedience, therapy dog.

5 Facts

Quiet indoors
Ideal for apartments
Moderate grooming
Bonds with one person
Playful

TIBETAN TERRIER

Origin: Tibet, antiquity. (Although Tibetan, it is not a terrier, despite the name.)

Original Purpose: Hunting and guarding; considered a "good luck" dog.

Personality: Very person-oriented, sensitive, happy, gentle, amiable.

Breed Traits: Agile. Natural watchdog. Excellent jumper.

Physical Attributes: 15 to 16 in (38 to 40.5 cm); 20 to 25 lb (9 to 11.5 kg). Any color.

Coat Type and Grooming: Long, profuse outercoat and soft, woolly undercoat. High maintenance; needs combing out frequently. Professional grooming is recommended. Minimal shedding.

Life Span: 10 to 14 years.

Health Concerns: Lens luxation.

Exercise: Low to moderate; can adjust to family activity level.

Housing: Adaptable to any living situation.

Sociability: Tends to bond to one person. Not good with children. Wary of strangers. Needs to be supervised with other pets.

Training: Average; may have housetraining problems.

Activities: Therapy dog.

5 Facts

Natural watchdog
Professional grooming
Adaptable
Bonds with one person
Sensitive

TOY FOX TERRIER

Origin: United States, 1900s.

Original Purpose: Companion.

Personality: Gregarious, friendly, intelligent, fearless, loyal, adaptable.

Breed Traits: Needs a lot of companionship from his family. High-energy outside but settles down inside the house. Can be barky.

Physical Attributes: 8.5 to 11.5 in (21.5 to 29 cm); 15 to 18 lb (7 to 8 kg). Colors are tricolor (black, tan, white); white, chocolate, and tan; white-and-tan; white-and-black.

Coat Type and Grooming: Short, straight, flat, hard, abundant, smooth, satiny; neck ruff. Low maintenance. Minimal shedding.

Life Span: 12 to 14 years.

Health Concerns: Legg-Perthes, patellar luxation, von Willebrand's.

Exercise: Moderate to high.

Housing: Makes an excellent apartment dog; can adapt to any living arrangement.

Sociability: Friendly and outgoing to everyone he meets. Enjoys children, but because of his size, a home with older children is preferred. Retains the hunting instincts of a terrier and will go after small animals in the garden.

Trainability: High. Using positive, reward-based training, he can be taught almost anything.

Activities: Agility, flyball, flying disc, obedience, therapy, service dog.

5 Facts

Gregarious
Needs companionship
Minimal grooming
Ideal for apartments
May bark

VIZSLA

Origin: Hungary, 1200s or earlier; some see Weimaraner and Pointers in the background. The breed is also known as the Hungarian Pointer.

Original Purpose: Tracking deer, quail, and hare.

Personality: Sensitive, fearless, stubborn, gentle, steady, lively.

Breed Traits: Noble, aristocratic; great sense of smell, energetic. Excellent watchdog; some are territorial. Some individuals may be timid. Does best with an active owner.

Physical Attributes: 21 to 25 in (53.5 to 63.5 cm); 44 to 66 lb (20 to 30 kg). Colors are golden rust, russet gold, dark yellow.

Coat Type and Grooming: Short, silky. Minimal care, just a quick brushing a few times a week. Heavy shedder year round.

Life Span: 11 to 14 years.

Health Concerns: Hip dysplasia, PRA, entropion, sebaceous adenitis.

Exercise: High; without sufficient exercise, he can be destructive.

Housing: Does best in the country with lots of room to run.

Sociability: Good with people. Usually friendly to children. Usually good with other pets.

Trainability: High; needs a sensitive touch.

Activities: Bird hunting, field trials, tracking, obedience, agility.

5 Facts

Needs active owner
Minimal grooming
Friendly
Not good for apartments
Energetic

WEIMARANER

Origin: Germany, early 1800s; the name comes from the court of Weimar; Bloodhound and Pointers in the ancestry.

Original Purpose: Gundog; hunting bear; later, retrieving fowl.

Personality: Bold, cheerful, alert, willful, determined, friendly, obedient.

Breed Traits: Hardy, noble, agile, strong. Requires company; does not do well alone. Protective of family. Some can be barkers. Needs a strong, thorough, experienced owner.

Physical Attributes: 22 to 27 in (56 to 68.5 cm); 54 to 80 lb (24.5 to 36.5 kg). Eyes are blue-gray or amber. Colors are shades of gray, including mouse and silver; this is why he is called "the gray ghost."

Coat Type and Grooming: Sleek, short, straight, and shiny. (There is also a longhaired version common in Europe.) Minimal care required. Moderate shedding.

Life Span: 10 to 12 years.

Health Concerns: Bloat, hip and elbow dysplasia, PRA, entropion, allergic dermatitis.

Exercise: High; if not given sufficient exercise, will become destructive.

Housing: Not well-adapted to city life; needs exercise and room to run.

Sociability: Likes children but may overwhelm small ones or elderly people. Can be aloof with strangers. Generally good with other pets, although some males dislike other males; may chase cats.

Trainability: Average; does best if taken to regular obedience classes.

Activities: Hunting, field trials, obedience, agility, tracking, flyball, search and rescue.

5 Facts

Active
Minimal grooming
High exercise requirements
Not for apartments
Needs company

WELSH SPRINGER SPANIEL

Origin: Wales, 1600s; may be the original version of the Springer Spaniel; Clumber Spaniel may be an ancestor.

Original Purpose: Flushing birds.

Personality: Affectionate, kindly, good-natured, adaptable, faithful.

Breed Traits: Compact, active. Barks to welcome guests. Likes a lot of attention. As an adult, calmer than many other spaniels. Very good water dog. Has a great nose. Can be a barker.

Physical Attributes: 17 to 19 in (43 to 48.5 cm); 35 to 44 lb (16 to 20 kg). Colors are dark red and white.

Coat Type and Grooming: Glossy, silky, medium-long. Moderate maintenance required; brushing twice a week. Ears need special attention. Professional grooming is optional; some trimming needed around the feet and ears. Moderate shedding.

Life Span: 12 to 14 years.

Health Concerns: Hip dysplasia, PRA, cataracts.

Exercise: Medium to high, especially as a puppy.

Housing: Adaptable to any living situation, with exercise.

Sociability: Good with people. Some are a little wary of children. Good with other dogs; may chase cats.

Trainability: High; quick learner but does need careful training.

Activities: Hunting, obedience, agility, tracking, field trials.

5 Facts

Good-natured
Moderate grooming
Adaptable
Quick learner
May bark

WELSH TERRIER

Origin: Wales, 1700s.

Original Purpose: Ratting; hunting otters, foxes, badgers.

Personality: Happy, independent, alert, fearless, calm, spirited.

Breed Traits: Milder than many other terriers. Superior watchdog. Enjoys water. May dig or bark.

Physical Attributes: 15 in (38 cm); 20 to 25 lb (9 to 11.5 kg). Color is tan with black or grizzle jacket.

Coat Type and Grooming: Wiry, short. Fairly high maintenance; grooming twice a week. Professional grooming is recommended; show dogs need stripping two or three times a year; clipping for pets. Light shedding.

Life Span: 12 to 14 years.

Health Concerns: Patellar luxation.

Exercise: Moderate to high.

Housing: Adapts well to any living situation.

Sociability: Tends to bond to one person. Good with older children but not good with toddlers. Wary of strangers. Good with other dogs (much better than most other terriers but can still get into quarrels); bad with cats and smaller animals.

Trainability: Average; early obedience training a must.

Activities: Earthdog trials, ratting, agility.

5 Facts

Spirited
Professional grooming
Adaptable
Bonds with one person
May bark

WEST HIGHLAND WHITE TERRIER

Origin: Argyleshire, Scotland, 1800s; shares ancestry with the Cairn, Scottish, and Skye Terrier.

Original Purpose: Hunting foxes, otters, and badgers; vermin extermination.

Personality: Tenacious, affectionate, proud, happy, spirited, friendly, independent.

Breed Traits: Active. Fine sense of hearing. Lovable family pet. Needs a lot of attention; does not do well alone, becoming quite destructive. Barkers and diggers. Should stay on a leash when not in a fenced area.

Physical Attributes: 10 to 11 in (25.5 to 28 cm); 14 to 21 lb (6.5 to 9.5 kg). Color is white, of course; however, at one time they came in a variety of colors.

Coat Type and Grooming: Dense, hard, straight outercoat; soft undercoat. Moderate maintenance required; brushing twice a week to prevent mats. An all-white coat is always more difficult to keep presentable. Professional grooming is recommended; stripping for show, clipping for pets. Light shedding when groomed correctly.

Life Span: 12 to 14 years.

Health Concerns: CMO, globoid cell leukodystrophy, anemia, skin problems (allergies), cataracts, diabetes, orthopedic problems (patellar luxation, Legg-Perthes, hip dysplasia), dilated cardiomyopathy.

Exercise: Moderate to high; can be destructive if not exercised thoroughly.

Housing: Can adapt well to apartments if given sufficient exercise.

Sociability: Bonds with the whole family. Playful but does best with older children; not good with toddlers unless socialized very early. Some wary of strangers, others are friendly. Some can be snappish if not respected. Can get overexcited or aggressive with other pets; not good with small animals or dogs.

Trainability: Low to average; these are very independent dogs.

Activities: Obedience, agility, earthdog trials.

5 Facts

Active
Needs attention
Professional grooming
Adaptable
May bark

WHIPPET

Origin: Northeast England, 1700s; ancestors may include Italian Greyhounds, terriers, or possibly Pharaoh Hounds.

Original Purpose: The only sighthound developed mainly for racing as opposed to hunting.

Personality: Pleasant, affectionate, friendly, obedient (for a sighthound), quiet, charming.

Breed Traits: Fast. Elegant. Many individuals make good watchdogs. Quiet, well-behaved, and calm in the house. Practically odor-free and naturally clean. Suffers in cold weather. A good breed for the first-time owner.

Physical Attributes: 18 to 22 in (45.5 to 56 cm); 21 to 35 lb (9.5 to 16 kg). A Greyhound in miniature; considered the smallest but one of the fastest sighthounds, outrunning a Greyhound in a sprint. They say that if your Whippet has the correct topline, you should be able to put a drop of water on the back of his skull and watch it run down the neck, along the back, and off the tip of the tail. Any color allowed.

Coat Type and Grooming: Short and dense. Minimal care required; once a week with a hound mitt. Very low shedding.

Life Span: 13 years.

Health Concerns: Phobias, eye problems (PRA, cataracts, lens luxation), color dilution alopecia, gastritis, mitral valve insufficiency, sensitivity to anesthesia.

Exercise: Moderate to high.

Housing: Adaptable to any living situation with sufficient exercise.

Sociability: Excellent with gentle children; most cannot handle rough play. May be aloof with strangers. Very friendly with other dogs but may chase rabbits.

Trainability: Average to high.

Activities: Therapy dog, lure-coursing.

5 Facts

Charming
Quiet in house
Minimal grooming
Aloof with strangers
Fast

WIRE FOX TERRIER

Origin: England, 1800s.
Original Purpose: Exterminating rats and mice.
Personality: Adventuresome, playful, mischievous, friendly, fearless, bold, independent.
Breed Traits: Solid, handsome, elegant, energetic, and dynamic. Superlative watchdog but not protective. May dig and bark.
Physical Attributes: 14 to 17 in (35.5 to 43 cm); 20 to 25 lb (9 to 11.5 kg). Show dogs tend to be smaller than pets. Color is basically white, with black and brown markings.
Coat Type and Grooming: Wiry, as the name indicates. High maintenance. Some professional care and hand-stripping for show dogs advised. Pets can be clipped. Light shedding.

Life Span: 12 to 14 years.
Health Concerns: Legg-Perthes, allergies.
Exercise: High.
Housing: Adaptable to any living environment.
Sociability: Good with older children. Wary of strangers. Not good with small pets; okay with opposite-sex dogs.
Trainability: Average; this dog requires firm handling.
Activities: Therapy dog, earthdog trials, obedience.

5 Facts

Good watchdog
High-maintenance coat
Adaptable
Energetic
May bark

WIREHAIRED POINTING GRIFFON

Origin: Originated in Holland but developed in France, 1800s.

Original Purpose: Gundog.

Personality: Independent, devoted, sensitive, gentle.

Breed Traits: Strong. Makes a good watchdog; can be protective if aroused. Does best in a quiet, relaxed family. Some are very hyper indoors. They are instinctive retrievers.

Physical Attributes: 20 to 23 in (51 to 58.5 cm); 50 to 60 lb (22.5 to 27 kg). Colors are solid or roan chestnut, gray chestnut, steel gray with brown.

Coat Type and Grooming: Short, straight, wiry outercoat; undercoat of fine down. Moderate maintenance required; some trimming. Professional grooming is recommended. Low to moderate shedding.

Life Span: 12 to 15 years.

Health Concerns: Hip dysplasia, eye problems (ectropion, entropion), hypothyroidism. Some individuals seem to have phobias.

Exercise: High.

Housing: This dog is happiest in the country, with room to run.

Sociability: Devoted to his family. Not a breed to have around small children; may attempt to dominate. Generally friendly with strangers. Good with other pets but tends to dominate; will chase cats.

Trainability: High; needs gentle handling.

Activities: Upland bird and waterfowl hunting, agility, flyball.

5 Facts

**Independent
Professional grooming
Devoted to family
Needs room to run
Sensitive**

XOLOITZCUINTLE

Origin: Mexico, antiquity.

Original Purpose: Companion; food; watchdog. Highly prized by the Aztecs for curative and mystical powers.

Personality: Cheerful, attentive, alert, loyal, devoted.

Breed Traits: Good watchdog. Calm and quiet in the home. Will bark to alert his owner but is not noisy otherwise. Excellent companion. Needs a lot of attention. Loves to snuggle.

Physical Attributes: Xolos come in three sizes: Standard, Miniature, and Toy. Standard Xolos are 17.5 to 23.5 in (25.5 to 35.5 cm); 20 to 31 lb (9 to 14 kg). Miniature Xolos are 13.75 to 18 in (35 to 45.5 cm); 13 to 22 lb (6 to 10 kg). Toy Xolos are 10 to 14 in (25.5 to 35.5 cm); 9 to 18 lb (4 to 8 kg). They come in any color or combination of colors.

Coat Type and Grooming: Xolos come in two varieties of coats: hairless and coated. The hairless has a total lack of hair on the body, although they do have short, coarse, thick hairs on the forehead and back of the neck. The coated variety has hair all over the body. Grooming for both varieties is average. The coated variety needs regular brushing. The hairless needs an occasional bath with a light application of lotion afterwards; he also needs sunscreen when spending time outdoors.

Life Span: 15 to 20 years.

Health Concerns: There are no reported breed-specific health concerns.

Exercise: Moderate to high. Although he may look fragile, this sturdy dog needs plenty of exercise and activity. When outdoors in cool weather, a sweater may be necessary.

Housing: Adaptable.

Sociability: Bonds to one person. Aloof and suspicious towards strangers. May try to dominate other dogs.

Trainability: Average to high. This breed is naturally in tune with his owner and a quick learner. He needs positive training and a good leader or may try to manipulate the household.

Activities: Agility, obedience.

5 Facts

Needs company
Clean with no doggy odor
Ideal for apartment life
Good with children
Gentle handling

YORKSHIRE TERRIER

Origin: Yorkshire, England, 1800s; may have Maltese in its background.

Original Purpose: Ratter.

Personality: Domineering, fiery, stubborn, alert, adventuresome, lively.

Breed Traits: Makes a good watchdog. Some are inappropriately aggressive. Some are barky. They enjoy being pampered but also like a chance to act like other dogs and run and play.

Physical Attributes: 7 to 9 in (18 to 23 cm); under 7 lb (3 kg). Pet dogs are usually larger than show dogs. Colors are dark steel blue on body; golden tan on face, chest, ears, and legs. Pet types have black markings that just don't turn blue. Yorkies are born black.

Coat Type and Grooming: Long, silky, straight hair. High maintenance; daily grooming needed. Professional grooming is recommended. Minimal shedding.

Life Span: 14 to 16 years.

Health Concerns: Heart problems (mitral valve insufficiency), rheumy eyes, liver disease (portacaval shunt, hepatitis), dermatitis, ear infections, enteritis, cancer, nephritis.

Exercise: Low.

Housing: Small enough for apartment life, but some are too vocal. Can get sufficient exercise in an apartment and will self-exercise.

Sociability: Good with well-behaved children but may not do well in a home with toddlers. Most are friendly, some are shy. Usually compatible with other pets.

Trainability: Average; can be hard to housetrain.

Activities: Companion, agility.

5 Facts

Fiery
Adaptable
Professional grooming
Lively
May bark

GLOSSARY

Acral lick dermatitis: A skin disorder caused by a dog's licking a localized area, usually on the legs. The original cause may be physical or psychological, but the area soon becomes traumatized.

Agility: A canine sport that tests a dog's ability to balance, climb, jump, and navigate obstacles.

Allergic dermatitis: A skin condition caused by an allergy.

Anal fissures: Also called perianal fistula, an area of inflammation, ulceration, and draining sores around the anus.

Anal sacs: A pair of sacs located on either side of the anus. They contain foul-smelling liquid.

Anemia: Lower-than-normal number of white blood cells.

Aortic stenosis: A narrowing of the aorta in the heart.

Arrhythmia: Abnormal heart rhythms; most common in larger breeds.

Arthritis: Inflammation of a joint, characteristic of geriatric dogs.

Aseptic meningitis: Meningitis (inflammation of the meninges) but not caused by an infectious agent.

Autoimmune hemolytic anemia: Severe anemia caused by an autoimmune problem.

Axonal dystrophy: Degenerative nerve disease.

Basenji enteropathy: Digestive malabsorption disease that results in protein loss, diarrhea, and consequent weight loss.

Belton: Flecked colors in the coat of English Setters (named after a village in Northumbria). Typically "orange" and "blue" belton (which is black and white), but also lemon belton, liver belton, and tricolor.

Biddable: Obedient, easily taught.

Biscuit: Grayish yellow.

Bloat: Condition in which gases in the stomach are produced in great amounts, which sometimes cannot be belched and may result in torsion (twisting) of the stomach, a condition that is rapidly fatal without prompt treatment. Characteristic of deep-chested breeds like Bloodhounds and Great Danes.

Blue merle: Mottled shades of blue, black, and gray with tan shadings.

Breed standard: The ideal dog, described in writing. Some breeds also have an "illustrated standard."

Brindle: A color pattern of black stripes on a brown coat. In Great Danes, gold with black cross stripes in a chevron pattern.

Broken coat: Rough coat, said of a variety of Jack Russell Terriers.

Cancer: Any malignant, cellular tumor.

Canine Eye Registration Foundation (CERF): International organization devoted to eliminating hereditary eye disease from purebred dogs.

Cardiomyopathy: Weakened, degenerated heart muscle; more common in large and giant breeds.

Cataract: A clouding of the lens causing blindness. Surgical correction is sometimes possible. Commonly affected breeds include Staffordshire Bull Terriers, Afghan Hounds, Cocker Spaniels, Bedlington Terriers, and Boston Terriers.

Cerebellar ataxia: Inherited fatal disease of the nervous system.

Chondrodysplasia: Abnormal growth of cartilage.

Cleft palate: Hole between the oral and nasal cavities.

CMO: See "cranioiomandibular osteopathy."

Collapsing trachea: Narrowing of the trachea, the main air passage to the lungs; occurs most often in small breeds.

Collie eye anomaly: An inherited trait that while it does not cause blindness, can lead to other painful eye conditions. Commonly affected breeds include Collies, Shelties, and Border Collies.

Collie nose: A crusting, depigmenting dermatitis of the nose and sometimes also of the lip and eyelid margins. Most commonly a result of exposure to sunshine.

Color dilution alopecia: A deformity of the hair seen in dogs with a blue or fawn coat, caused by the dilution gene at the D locus.

Coonhound trials: Events in which coonhounds are tested on their ability to tree a raccoon.

Conjunctivitis: Inflammation of the conjunctiva.

Copper toxicosis: Accumulation of copper in the liver, resulting in chronic hepatitis.

Corded: Coat type in which the hairs intertwine to form long mats, resulting in a mop-like appearance.

Corneal ulcer: A sore in the cornea that may be caused by trauma or infectious agents.

Coursing: Visual pursuit; the hunting style of gaze or sighthounds like Afghans and Salukis.

Craniomandibular osteopathy: Proliferative bone disease that typically affects the lower jawbone. Affects young dogs, mostly certain terriers.

Cropping: Surgical shaping of the ears. Outlawed in England and several other European countries.

Cruciate ligament ruptures: A tear in the ligament of the knee.

Cushing's disease: Abnormality of the adrenal glands leading to mineral and water imbalances.

Dapple: Mottled or variegated coat pattern.

Degenerative myelopathy: A slowly progressive condition that affects the spinal cord, causing paralysis.

Dermatitis: Skin inflammation.

Dermatomyositis: Inflammation of skin and muscles.

Dermoid sinus: An abnormal and heritable opening (sinus) into the skin along the ridge on the dog's back that can get infected. Sometimes goes into the spinal cord. Seen mostly in Rhodesian Ridgebacks, occasionally in Boxers and Shih Tzu. Surgical correction is sometimes possible.

Detached retina: Separation of the inner layers of the retina from the pigment epithelium, which remains attached to the choroid. It occurs most often as a result of degenerative changes in the eye.

Dewclaw: An extra claw near the knee or below the hock, often removed when the puppy is a few days old.

Diabetes: An abnormality in sugar metabolism, leading to excess sugar in the blood.

Distichiasis: Eyelashes that project in towards the surface of the eye.

Docking: Removal of the tail.

Drafting: A canine sport involving pulling.

Dry eye: A condition in which the tear glands do not function properly.

Ear infections: This common ailment can be caused by ear mites, allergies, or the yeast organism mallesezia canis. Lop-eared dogs are more susceptible than are dogs with upright ears.

Ectropion: Inherited condition in which the lower eyelid rolls away from the eyeball; opposite of entropion.

Elbow dysplasia: A name for several conditions of the elbow joint, found mostly in young, rapidly growing large-breed dogs; usually a laxity of the joint.

Enteritis: Inflammation of the intestinal mucosa.

Entropion: Turning inward of the eyelid. This condition may be congenital or acquired and causes eye irritation and other vision problems.

Epilepsy: Seizure disorder of unknown cause.

Exocrine pancreatic insufficiency: Pancreas fails to produce needed digestive enzymes, leading to incomplete digestion and absorption of nutrients.

Factor IX deficiency: A clotting disorder.

Fanconi's syndrome: Kidney disease resulting from reabsorption defects.

Fawn: A brown color ranging from light tan to mahogany; sometimes called Isabella.

Feathers: Long hairs, usually on the legs, but also on the ears and beneath the tail.

Field trials: An event testing the ability of sporting dogs and scenthounds to locate game.

Fleabite dermatitis: Skin inflammation caused by an allergic reaction to flea bites.

Flyball: A canine sport in which dogs race to retrieve balls.

Flying disc competition: Canine "Frisbee."

Gastric torsion: See "bloat."

Gastritis: Inflammation of the lining of the stomach.

Gazehound: A sighthound, such as a Greyhound or Whippet.

Gingivitis: Inflammation of the gums.

Glaucoma: Increased fluid pressure in the eye. Commonly affected breeds include Cocker Spaniels, English Cocker Spaniels, Welsh and English Springer Spaniels, Beagles, and Basset Hounds.

Globoid cell leukodystrophy: Inherited lysosomal storage leading to paralysis.

Glycogen storage disease: An inherited disorder marked by abnormal storage of glycogen in the body tissues.

Grizzle: White mixed with black or red.

Harlequin: White with irregular black patches; usually referring to Great Danes.

Heartworm disease: Dirofilaria, a condition in which the pulmonary artery is infested with heartworms.

Heatstroke: Elevation of body temperature to dangerous levels.

Hemophilia: A bleeding disorder.

Hepatitis: Infection or inflammation of the liver.

Herding: A canine sport in which sheepdogs are tested on their ability to handle sheep.

Hernia: Abnormal protrusion of part of an organ or tissue through the structures normally containing it.

Hip dysplasia: An inherited condition in which the head of the femur (hip joint) does not fit properly into the socket. It can be mild, requiring nothing more than occasional medication for pain or inflammation. On the other hand, severe cases need surgery.

Histiocytosis: Rapidly progressive cancer resulting in abnormal white blood cells infiltrating many parts of the body.

Hot spots: Acute moist dermatitis.

Hounds: A hunting dog who tracks prey by scent or sight.

Hydrocephalus: Excessive accumulation of fluid in the brain.

Hypertrophic osteodystrophy: Disease of young, large-breed dogs. Inflammation of bone and derangement of normal bone development.

Hypothyroidism: A malfunction of the thyroid gland resulting in underproduction of thyroxine, which controls the metabolic rate; most common in adult dogs.

Intervertebral disk disease: Abnormality of the soft cartilaginous disks that cushion the vertebrae. Most common in Dachshunds and Corgis.

Isabella: Fawn or medium brown color, used referring to Dobermans and some other breeds.

Juvenile cataracts: Cataracts developing in very young (under 6 months) dogs.

Legg-Perthes disease: Abnormal femur head, resulting from lack of adequate blood supply.

Lens luxation: Weakening of one or more of the ligaments holding the lens in place. Commonly affected breeds include Smooth and Wire Fox Terriers, Jack Russell Terriers, and Tibetan Terriers.

Line-breeding: The breeding of related individuals.

Liver: Medium to deep mahogany brown coat.

Lure-coursing: A canine sport in which sighthounds chase lures.

Lymphedema: Lymph system not draining properly; can lead to swelling.

Merle: Dark irregular blotches of color on a lighter background of the same color. Usually refers to longhaired dogs. In shorthaired dogs, the same pattern is often called dappled.

Mitral valve insufficiency: Degeneration of a heart valve.

Nephritis: Inflammation of the kidney.

Nodular dermatofibrosis: A syndrome primarily of German Shepherds in which fibrous nodules form in and beneath the skin.

Obedience: A canine sport that tests a dog's ability to follow commands.

OCD: See "osteochondrosis."

Orthopedic Foundation for Animals (OFA): Organization dedicated to eliminating orthopedic diseases from purebred dogs.

Osteochondrosis: A disorder of young, usually large-breed dogs. The cartilage fails to develop into mature bone.

Osteosarcoma: A kind of bone cancer.

Outcrossing: Mating of unrelated dogs of the same breed.

Pancreatitis: Inflammation of the pancreas; tends to occur in young overweight dogs, often after ingesting a fatty meal.

Panosteitis: Bone inflammation leading to uneven bone growth; self-limiting.

Patella: Kneecap.

Patellar luxation: Loose kneecaps.

Patent ductus arteriosus (PDA): Congenital defect in which the ductus arteriosus, an embryonic blood vessel in the heart, does not close as it should, soon after birth. Limits the amount of blood circulating to the tissues and produces a murmur.

PDA: See "patent ductus arteriosus."

Pedigree: A diagram of a dog's ancestry. A good breeder will provide a three-generation pedigree to customers; a longer one may be purchased from the AKC.

Phobia: A severe, irrational fear.

Piebald: A color pattern of brown and white patches.

Portacaval shunt: Failure of the embryonic liver blood vessel to close properly after birth.

PRA: See "progressive retinal atrophy."

Progressive neuronal abiotrophy: A form of familial neuronal abiotrophy, an inherited malformation of nerve cells. Also called the Chinese Beagle syndrome.

Progressive retinal atrophy (PRA): Progressive destruction of light-sensitive tissue at the back of the eye. Most commonly affected breeds include Collies, Shelties, and Cocker Spaniels.

Protein-losing enteropathy: Excessive loss of plasma proteins into the intestinal lumen. Associated with a number of bowel disorders.

Protein-losing nephropathy: Excretion of excessive amounts of protein in the urine.

Pug Dog encephalitis: Inflammation of the brain and its covering, possibly caused by a virus, leading to symptoms such as depression, circling, head pressing, and blindness.

Pulmonary stenosis: Congenital narrowing of the opening in a heart valve due to thickening of the heart muscle. Characterized by abnormal blood flow between the right ventricle and pulmonary artery; can result in heart failure.

Puppy: A dog under 12 months of age.

Purebred: A dog whose sire and dam are of the same breed.

Rage syndrome: Sudden episode of unprovoked aggression.

Renal dysplasia: Malformed kidneys.

Retinal dysplasia: Abnormal development of the retina.

Roan: Solid color with a sprinkling of white hairs.

Sable: Black-tipped hairs on a lighter background.

SAS: See "subaortic stenosis."

Scenthound: A hound who follows game by its scent.

Schutzhund: A canine sport that tests the dog's ability to guard and protect.

Seal: Coat appears black but has a reddish cast.

Search and rescue: An activity in which dogs locate lost or missing persons.

Sebaceous adenitis: Inflammation of the sebaceous glands.

Sebaceous cysts: A benign condition in which fluid collects in a sac under the skin.

Sebaceous gland tumor: A wart-like growth, usually benign, that can appear anywhere on the body.

Seizure: A fit or convulsion.

Service dog: A dog used to guide the blind or in other ways help the disabled.

Sighthound: A hound who locates and chases game by sight.

Skijoring: A canine sport in which dogs pull humans on skis.

Sledding: A canine sport in which dogs pull sleds.

Smooth coat: Close-lying, short coat.

Spitz dogs: Members of a number of (usually) arctic breeds characterized by short-bodied, stocky builds and heavy double coats. Examples include the Chow Chow, Alaskan Malamute, Siberian Husky, Finnish Spitz, and Norwegian Elkhound.

Stag red: Black hairs intermingling with a predominantly red coat.

Stripping: Plucking of dead hairs to maintain coat quality. A labor-intensive task done mostly on show dogs; pet dogs are clipped instead, a much easier task, but one resulting in a softer coat.

Subaortic stenosis (SAS): Heart condition resulting from a narrowing just below the aortic valve.

Terrier: A group of dogs used originally for hunting vermin.

Therapy dog: A dog used to visit and comfort elderly, sick, or disabled persons.

Thrombopathia: A bleeding disorder.

Ticking: Small, irregular spots in an otherwise white coat.

Toy: Dogs characterized by small size.

Tracheal collapse: Loss of rigidity of the trachea.

Tracking: A canine sport in which dogs follow scent to locate an article.

Tricolor: Black with white markings and tan shadings.

Umbilical hernia: A protrusion of the navel.

Urinary tract stones: Hard accumulations of crystals usually found in the bladder.

Ventricular septal defect (VSD): A hole in the inner wall of the heart.

VSD: See "ventricular septal defect."

Von Willebrand's disease: A congenital bleeding disorder characterized by a prolonged bleeding time and slow clotting. Caused by a deficiency in clotting factor VIII.

Weight-pulling: A canine event in which dogs pull weights competitively.

Wheaten: Pale yellow or fawn coat.

Whitelies: White body color with red or dark markings, used to describe the Pembroke Welsh Corgi.

Withers: Top of the shoulders.

Wobblers: Cervical vertebral instability due to spinal cord compression, resulting in neck pain and difficulty in walking.

RESOURCES

PUBLICATIONS
Books
Anderson, Teoti. *Puppy Care & Training.* New Jersey: TFH Publications, Inc., 2007.

Anderson, Teoti. *The Super Simple Guide to Housetraining.* New Jersey: TFH Publications, Inc., 2004.

Becker, Susan C. *Living With a Deaf Dog: A Book of Advice, Facts and Experiences About Canine Deafness.* Ohio: S.C. Becker, 1997.

Boneham, Sheila Webster, Ph.D. *The Multiple-Dog Family.* New Jersey: TFH Publications, Inc., 2009.

Boneham, Sheila Webster, Ph.D. *The Dog Training Handbook.* New Jersey: TFH Publications, Inc., 2008.

Copeland, Sue and John A. *Hamil. Hands-On Dog Care.* California: Doral Publishing, 2000.

Dainty, Suellen. *50 Games to Play With Your Dog.* New Jersey: TFH Publications, Inc., 2007.

DeGioia. *The Mixed Breed Dog.* New Jersey: TFH Publications, Inc., 2007.

DeVito, Russell-Revesz, Fornino. *World Atlas of Dog Breeds, 6th Ed.* New Jersey: TFH Publications, Inc., 2009.

Downing, Robin. *Pets Living With Cancer: A Pet Owner's Resource.* American Animal Hospital Association, 2000.

Gagne, Tammy. *The Happy*

Adopted Dog. New Jersey: TFH Publications, Inc., 2009.

King, Trish. *Parenting Your Dog: Complete Care and Training for Every Life Stage.* New Jersey: TFH Publications, Inc., 2010.

Knueven, Doug, DVM. *The Holistic Health Guide for Dogs.* New Jersey: TFH Publications, Inc., 2008.

Kennedy, Stacy. *Complete Guide to Puppy Care.* New Jersey: TFH Publications, Inc., 2011.

Mammato, Bobbie and Susie Duckworth. *Pet First Aid: Cats and Dogs.* Missouri: CV Mosby Publishing Company, 1997.

Morgan, Diane. *Feeding Your Dog for Life: The Real Facts About Proper Nutrition.* California: Doral Publishing, 2002.

Morgan, Diane. *The Living Well Guide for Senior Dogs.* New Jersey: TFH Publications, Inc., 2007.

Morgan, Diane. *Complete Guide to Dog Care: Everything You Need to Know to Have a Happy, Well-Trained Dog.* New Jersey: TFH Publications, Inc., 2011.

Tousley, Marty and Katherine Heuerman. *Final Farewell: Preparing for and Mourning the Loss of Your Pet.* Arizona: Our Pals Publishing Co., 1997.

Magazines
AKC Family Dog
American Kennel Club
260 Madison Avenue
New York, NY 10016
Telephone: (800) 490-5675
E-mail: familydog@akc.org
www.akc.org/pubs/familydog

AKC Gazette
American Kennel Club
260 Madison Avenue
New York, NY 10016
Telephone: (800) 533-7323
E-mail: gazette@akc.org
www.akc.org/pubs/gazette

ORGANIZATIONS
Animal Welfare and Rescue
American Humane Association (AHA)
63 Inverness Drive East
Englewood, CO 80112
Telephone: (303) 792-5333
Fax: (303) 792-5333
www.americanhumane.org

American Society for the Prevention of Cruelty to Animals (ASPCA)
424 E. 92nd Street
New York, NY 10128-6804
Telephone: (212) 876-7700
www.aspca.org

Canadian Federation of Humane Societies (CFHS)
102-30 Concourse Gate
Ottawa, ON K2E 7V7
Canada
Telephone: (888) 678-CFHS
Fax: (613)723-0252
E-mail: info@cfhs.ca
www.cfhs.ca

The Humane Society of the United States (HSUS)
2100 L Street, NW
Washington, DC 20037
Telephone: (202) 452-1100
www.humanesociety.org

Partnership for Animal Welfare
P.O. Box 1074
Greenbelt, MD 20768
Telephone: (301) 572-4729
E-mail: dogs@paw-rescue.org
www.paw-rescue.org

Royal Society for the Prevention of Cruelty to Animals (RSPCA)
Wilberforce Way

Southwater, Horsham,
West Sussex RH13 9RS
United Kingdom
www.rspca.org.uk

Behavior

American College of Veterinary Behaviorists (ACVB)
College of Veterinary Medicine
Texas A&M University
College Station, TX 77843-4474
E-mail: info@dacvb.org
www.dacvb.org

Animal Behavior Society (ABS)
Indiana University
402 N. Park Ave.
Bloomington, IN 47408-2603
Telephone: (812) 856-5541
Fax: (812) 856-5542
E-mail: aboffice@indiana.edu
www.animalbehaviorsociety.org

Breed Clubs

American Kennel Club (AKC)
8051 Arco Corporate Drive, Suite 100
Raleigh, NC 27606
Telephone: (919) 233-9767
Fax: (919) 233-3627
E-mail: info@akc.org
www.akc.org

Canadian Kennel Club (CKC)
200 Ronson Drive, Suite 400
Etobicoke, Ontario
M9W 6R4
Canada
Telephone: (416) 675-5511
Fax: (416) 675-6506
E-mail: information@ckc.ca
www.ckc.ca

The Fédération Cynologique Internationale (FCI)
13 Place Albert 1er
B-6530 Thuin
Belgium
E-mail: info@fci.be
www.fci.be

The Kennel Club
1-5 Clarges Street
Picadilly, London
W1J 8AB
United Kingdom
Telephone: 0844 463 3980
Fax: 020 7518 1058
www.thekennelclub.org.uk

United Kennel Club (UKC)
100 E. Kilgore Road
Kalamazoo, MI 49002-5584
Telephone: (269) 343-9020
Fax: (269) 343-7037
www.ukcdogs.com

Grooming

The International Society of Canine Cosmetologists (ISCC)
2702 Covington Drive
Garland, TX 75040
Fax: (972) 530-3313
E-mail: iscc@petstylist.com
www.petstylist.com

National Dog Groomers Association of America, Inc. (NDGAA)
P.O. Box 101
Clark, PA 16113
Telephone: (724) 962-2711
Fax: (724) 962-1919
E-mail: ndgaa@nationaldoggroomers.com
www.nationaldoggroomers.com

Health

The American Animal Hospital Association (AAHA)
12575 W. Bayaud Ave.
Lakewood, CO 80228
Telephone: (303) 986-2800
Fax: (303) 986-1700
E-mail: info@aahanet.org
www.aahanet.org

American Kennel Club Canine Health Foundation (AKCCHF)
P.O. Box 900061
Raleigh, NC 27627-7941

Telephone: (888) 682-9696
E-mail: caninehealth@akcchf.org
www.akcchf.org

Canine Health Information Center (CHIC)
2300 E. Nifong Blvd.
Columbia, MO 65201-3806
Telephone: (573) 442-0418
Fax: (573) 875-5073
E-mail: chic@offa.org
www.caninehealthinfo.org

Canine Eye Registration Foundation (CERF)
VMDB/CERF
1717 Philo Road
Urbana, IL 61803-3007
Telephone: (217) 693-4800
E-mail: CERF@vmdb.org
www.vmdb.org

Orthopedic Foundation for Animals, Inc. (OFA)
2300 E. Nifong Blvd.
Columbia, MO 65201-3806
Phone: (800) 442-0418
E-mail: ofa@offa.org
www.offa.org

Pet Sitting

The National Association of Professional Pet Sitters (NAPPS)
15000 Commerce Parkway, Suite C
Mt. Laurel, NJ 08054
Telephone: (856) 439-0324
E-mail: NAPPS@ahint.com
www.petsitters.org

Pet Sitters International
201 East King Street
King, NC 27021
Telephone: (336) 983-9222
Fax: (336) 983-5266
E-mail: NAPPS@petsiters.org
www.petsit.com

Sports

Agility Association of Canada (AAC)
RR#2

Lucan, Ontario N0N 2J0
Canada
Telephone: (519) 657-7636
www.aac.ca

North American Dog Agility Council (NADAC)
P.O. Box 1206
Colbert, OK 74733
E-mail: info@nadac.com
www.nadac.com

North American Flyball Association (NAFA)
1333 West Devon Avenue, #512
Chicago, IL 60660
Telephone/Fax: (800) 318-6312
E-mail: flyball@flyball.org
www.flyball.org

United States Dog Agility Association (USDAA)
P.O. Box 850955
Richardson, TX 75085-0955
Telephone: (972) 487-2200
Fax: (972) 231-9700
E-mail: info@usdaa.com
www.usdaa.com

Therapy

The Bright and Beautiful Therapy Dogs, Inc.
80 Powder Mill Road
Morris Plains, NJ 07950
Telephone: (888) PET-5770
Fax: (973) 292-9559
E-mail: info@golden-dogs.org
www.golden-dogs.org

Delta Society
875 124th Ave. NE, Suite 101
Bellevue, WA 98005
Telephone: (425) 679-5500
Fax: (425) 679-5539
E-mail: info@deltasociety.org
www.deltasociety.org

Therapy Dogs Inc.
P.O. Box 20227
Cheyenne, WY 82003
Telephone: (877) 843-7364

E-mail: therapydogsinc@
qwestoffice.net
www.therapydogs.com

Therapy Dogs International
88 Bartley Square
Flanders, NJ 07836
Telephone: (973) 252-9800
Fax: (973) 252-7171
E-mail: tdi@gti.net
www.tdi-dog.org

Training

Association of Pet Dog Trainers (APDT)
101 North Main St., Suite 610
Greenville, SC 29601
Telephone: (800) PET-DOGS
Fax: (864) 331-0767
E-mail: information@apdt.com
www.apdt.com

Certification Council for Pet Dog Trainers (CCPDT)
1350 Broadway, 17th Floor
New York, NY 10018
Telephone: (212) 356-0682
E-mail: administrator@ccpdt.org
www.ccpdt.org

Veterinary

Academy of Veterinary Homeopathy (AVH)
P.O. Box 232282
Leucadia, CA 92023-2282
Telephone/Fax: (866) 652-1590
www.theavh.org

American Academy of Veterinary Acupuncture (AAVA)
P.O. Box 1058
Glastonbury, CT 06033
Telephone: (860) 632-9911
Fax: (860) 659-8772
E-mail: office@aava.org
www.aava.org

American Animal Hospital Association (AAHA)
12575 W. Bayaud Ave.
Lakewood, CO 80228

Telephone: (303) 986-2800
Fax: (303) 986-1700
E-mail: info@aahanet.org
www.aahanet.org

American College of Veterinary Internal Medicine (ACVIM)
1997 Wadsworth Blvd., Suite A
Lakewood, CO 80214-5293
Telephone: (800) 245-9081
Fax: (303) 231-0880
E-mail: ACVIM@ACVIM.org
www.acvim.org.

American College of Veterinary Ophthalmologists (ACVO)
P.O. Box 1311
Meridian, ID 83680
Telephone: (208) 466-7624
Fax: (208) 466-7693
E-mail: office10@acvo.org
www.acvo.org

American Holistic Veterinary Medical Association (AHVMA)
PO Box 630
Abingdon, MD 21009
Telephone: (410) 569-0795
Fax: (410) 569-2346
E-mail: office@ahvma.org
www.ahvma.org

American Veterinary Chiropractic Association (AVCA)
442154 E 140 Road
Bluejacket, OK 74333
Telephone: (918) 784-2231
Fax: (918) 784-2675
E-mail: avcainfo@junct.com
www.animalchiropractic.org

American Veterinary Dental Society (AVDS)
P.O. Box 803
Fayetteville, TN 37334
Telephone: (800) 332-AVDS
Fax: (931) 433-6289
E-mail: avds@avds-online.org
www.avds-online.org

American Veterinary Medical Association (AVMA)

1931 North Meacham Road, Suite 100
Schaumburg, IL 60173-4360
Telephone: (800) 248-2862
Fax: (847) 925-1329
E-mail: avmainfo@avma.org
www.avma.org

International Veterinary Acupuncture Society (IVAS)
1730 South College Ave., Suite 301
Ft. Collins, CO 80527-1395
Telephone: (970) 266-0666
Fax: (970) 266-0777
E-mail: office@ivas.org
www.ivas.org

US Food & Drug Administration's Center for Veterinary Medicine (CVM)
Communications Staff (CVM)
Food and Drug Administration
7519 Standish Place, HFV-12
Rockville, MD 20855
Telephone: (240) 276-9300
E-mail: ASKCVM@fda.hhs.gov
www.fda.gov/cvm/default.htm

Veterinary Cancer Society (VCS)
P.O. Box 1763
Spring Valley, CA 91979
Telephone: (619) 741-2210
Fax: (619) 741-1117
E-mail: vcs@cox.net
www.vetcancersociety.org

WEBSITES

General
Animal Planet
www.animal.discovery.com
The domestic dog section has a great guide to dogs, a breed selector, training information, and more.

Nylabone®
www.nylabone.com
Nylabone premium chews, toys, and other products promote good canine dental hygiene, enhance overall mental fitness, encourage positive behavior, provide comfortable shelter, and allow for safe, pleasant travel.

TFH Publications, Inc.
www.tfh.com
Comprehensive and authoritative animal reference books and learning vehicles for pet owners that ensure the optimum human–companion animal experience.

Activities
Carting With Your Dog
www.cartingwithyourdog.com
Information and resources on carting.

DogPlay
www.dogplay.com
Excellent guide to activities that you can do with your dog.

Dog Works, Inc.
www.dogworks.com
A great source for canine carting and watersports equipment.

Hike With Your Dog
www.hikewithyourdog.com
Direct links to more than 2,000 dog-friendly parks, plus dog regulations for national parks in the US and Canada.

Skyhoundz
www.skyhoundz.com
Products and events for disc dog enthusiasts.

Sled Dog Central
www.sleddogcentral.com
Sled dog information resource.

SportsVet.com
www.sportsvet.com
Website dedicated to athletic and working dogs. A great site for health and care information for your canine athlete.

Legal
American Dog Owner's Association
www.adoa.org
Information and ideas about preserving dog owners' rights, and information about responsible dog ownership.

Animal Legal Defense Fund
www.aldf.org
Advancing the lives of animals through the legal system.

Dog Watch
www.dogwatch.net
Provides information on canine breed-specific legislation in North America and abroad.

National Animal Interest Alliance
www.naiaonline.org
Provides expert information on animals and public policy.

People With Pets
www.peoplewithpets.com
A free nationwide apartment locator service for people with pets.

Lost and Missing Pets
Last Chance for Animals
www.stolenpets.com
Learn about how to combat the problem of stolen pets who are sold to research institutions.

Missing Pet Network
www.missingpet.net
Website run by a group of volunteers sponsored by the USDA Animal Care Office, who help people find missing pet animals.

Pets 911
www.pets911.org
Contains a nationwide list of animal control facilities, humane societies, and veterinarians; searchable by zip code.

INDEX

Boldfaced numbers indicate illustrations.

A

AAHA (American Animal Hospital Association), 13
acral lick dermatitis, 241
activities. *see* sports and activities
adaptability, 14
adoption
  pros and cons of, 32–33
  from rescues and shelters, 31–32
adult dogs *vs.* puppies, 13, 18, 32–33
Affenpinscher, 68
Afghan Hound, 42, **50,** 69
age of puppy, 22
aggression, 32
agility, 52, 241
ailments, 13, 64–65
Airedale Terrier, 70
AKC (American Kennel Club)
  breed groups of, 67
  championships of, 19–20
  events sponsored by, 26, 30, **30,** 67
  registration with, 20, 26, 30
Akita, 71
Alaskan Malamute, 72
allergic dermatitis, 241
allergies
  canine, 25, 64
  human, 7, 47, 64
alopecia, color dilution, 242
American Animal Hospital Association (AAHA), 13
American English Coonhound, 73
American Eskimo Dog, 74
American Foxhound, 75
American Kennel Club (AKC)
  breed groups of, 67
  championships of, 19–20
  events sponsored by, 26, 30, **30,** 67
  registration with, 20, 26, 30
American Society for the Prevention of Cruelty to Animals (ASPCA), 31
American Staffordshire Terrier, 76
American Water Spaniel, 77
anal fissures, 241
anal sacs, 241
Anatolian Shepherd Dog, 78
anemia, 241

anesthesia, sighthounds and, 24–25, 64
animal welfare and rescue organizations, 246–247
aortic stenosis, 241
apartment living, 9–10, 11–12, 48, 65
application process, 27–28
arrhythmia, 241
arthritis, 241
aseptic meningitis, 241
ASPCA (American Society for the Prevention of Cruelty to Animals), 31
ataxia, cerebellar, 241
Australian Cattle Dog, 41, 79
Australian Shepherd, 80
Australian Terrier, 81
autoimmune hemolytic anemia, 241
axonal dystrophy, 241

B

backyard breeders, 19–20
BAER (brainstem auditory evoked response) test, 25
barking, 48–49, 62
Basenji, 82
Basenji enteropathy, 241
Basset Hound, **48,** 83
Beagle, 84
Bearded Collie, 85
Beauceron, 86
Bedlington Terrier, 87
behavior, resources for, 247
behavioral traits, 37
  of breed groups, 38–41
  matching lifestyle to, 41–43
behavior problems, 20, 32
Belgian Malinois, 88
Belgian Sheepdog, 89
Belgian Tervuren, 90
belton, 241
Bernese Mountain Dog, 91
Bichon Frise, 92
biddable, 241
bill of sale, 29
biscuit, 241
Black and Tan Coonhound, 93
Black Russian Terrier, 94
bleeding disorders, 64, 65
bloat, 241
Bloodhound, 95
blue merle, 241
"blue slip," 26, 30
Bluetick Coonhound, 96

books, 246
Border Collie, 37, **52,** 60, 97
Border Terrier, 98
Borzoi, 99
Boston Terrier, 100
Bouvier des Flandres, 101
Boxer, 102
Boykin Spaniel, 103
brainstem auditory evoked response (BAER) test, 25
breathing problems, 64
breed
  purpose of, 37, 60
  reasons not to choose, 43
  researching, 42–43
breed clubs, 22–23, 247
breeders, 21–31
  application process of, 27–28
  backyard, 19–20
  co-ownership with, 30–31
  criteria for judging, 22–27
  finding, 22
  paperwork from, 23, 29–31
  puppy selection at, 28–29
breed groups
  behavioral traits in, 38–41
  matching lifestyle to, 41–43
breeding, line-, 25, 64, 243
breeding program, 23
breed profiles, using, 59–67
breed rescues, 31–33, 246–247
breed standard, 42, 60–61, 241
breed traits, 61–62
Briard, 104
brindle, 241
Brittany, 105
broken coat, 241
Brussels Griffon, 106
Bulldog, 39, 107
  French, **49,** 140
Bullmastiff, 108
Bull Terrier, 109
  Miniature, 176
  Staffordshire, 223
"Bully-breeds," 39

C

Cairn Terrier, 110
Canaan Dog, 111
cancer, 241
Cane Corso, 112
Canine Eye Registration Foundation (CERF), 25, 64, 241

French Bulldog, **49,** 140
friendly dogs, 51
friends, getting dog from, 21
"full-blooded" dog, 19

G
Garbrick, Alisa, 33
gastric torsion, 241
gastritis, 243
gazehound, 243. *see also* sighthounds
genetic code, 36
genetic diseases
    breed profiles of, 64
    coloration and, 20
    testing for, 24–25, 64–65
German Pinscher, 141
German Shepherd Dog, 142
German Shorthaired Pointer, 143
German Wirehaired Pointer, 144
Giant Schnauzer, 145
gingivitis, 243
glaucoma, 243
Glen of Imaal Terrier, 146
globoid cell leukodystrophy, 243
glossary, 241–245
glycogen storage disease, 243
Golden Retriever, **51,** 147
Gordon Setter, 60, 148
Great Dane, 149
Greater Swiss Mountain Dog, 150
Great Pyrenees, 151
Greyhound, 39, 152
    Italian, 162
grizzle, 243
grooming, 63–64
    need for, 42, 47
    professional, 14, 63–64
    resources for, 247
    shedding and, 64
    of terriers, 42, 63
guard dogs, 37

H
harlequin, 243
Harrier, 153
Havanese, 154
health
    checkups for, 14–15
    dog ownership and human, 7
    of puppy, 24–25, 29
    of rescue or shelter dog, 32, 33
    resources for, 247, 248–249
health contract, 23, 29
health problems

breed profiles of, 64–65
    top ten, 13
heartworm disease, 243
heat intolerance, 49
heatstroke, 243
height, 62
hemolytic anemia, autoimmune, 241
hemophilia, 243
hepatitis, 243
herding, 243
Herding Group, 38, 67
    Australian Cattle Dog, 41, 79
    Australian Shepherd, 80
    Bearded Collie, 85
    Beauceron, 86
    Belgian Malinois, 88
    Belgian Sheepdog, 89
    Belgian Tervuren, 90
    Border Collie, 37, **52,** 60, 97
    Bouvier des Flandres, 101
    Briard, 104
    Canaan Dog, 111
    Cardigan Welsh Corgi, 113
    Collie, **53,** 123
    Entlebucher Mountain Dog, 135
    Finnish Lapphund, 137
    German Shepherd Dog, 142
    Icelandic Sheepdog, 156
    Norwegian Buhund, 182
    Old English Sheepdog, 187
    Pembroke Welsh Corgi, 192
    Polish Lowland Sheepdog, 197
    Puli, **55,** 202
    Pyrenean Shepherd, 203
    Shetland Sheepdog, **49,** 214
    Swedish Vallhund, 226
hereditary problems. *see* genetic
    diseases
hernia, 243, 245
hip dysplasia, 24–25, 64–65, 243
histiocytosis, 243
home
    leaving dog alone at, 12–13, 50
    puppy-proofing, 11
    suitability of, 15, 48–49, 65
hot climate, 49
hot spots, 243
Hound Group, 38–39, 40, 67
    Afghan Hound, 42, **50,** 69
    American English Coonhound, 73
    American Foxhound, 75
    Basenji, 82
    Basset Hound, **48,** 83

Beagle, 84
    Black and Tan Coonhound, 93
    Bloodhound, 95
    Bluetick Coonhound, 96
    Borzoi, 99
    Dachshund, 125
    English Foxhound, 131
    Greyhound, 39, 152
    Harrier, 153
    Ibizan Hound, 155
    Irish Wolfhound, 161
    Norwegian Elkhound, 183
    Otterhound, 188
    Petit Basset Griffon Vendéen, 193
    Pharaoh Hound, 194
    Plott, 195
    Redbone Coonhound, 204
    Rhodesian Ridgeback, 205
    Saluki, 208
    Scottish Deerhound, 211
    Whippet, 236
hounds, 243
    getting two, 29
    natural characteristics of, 41
house-raised dog, 25
housetraining, 15
humane societies, 31, 246–247
Humane Society of the United States
    (HSUS), 31
hydrocephalus, 243
hypertrophic osteodystrophy, 243
"hypoallergenic" dog, 47
hypothyroidism, 243

I
Ibizan Hound, 155
Icelandic Sheepdog, 156
identification, 29
intelligence, 61
Internet resources, 19–21, 249
intervertebral disk disease, 243
Irish Red and White Setter, 157
Irish Setter, 158
Irish Terrier, 159
Irish Water Spaniel, 160
Irish Wolfhound, 161
Isabella, 242, 243
Italian Greyhound, 162

J
Japanese Chin, 163
jogging, 52
juvenile cataracts, 243

AUTHOR

Diane Morgan teaches literature and writing at Indian River State College. She has authored numerous books on canine care and nutrition and has also written many breed books, horse books, and books on Eastern philosophy and religion. Diane lives in Vero Beach, Florida, with several dogs, two cats, some fish, and a couple of humans.

At Animal Planet, we're committed to providing quality products designed to help your pets live long, healthy, and happy lives.